100 Tales
of Old Texas

Murphy Givens

100 Tales
of Old Texas

One Hundred Stories
From the Annals of Texas History

Selected, Edited and Annotated by
Murphy Givens

Corpus Christi, Texas

Library of Congress Control Number 2020917465

100 Tales of Old Texas

Edited by: Givens, Murphy

Includes bibliography.

1. Texas — History.
2. Texas Revolution — History.
3. Civil War, Texas — History.
4. Reconstruction, Texas — History
5. Ranching, Texas — History

ISBN   978-1-7339524-3-9

Published by Nueces Press, Corpus Christi, Texas.

Cover design by Jeff Chilcoat

CONTENTS

Contents   v

Photos and Illustrations   viii

Publisher Note   x

Preface   xi

1 Ambush: Jesse Burnam   1

2 Letter from Texas: W.B. DeWees   5

3 Fresh Meat: Noah Smithwick   13

4 From Monclova to San Patricio: Benjamin Lundy   16

5 David Crockett, Houseguest: John Swisher   22

6 Fighting at the Alamo: José María Rodríguez   27

7 Raid on Parker's Fort: James T. DeShields   31

8 Back from the Dead: Bigfoot Wallace   38

9 Hog-Killing Weather: Mary Austin Holley   44

10 Snap Judgement: John J. Linn   48

11 A Deliberate Falsehood: Z. N. Morrell   52

12 The Death of Chief Bowles: John H. Reagan   57

13 Gen. Lamar Did Not Dance Well: Mary Maverick   63

14 Capt. Denton's Grave: Andrew A. Davis   66

15 A Place of Some Importance: William Bollaert   71

16 The March to Perote: James L. Trueheart   73

17 The Pigs of Galveston: Mrs. Houstoun   81

18 Riding Match: J. W. Wilbarger   84

19 The First Wine: Henry Castro   89

20 Letter to Roasting Ear: Thomas G. Western   93

21 Army Lands on North Beach: Ethan Allen Hitchcock   95

22 Traders from Camargo: N. S. Jarvis   100

23 Grant Cast as Desdemona: James Longstreet   103

24 Breaking Wild Mules: Ulysses S. Grant   108

25 Leaving for the Border: Daniel P. Whiting   109

26 Lost in a Blizzard: James Buckner Barry   114

27 Mustang Country: Thomas A. Dwyer   121

28 Going West: John H. Peoples   124

29 No Bells Tolled: E. Domenech   127

30 Dinner at Eberly House: Jane Cazneau   130

31 Letters from the Border: Henry Redmond   133

32 A Fair Celebration: J. Williamson Moses   136

33 A Comanche Horse Race: Richard Irving Dodge   140

34 Koweaka's Choice: Rupert Norval Richardson   144

35 It Takes All Sorts: Frederick Law Olmsted   149

36 Gone for a Soldier: Lydia Spencer Lane   153

37 Pine Knots: August Santleben   158

38 My Old Turnip: Nelson Lee   161

39 Hard Licks: Robert Adams   168

40 Hunting a Panther: Thomas Noakes   171

41 Growing Up at Banquete: Eli T. Merriman   174

42 Law and Order in El Paso: William W. Mills   179

43 Wizard Oil Times: Andrew Anderson   185

44 Houston Feared No Mobs in Texas: Thomas North   190

45 Some of the Boys Never Came Home: W. F. Cude   195

46 The Vigilance Committee: R. H. Williams   199

47 Sibley's Retreat: Theophilus Noel   205

48 Matagorda Cowboy: Charles A. Siringo   210

49 Battle of Corpus Christi: Francis R. Lubbock   213

50 Strife and Struggle: Rosalie Priour   218

51 Elysium: Arthur James Lyon Fremantle   225

52 The Lost Blanket: John C. West   230

53 Capture of Fort Semmes: Edwin B. Lufkin   234

54 Burying the Dead: A. J. H. Duganne   237

55 Dinner Party: Charles C. Nott   241

56 Chasing Deserters: Cliff Cates   247

57 Going Home: Joseph P. Blessington   250

58 Visiting the Deaf: Elizabeth Bacon Custer   252

59 Out of Sorts: H. H. McConnell   256

60 Names of the Dead: Joseph Almond   260

61 In Shallow Graves: Anna Moore Schwien   265

62 Diary of a Trail Drive: Jonathan Hamilton Baker   268

63 Up the Chisholm Trail: John Taylor Allen   275

64 Land Was Dirt Cheap: W. G. Sutherland   279

65 Outlaws and Gunfighters: Carroll C. Holloway   283

66 My Last Stampede: James T. Johnson   293

67 The Art of Dave Gambel: Ruth Dodson   296
68 Shooting a Dog: E. H. Caldwell   300
69 Shoot the Scoundrel: John Wesley Hardin   303
70 Turkey Roost Country: Billy Dixon   309
71 Outrage in Refugio: William L. Rea   315
72 The Lynching of Moss Top: John B. Dunn   318
73 Boots and Saddles: Dr. Robert T. Hill   322
74 Disaster at Indianola: V. L. Manci   329
75 Cooley's Revenge: James B. Gillett   334
76 Reluctant Bulls: Mrs. O. B. Boyd   340
77 Doctor Turns Cowboy: Henry F. Hoyt   342
78 The Kickapoo Raid: Jean Stuart   350
79 Hanging Day: William John L. Sullivan   353
80 Stone for an Indian Chief: Clarence Wharton   356
81 Island Ranch: Pat Dunn   360
82 A Photo for Quanah Parker: Zoe Tilghman   366
83 This Land Is Mine: Robert Maudslay   371
84 Geronimo in San Antonio: Mary Handy   378
85 Crossing the Reef: Leona Gussett   382
86 The King of Ranches: Richard Harding Davis   385
87 The Bill Collector: Owen P. White   389
88 Big Day in Havana: T. F. Fitzsimmons, Robert Hall   393
89 Valley of Long Hollow: J. Frank Dobie   396
90 Selling Texas Lands: George H. Paul   401
91 The 'Good Indian': Robert G. Carter   408
92 Horses, Buggies and Cadillacs: Carlyle Leonard   412
93 Mr. Johnson Killed My Cat: Theodore Fuller   417
94 Flu Diary: Anita Lovenskiold   421
95 The Water Kept Rising: Anna Priscilla Sorelle   425
96 Oh! Momma!: Lucy Caldwell   429
97 The Talking Skeleton: Ike Elliff   436
98 Storm on the Island: Louis Rawalt   442
99 Get-Away Money: Bill Duncan   448
100 Fields and Fences: Roy Bedichek   451
Bibliography   460
Other books from Nueces Press   471

PHOTOS AND ILLUSTRATIONS

2 Military Plaza, San Antonio — 10

3 Noah Smithwick — 14

4 Benjamin Lundy — 18

5 David Crockett, John Swisher — 23, 24

6 Alamo — 29

8 Bigfoot Wallace — 41

9 Mary Austin Holley — 46

10 John J. Linn — 49

11 Z. N. Morrell — 54

12 John H. Reagan — 59

13 Mary Maverick and children — 65

16 James Trueheart — 76, 78

18 Henry Kinney — 85

21 Zachary Taylor, Ethan Allen Hitchcock — 96, 98

23 U.S. Grant — 105

25 Daniel P. Whiting, Camp at Corpus Christi — 110, 111

27 Wild Mustang — 122

30 Indianola street scene — 131

32 J. Williamson Moses — 138

35 Frederick Law Olmsted — 150

36 San Antonio street scene — 156

40 Thomas J. Noakes — 172

41 Eli Merriman — 176

42 El Paso Grievance Board — 180

43 Andrew Anderson, Market Hall — 187, 188

44 Sam Houston — 192

47 Henry H. Sibley — 207

49 Battle of Corpus Christi, Francis Richard Lubbock — 215, 216

50 Rosalie Hart Priour — 220

54 Camp Groce — 238

55 Camp Ford "Shebang" — 243

58 George A. Custer — 253

61 Anna Moore Schwien..266
62 Trail Drive...271
63 Stampede..277
65 Belle Starr, Cole Younger.............................285, 287
67 Ruth Dodson..298
68 E. H. Caldwell...301
69 John Wesley Hardin..306
72 John B. Dunn...319
73 Fort Griffin..326
75 John B. Jones...337
77 Dr. Henry F. Hoyt...345
80 Chief Satanta...358
81 Pat Dunn, Ranch House.................................362, 363
82 Quanah, Cynthia Ann Parker.........................369, 370
83 Robert Maudslay..375
84 Geronimo, Fort Sam Houston.......................379, 380
85 Wagon on Reef Road..384
86 Main House at King Ranch......................................386
89 Pasture Windmill..398
90 George H. Paul, Excursion Train....................402, 403
91 Funeral of Quanah Parker.......................................410
92 Pitts Livery..413
96 Nueces Hotel...432
97 Nueces County Courthouse....................................439
98 Don Patricio Causeway..446
100 Fence Post...455

PUBLISHER'S NOTE

Texas has a long and rich history. More books are added every year as historians and scholars contribute their writings to the mix. In addition to these new works, libraries and collections have many old books, which were originally printed in small quantities many years ago. Most of us are unable to read everything written on our state's history, especially these old works. In addition, we tend to specialize in a period, event or locale and never read many books on other Texas subjects. Unfortunately, we miss much of Texas' interesting history with this approach.

Over the last 12 years, I have worked with Murphy Givens to bring South Texas history to print in a total of 13 books. Some were written by others and needed to be edited and published, some were original works and others were compilations of Murphy's newspaper columns. This book is different. It focuses on old Texas histories and brings excerpts selected by Givens to life in one volume.

As I read through Murphy's manuscript, I recognized some of these writings, but most of them were new to me. We believe you will enjoy finding new adventures in Texas history through this volume, the latest book from Nueces Press.

Jim Moloney
Nueces Press

PREFACE

Since 2001 I have written or edited (or co-written and co-edited) 14 books on Corpus Christi area history. The last one was "Streets of Corpus Christi" published in 2019 by Jim Moloney and Nueces Press. Last year, with time on my hands, I began to cast around for a new project. My first idea was to assemble first-hand historical accounts of Corpus Christi by people who were there and could tell what they saw. Well, as every writer and editor will discover, the material sometimes takes over and the author is dragged along, either willingly or by his heels.

In this case, I found myself collecting stories from all over Texas, and even beyond, since Texas stories tend to overlap adjacent states.

What I was not looking for were the big familiar stories of Texas history: the fall of the Alamo, the massacre of Fannin's men, Houston's surprise victory at San Jacinto. I was looking for little unfamiliar stories of the settlers and their way of life on the frontier, of encounters with Indians, of cowboys and Indians and outlaws, stories of the human condition. Mainly, I was looking for stories that appealed to me, that touched my emotions in some way or added to my own understanding of the past.

J. Frank Dobie, who is included in this collection, wrote in his preface to "Guide to Life and Literature of the Southwest" that he was not much interested in what happened in Abilene, Kansas in 1867 when the first Texas herds found a market there, as he was in picking out of Abilene in 1867 some one thing that revealed the character of the men who went up the Chisholm Trail.

That was true for me as I looked for old out-of-print books that had a story worth telling to today's readers.

What I found, to pick and choose from among the 100 selections, were: Jesse Burnam, a militia captain, on setting up an ambush of hostile Karankawas in Austin's colony; Noah Smithwick on how he came to relish horsemeat; Benjamin Lundy on traveling from Monclova, the capital of Texas, to San Patricio; Bigfoot Wallace on surviving captivity by Comanches; John Reagan on the killing of Chief Bowles; James Trueheart on the march to Perote Prison; U.S. Grant on breaking wild mules; Abbé Domenech on the horrific cholera outbreak in 1849; Richard Dodge on a horse race at Fort Chadbourne; Nelson Lee on how he was saved from torture and death by his pocket watch; William Mills on settling differences in El Paso in 1858; R. H. Williams on the dark deeds of the San Antonio Vigilance Committee; Theophilus Noel on Sibley's disastrous retreat from New Mexico; A. J. H. Duganne and Charles Nott on Texas Confederate prison camps; Elizabeth Custer on visiting the deaf institute in Austin; John Wesley Hardin on shooting Jack Helm, "the best act of my life"; Clarence Wharton on how a monument came to be erected to Kiowa chief Satanta; Zoe Tilghman on Quanah Parker's photo of his mother, Cynthia Ann Parker; Owen White on collecting bills at brothels in El Paso; J. Frank Dobie on growing up on his father's ranch in Live Oak County; and, lastly, Roy Bedichek describes the great despoiling of the land of Texas.

The pieces collected for "100 Tales of Old Texas" were taken from 100 sources; readers will find a bibliography near the end of the book. Many fine works of the past are out of print now, unavailable and unknown. Except for the Corpus Christi stories with which I was already familiar, my search for material was conducted in the digital archives, mainly Hathitrust Digital Research Library, a valuable resource.

All the pieces selected have been published in books, magazines or newspapers but are now in the public domain. All included here have been edited, at least minimally, and anyone with the original works will be able to find textual differences. As the editor, I was compelled to take liberties as I struggled to regain mastery of the material. I wish to thank Mary Jo O'Rear, Claude D'Unger, and Jim Moloney for reading the manuscript and offering their valuable suggestions.

—Murphy Givens, January, 2020

1

AMBUSH

Jesse Burnam

SETTLER, MILITIA CAPTAIN

In the war of 1812 I contracted a disease and the physicians advised me to seek a warmer climate. I started from Tennessee with nine families, besides my own, and settled at Pecan Point on the Red River. From there I went down into the interior of Texas. I had three horses and loaded what I could on them, my wife Mary Temperance bringing her spinning wheel.

We got out of bread before we stopped. Being too feeble to hunt, I hired an old man to keep us in meat. I had fixed up a camp so my family could be comfortable. My man failed to kill a deer and we were out of food for two days. I heard one of my children crying from hunger. I had been lying there, hoping to hear the old man's gun. I was still too weak to hunt but I got up and began loading my gun. I didn't feel as though I could walk but I started on my first hunt in Texas. I had not gone far when I saw two deer, a fawn and its mother. I shthe fawn first, knowing the doe would not run far, then I shot and killed her. "Oho!" said I to myself. "Two deer in one day! And on my first hunt!"

I took the fawn to my children and took William, my oldest boy, and a horse after the doe. My wife had dressed a skin and made William a shirt, but it lacked one sleeve, so she dressed the fawn skin that day and made the other sleeve.

We stayed in that camp four or five months then moved down on the Colorado. It was the league Austin surveyed for me, my name being number 13 on the list of Austin's Colony. All the colony had moved further down, so it was the highest point upon the river of any of the settlements, and the most exposed to Indians. All the neighbors moved down for protection, and at last I had to go, but did not stay long. I went back and built a block house to fight from.

We were still out of bread. It had been nine months since we had seen any. A man from lower down the country came up and told me he had corn that he had planted with a stick. There were no plows then in the colony. I gave him a horse for 20 bushels and went 60 miles after it with two horses. I brought eight bushels back. Before I left home, I had prepared a mortar to grind it in and a sieve made of deerskin with holes punched in it and stretched over a hoop.

Our honey we kept in a deerskin, for we had no jars, jugs or cans. I would take the skin off a deer whole, except having to cut it around the neck and legs. I would tie up all the holes very tight and hang it up by the forelegs. We had quite a nice can. We always kept it pretty well filled.

About this time my oldest daughter's dresses were worn out, before we could get any cotton to spin, and she wore dressed buckskin. I had pants and a hunting shirt made of deerskin. My wife dyed the skin brown and fringed the hunting shirt. It was considered the nicest suit in the colony.

The first fight we had with the Karankawas in Austin's colony was in the spring of 1823 at Skull Creek. We were commanded by Bob Kuykendall, who had 18 men in the fight. We killed 14 Indians and wounded seven. We lost not a man in the fight. I killed one Indian and wounded two. I served as a lieutenant under Kuykendall and after two or three months took his place as captain.

A YEAR AFTER the Skull Creek fight, I was informed by Capt. White, an old trader who ran a boat, that there were Indians at the mouth of the Colorado River. He lived at La Bahia and had started from there and embarked at Port Lavaca with his boat loaded with salt to trade for corn. He steered up the Colorado to the Old Landing, just above the mouth. The Karankawas camped there wanted to trade with him.

After leaving his boat at a landing on the river, he went up Peach Creek to the Kincheloe settlement in search of corn. There he told of the Indians being at the mouth of the river. These Indians were hostile to whites.

The settlers at Kincheloe sent a runner to me, 60 miles above, and I got the news as I was on my way to the field to plow. Taking my harness off and putting my saddle on, I was ready in half an hour. Having but two neighbors near me, I left them and went to Judge Cumming's, 15 miles below, and from this settlement I took seven men, half of the men there. I always left half the men at home for protection. I then went to the Kincheloe settlement and from there took five, which gave me 12 men.

In the meantime, Capt. White made a deal to trade his salt for corn, with the corn to be delivered and the salt received at the place where the boat was landed. We started on our trip with each man carrying a sack of corn on his horse, with 60 miles to go. We camped at Jenning's camp, where Capt. Rawls joined me with another 12 men. We rode down to the landing and were very sleepy and tired when we reached it, after traveling 120 miles.

3

Capt. White had agreed to inform the Indians of his return by making a campfire, which was to be his signal to them. He gave the signal about daybreak. I left 12 of my men at the boat, for fear the Indians might come from a different direction, while I took the other 12 and went on foot down the river to the Indians' landing place, a hundred yards below where White was camped.

The sun had been up half an hour when the Indians came rowing up the river. They came slowly and cautiously, as though they expected some danger. The river banks were low, but there was enough brush to conceal us.

As the Indians were landing, I fired on them. This was the signal for my men to fire. My signal shot killed one man and in less than five minutes we killed eight Indians. The other two swam off with the canoe, which they kept between us and them. As one of the Indians raised his head to guide the canoe, he received a mortal shot in the head from one of my men. I returned home without the loss of a man.*

JESSE B. BURNAM was born in Kentucky on Sept. 15, 1892. His father died when he was young and his mother moved the family to Tennessee. When he was 20, he married Mary Temperance Nall. He moved the family to Texas in 1821 and settled in Fayette County, where he established a trading post and ferry on the Colorado River. He led the Austin Colony settlers in action against Karankawas and was a member of the provisional government of the Republic. His wife died in 1833, leaving him with nine children, and he married Nancy Ross, who bore him another seven children. He died on April 30, 1883 and was buried in the Burnam-Smithart Cemetery.

---

* Events cited as justification for Burnam's ambush were related in Henderson Yoakum's "History of Texas" (p. 226) and in W. B. DeWees' "Letters from an Early Settler of Texas" (p. 50).

2

LETTER FROM TEXAS

W. B. DeWees
PIONEER SETTLER

Colorado River, Coahuila and Texas. March 15, 1823.

Dear Friend: — About six months ago, in company with two families, I came to this river in a vast and unknown land. We struck the river at the crossing of the old La Bahia road. Here we found no traces of civilization, nothing to lead us to suppose that the foot of white man had ever trod these plains. Around all was wild, all was silent. Before us flowed the beautiful Colorado, while around us lay the prairies, green and lovely. This is truly an enchanting spot in what looks to be a new country.

On the side of the river opposite us is a high bluff, which at the season of our arrival here was beautiful beyond description. Here the tall green grass was waving in the wind, bent down as if desiring to kiss the water's edge.

The water was low but clear and beautiful. Surrounding this rocky bluff were lofty trees, apparently for miles around. On this side, above us, is a timber country with a high bluff covered with pine. These reminded me of the beautiful high cliffs of the Cumberland River, where I whiled away the merry hours of childhood's days in peace and innocence.

It being late in the evening when we arrived, we immediately made camp. While we were making rations for roasting a piece of venison, we were surprised by the barking of a dog, apparently half a mile above us on the opposite side of the river.

NOT KNOWING WHETHER IT WAS the dog of an Indian or white man, we shouldered our rifles and went up opposite the place from whence the sound proceeded. There we were delighted by the sight of a small log cabin, on the west bank of the river.

We shouted in order to learn who was living there. We ascertained them to be two old adventurers by the names of Buckner and Powell. They informed us that there was no way of crossing the river, but that about 12 miles below, on our side of the river, a few families had settled.

Next morning, we started from the place of our encampment to join these families. Our route lay through a beautiful country, the creeks were bounded by tall cedars, the land was hilly, and well covered with timber.

On our arrival at the settlement we found five or six families., among whom was my old friend, Jesse Burnam, whom I had previously known in Arkansas as well as in Kentucky. Others there were the Gillelands, Kuykendalls and Boatwrights (related by marriage). They were engaged in building cabins. I spent some time looking about the country and hunting.

In a short time after our arrival in this settlement tidings came that a vessel had landed at the mouth of the Colorado. All the crew with the exception of one man had left her and had come up the river searching for settlements. During their absence, the Karankawa Indians attacked the vessel, murdered the guardsman and plundered the vessel of whatever they wished.

We collected all the men we could, and these amounted to about 25, and elected Bob Kuykendall captain and took up our line of march for the mouth of the river. This was the second vessel that had landed at the mouth of the Colorado, with emigrants to Coahuila and Texas. Jennings, Hannah, Massey, and Philip Dimmitt had landed there some time previous, had unloaded their vessel; and taken their goods and provisions 25 miles up the river, where they had built themselves a cabin and stored away their goods. Jennings was dead and the rest of the company had left for the west.

ON OUR WAY DOWN we found three settlers had encamped on the west bank of the river, about 40 miles above the bay opposite the head of a large prairie, which extends from there to the bay. There was an old man by the name of Wilson, with two others, named Moss and Parks, camped together. None of them had any family; Wilson had a few Negroes. They appeared to have plenty of pickled pork, coffee, and such things. We thought this was strange, as they were from Arkansas and had come by land.

We kept on our course till we arrived at the cabin mentioned above, where Dimmitt and company had stored their goods. The Indians had, judging from appearances, been here a day or two previous, had broken open the cabin, taken everything therefrom, forced open boxes of goods, chests of carpenters' tools and farming utensils, and after having destroyed their contents, had left them scattered upon the earth. Barrels of whisky had been rolled out of the cabin and left standing there unopened.

After camping, the captain placed sentinels. We began to feel a little desirous to know what kind of whisky the barrels contained. We removed the bung from one of them and drew some of the whisky and each of us took a sip. Soon a gourd was filled and sent round to the sentinels. The sentinels shortly became querulous, refused to stand guard any longer, and came into camp. The captain, being fond of a wee bit of drink himself, had kissed the gourd quite often and, full of courage, decided we could whip all the Indians in that part of the country, that there was no need for sentries to stand guard, and that we could stay at the fire all night.

WE KEPT UP THE FROLIC till nearly daylight. Some of the company now and then exclaimed that they wished the Indians would attack us, that we might show them how the Americans could fight.

The next morning, we exerted ourselves to continue our course to the month of the river, of course feeling very dull and drowsy.

On arriving at the vessel, we found it had been robbed of a large portion of the cargo. We could find nothing of the body of the murdered man and came to the conclusion that the Indians, who were cannibals, must have devoured it.

We could find nothing of any Indians and no signs of them having been there for several days. Knowing this tribe to be inhabitants of the coast, we supposed that they had fled into the bay in their canoes and escaped out of our reach. On our return we discovered a small trail having the appearance of a slide drawn by a horse, going to and from the vessel.

Being curious to know the origin of this, we followed it down to the bay shore, till we came to a little grove, where we found a large part of the plunder had been secreted.

Knowing that this was not done after the manner of the Indians, our suspicions naturally fell upon those men from Arkansas, whom we had discovered with such large supplies of provisions.

We now gave up the pursuit of the Indians and started for home. When we arrived at Wilson's camp, we interrogated him and his companions about this plunder.

Being unable to obtain from them any satisfactory answer, we continued our journey home.

Upon our return home, some of the men decided to make further investigation of this robbery. They formed a court by electing a magistrate, a sheriff, and other necessary officers. The sheriff was sent down to take the men prisoners. Parks, on being arrested, said if they would not hurt him he would turn evidence and confess the whole matter. The sheriff agreed to this. Parks' evidence was as follows:

Wilson, Moss, and himself had agreed to rob the vessel of what they wanted, believing it would be laid to the Indians, as they had already robbed it of part of the cargo. Wilson was to furnish the horse while he (Parks) and Moss were to do the work. After giving this evidence Parks was released.

WILSON WAS TRIED and sentenced to be sent to the city of San Antonio de Bexar and there deposited in a calaboose to await further trial. Moss being some distance below his cabin the sheriff went for him.

In a short time the sheriff returned alone, stating that Moss had escaped from his custody. But, by the by, he brought with him a fine gold watch, worth $150, which had belonged to Moss. He said Moss had no convenient way of carrying it and had given it to him to carry and then escaped. Moss has not been seen or heard from since.

Moses Morrison, Nelson and myself were selected to convey the prisoner Wilson to Bexar. Wilson was put in irons and we set out for San Antonio. We left the Colorado about 12 miles below the old La Bahia road and took our course through the woods and prairie, intending to strike the San Antonio road where it crosses the San Marcos River. This we succeeded in doing.

After striking the road we got on quite well and in three days entered San Antonio de Bexar. We delivered our prisoner to the proper authorities and saw him safely

Sketch of Military Plaza in San Antonio

lodged in a calaboose. Being very much pleased with San Antonio, we remained there about a week.

San Antonio de Bexar is a very ancient Spanish town, situated in a beautiful plain at the head of the San Antonio River, 150 miles from the coast. It contains about 5,000 inhabitants. The houses are built mostly of stone, one story in height, with terraced roofs. The streets are rather narrow.

There are two large magnificent churches in town. There is a standing army of 1,000 soldiers constantly stationed there. The soldiers are paid every week, and money is more plentiful there than at any place I was ever at.

The population is entirely Mexican, with the exception of three or four French and American merchants. Below the town are missions every three miles for the distance of 15 miles. These missions contain about three acres of land surrounded by a stone wall. In the midst of this stands a large splendid Catholic church. At each mission there is from 100 to 150 inhabitants.

The land in this country is very rich. There is but little timber and the water is not to be surpassed in any country. This part of the country is generally covered with mesquite timber resembling in appearance an old apple orchard. The mesquite grass grows thick and about three feet high, and looks very much like a blue grass pasture.

The Guadalupe and San Marcos rivers are as beautiful streams as I ever saw in my life, and as finely timbered. The river San Antonio is formed entirely from large cool springs breaking out from a small rocky mountain. The whole country for about 20 miles down is irrigated by this river. The water is conducted from the head of the river, on both sides, in ditches through the plantations. In the town it is conducted from the large ditches into smaller ones and carried through every street of the town, so that every garden and every farm can be watered.

WE WERE UNABLE TO CONVERSE with the people of this place, as we did not understand their language, but they treated us with great hospitality.

During our stay in this town, a party of Camanche Indians came into the town on a treaty expedition. They brought in dried buffalo meat, deer skins and buffalo robes, which they wished to exchange for sugar, beads, etc. These Indians were very friendly with the Mexicans, but friendly as they were, they seem to have the Mexicans rather under their control, making them stand back, if any Americans wished to trade with them.

Soon after our return to the Colorado, we learned that Wilson, whom we had lodged in the calaboose, had made his escape. After having rested a few days, we went to the officers of the court, by whom we had been employed in expectation of receiving some remuneration for our services, but to our sad disappointment we found that the property of Wilson had been divided among the officers during our absence and there was nothing left for us, after the other expenses had been paid.

The country through which the Colorado River runs, from here to the mouth, is a very beautiful prairie country. I have only explored the western bank. It is one entire prairie from here to the bay, with the exception of a few creeks. The prairie frequently bluffs up to the river and between these bluffs are rich bottoms of timber, though not extensive. The river empties into the bay of Matagorda, about 45 miles from Pass Cavallo. On the whole, I believe I like this part of the country as well as any I have ever seen. I think I will remain here for some time.

—Yours affectionately,
W.B.D.

————

WILLIAM BUFORD DEWEES was born in Virginia on Sept. 8, 1799. In late 1821 he accompanied a group of four families from Arkansas to the Austin colony; the party arrived on the lower Brazos River on Jan. 1, 1822. On Aug. 3, 1824, DeWees received title to a league of land on the Colorado River about ten miles below Columbus. He later obtained title to a second half league on the west bank and became known as a founder of Columbus. The census of 1825 listed him as a gunsmith and he appears as a blacksmith in the census of 1826. Beginning in 1837 he held a series of public offices in Colorado County, including justice of the peace, associate land commissioner, and associate justice of the county court. DeWees married Lydia Beason, who died in 1849, then married a German immigrant named Angelica Besch. In the early 1850s he collaborated with Emmaretta Cara Kimball Crawford that purported to be a compilation of his letters to a friend in Kentucky. The book of dictated reminiscences was published in 1852. DeWees died in Colorado County on April 14, 1878. A Texas historical marker for DeWees is located on the corner of Bowie and Washington streets in Columbus, Texas.

3

FRESH MEAT

Noah Smithwick
BLACKSMITH

When life in the colonies became stale and not so profitable as I could wish, I sold out my shop at Josiah Bell's Landing and invested the proceeds in tobacco. In company with Joe McCoy, Jack Cryor and John F. Webber we set out for Mexico on a smuggling trip.

We had a thousand pounds of leaf tobacco done up in bales of hundred pounds each, which we packed on mules. The first town we struck on the Rio Grande was Laredo. Some other trader had got there ahead of us and stocked the market. We proceeded on up the river to find new territory.

On the way up one of those inconvenient Texas rains set in and we were compelled to strike camp and cover up our tobacco. We ran out of food. There were no settlements near and no game but wild horses, which the very thought of eating sickened me. There was a prospect of famine, at least for me. The other boys had been in Texas long enough to get rid of any fastidious notions about clean and

Smithwick, blind at age 91

unclean beasts. When provisions ran out, they killed a mustang and were provisioned for a siege. But I turned away from the horse meat with disgust and told them I would rather starve than eat it. I fasted two days and still the rain god, as if enjoying the situation, continued to pour out his moist blessing with no sign of cessation.

On the third day of my fast, I sat hungry and disconsolate by the campfire while Webber was frying out some horse fat to use to grease our packs and lariats. At length, when the fat was all fried out, Webber lifted out the "cracklings," brown, light and crisp, laying them on a rock to the windward of me.

I sniffed the air hungrily. Finally, when I thought the action was unperceived, I reached over and possessed myself of a crackling. I bit off a piece and found that it had no bad taste. On the contrary, it seemed to me that no meat ever tasted better.

My prejudice took wings and I went for a fresh horse steak, which I could scarcely wait to cook, as famished as I was. When I was revived by horse-meat, the boys said I was "broke in." From then on, I ate horse with the rest of them, though I can't say that I should do so of choice.

We sold all our tobacco at San Fernando, getting a good price, $2 a pound for some of it, but with what the soldiers stole and what we spent on expenses, we didn't have more profit than the law allowed to take out duty free. So we had no difficulty leaving the state. Traders who did a large business, though, found the export duty onerous and resorted to many devices to evade it. In due course we reached San Felipe de Austin, no richer than when we left, but wiser, and we had had "heaps of fun."

NOAH SMITHWICK was born in North Carolina on Jan. 1, 1808. He left for Texas when he was 19. He worked as a blacksmith and gunsmith at San Felipe and was in at the birth of Texas. During the revolution, he fought and made weapons for Texas soldiers. He left Texas in 1861, as an opponent of secession, and moved to California. His wife, Thurza Blakey Smithwick, died in 1871. He dictated his memoirs to a daughter shortly before he died. J. Frank Dobie described his book as "the best of all books dealing with early Texas." Smithwick died on Oct. 21, 1899. He was buried at Santa Ana Cemetery in Orange County, Calif.

4

FROM MONCLOVA
TO SAN PATRICIO

Benjamin Lundy
PIONEER ABOLITIONIST

Jan. 23, 1834: I left Monclova, capital of the state of Coahuila and Texas, in the afternoon in the company of Mr. J. Davis and two Mexican servants. Davis is going to La Bahia (Goliad) to purchase some goods. He has nine mules and two horses, in addition to those we ride, and $3,000 in specie. I intend to accompany him to San Patricio on the Nueces.

I saw a wolf on the road two or three miles from Monclova. We camped near the upper part of the Salado River.

Jan. 24: Proceeding on our way, we saw several wolves. About midday we passed a small village called El Tapato. Not long after leaving the village we came to a spring famous for the heat of its waters. It is enclosed in a large stone wall. I could not hold my hand in the water very long, the heat was so great.

Jan. 25: We set off in the morning and turned off from the Santa Rosa cart road, passed between two lofty mountains, and entered the vast plain of the Rio Bravo del Norte, otherwise called the Rio Grande. Here we found immense quantities of flowers — whole acres were thickly covered and as beautiful as any flowerbed I ever saw. We saw today a large brown Mexican tiger.

Jan. 26: The morning being drizzly, we prepared to lay in for a while. The weather continued rainy and we remained for two days.

Jan. 28: The rain having ceased we resumed our journey. We saw deer and rabbits in great number. There was no road, except the numerous paths of the wild mustang. We saw hundreds of these animals at a distance. One fine drove of about 40 passed so near that our loose horses seemed much inclined to join them. We camped for the night in the open plain.

Jan. 29: We saw a large herd of cattle which were nearly as wild as the horses. Before noon we came again to the river Salado and crossed it in a large canoe dug out of a huge cypress tree. Our horses were taken over at a ford some distance below. At a ranch near the ferry we got some good cheese for three cents a pound.

Jan. 30: We proceeded along our way till about four p.m. when we struck the wagon road from La Punto to Laredo on the Rio Bravo. As we approached the Rio Bravo, the land improved in quality. We saw less mesquite and prickly pear and more grass of a very fine quality.

Jan. 31: Last night was the coldest that has occurred since we began the trip. About midday we met a gentleman on the road who told us we were about seven leagues from Laredo. In the afternoon we camped for the night. We have found that horses and mules can't endure hard traveling

Benjamin Lundy, abolitionist from New Jersey

when they are fed on grass only. During the day we saw no animals, except a few rabbits and one large, saucy wolf.

Feb. 1: The land we passed today is beautiful and very rich. At length we came in sight of Laredo and at noon we reached the ferry. We crossed the stream which has as much water as the Ohio below Wheeling. Laredo is a poor-looking
place, with about 2,000 inhabitants. The people are friendly and clever, but not one of them can speak English.

Feb. 2: We left Laredo to strike across the plains in the direction of San Patricio. We were in company with some persons going that way with several mule-loads of sugar which they bought at Monterrey for three cents a pound. It is good brown sugar in rolls. Four men and a boy, with 15 loaded mules, went on before us. We shall have to travel slowly, as each mule carries a load of 300 pounds.

Feb. 3: During the evening our horses were heard running and our people became alarmed, fearing Indians were in the neighborhood. Guns were examined and scouts sent out, but no enemies were sighted. I slept soundly, but I can't answer for the rest of the company.

Feb. 4: We came to a large tract of land which could be well-adapted to farming and grazing. The mesquite growing on it gave the appearance of a peach orchard in New Jersey. I fell into a reverie concerning the future condition of the descendants of Africa.

Feb. 5: It being rainy, we lay by. I am glad that it rains here in the old-fashioned manner, with good big drops. At Monclova there was no rain, just a vague mist under a moist sky.

WHILE DETAINED by the rain, I whittled out buttons from hedge-thorn. It is said that a Yankee can make a wooden clock with his pen-knife. When the weather cleared up, we resumed our route.

Feb. 6: After traveling several miles we ascended a high ridge, about 300 feet above the plain. It is the highest land between the Rio Bravo and Rio Nueces. From its summit, on a clear day, one can see 120 miles. After leaving the mountain, by a gradual descent, we entered a fine rich valley.

Feb. 7: We were detained again by rainy weather. In the two weeks since we left Monclova, we have come 240 Mexican miles. A Mexican mile is about eight percent shorter than an English mile.

Feb. 8: Immense herds of wild horses were seen at a distance today. As we approached their watering holes, the paths were as well-beaten as a public road.

Feb. 9: We had a smart thundershower before daylight and the business of drying out clothes kept us from getting started till nearly noon.

Feb. 10. It is said that we are about 15 Mexican miles from San Patricio. We came to a creek called Duke Agua or sweet water (Agua Dulce), which flows into the Nueces. There was no timber on it, but it was evident that trees would soon grow up if fires were kept down.

It is wonderful to think of the vast quantity of extremely rich land which has been presented to our view in the last few days. It is an enchanting prospect to a northern man, for today, the tenth of February, a great number of flowers overspread the country.

We did not reach San Patricio this evening, owing to the dilatoriness of our company in starting. At length we reached the river Nueces. The timber of the valley of the river is far more abundant than I had anticipated. Many beautiful groves decorate the landscape.

Feb. 11: Having come to the ford opposite San Patricio, we ferried over our baggage and entered the town. We rode through the town and camped a quarter of a mile to the north.

The town of San Patricio is beautifully situated. It is on the east side of the Nueces, a mile from the river. I have rarely seen a prettier location. The place contains about 30 families, nearly all Irish. The houses are composed of pickets with thatched roofs. There are a few blacksmith and wheelwright shops and three or four small stores.

I called on an old gentleman by the name of O'Brien. He came out with me from New Orleans to Brazoria on the schooner "Wild Cat." He and his youngest daughter were all who reached San Patricio out of the 10 persons who left Brazoria. Of the rest, five died of cholera, one became insane, and two others went back to New Orleans.

AT THE REQUEST of my friend O'Brien, I stayed with him for the night. His daughter made us a pot of tea, the first I had seen in a long while.

Feb. 12: I concluded to go with Davis to Aransas Bay, which is 50 or 60 miles from this place. A French gentleman from La Bahia joined us and we went ahead of the muleteers.

Feb. 13: Having crossed the Aransas River, we reached the river of Missions and soon came in view of the church, near which we camped. This is an old deserted Spanish mission. There are half a dozen Irish f**amilies here.

Feb. 16: Having laid by yesterday and the day before, I concluded to go with Davis to Aransas Landing. He expects to purchase goods from two vessels from New Orleans which are anchored there.

We traveled several miles to Copano, or Aransas Landing. The Aransas is a very beautiful bay. I saw there, at the port of Copano, many emigrants, mostly Irish, going to the colonies in the interior. There were also about 20 Indians — men, women and children — of the Karankawa tribe. On one occasion, these Indians brought in a fine deer and sold it to a merchant for two bottles of whiskey, a pound and a half of cheap tobacco, and three or four hard biscuits. They seemed pleased with their bargain.

There were some unanticipated delays and I was obliged to remain at the port of Copano, or Aransas Landing, for 12 days.

Feb. 27: We hoisted sail at three p.m. and the "Philadelphia" got underway.

BENJAMIN LUNDY was an ardent abolitionist and Quaker from New Jersey who visited Texas and northern Mexico with an idea of establishing a colony for fr*ee slaves in the area of today's Corpus Christi. Lundy traveled throughout South Texas in 1833-34. His plan to found a farming colony for free blacks was put on hold during the Texas Revolution. Lundy died on August 22, 1839.

5

DAVID CROCKETT, HOUSEGUEST

John Milton Swisher

SOLDIER, CIVIL SERVANT

After the surrender of General Cos, on Dec. 10, 1835, the main army of Texas was disbanded, leaving about 100 men to garrison the Alamo. In January 1836, David Crockett, who had just left Tennessee and come to Texas for the purpose of assisting the struggling Texans, stayed at the Swisher residence at Gay Hill* to rest after his long journey.

It happened that on the day Colonel Crockett arrived, I had been out hunting with a party of friends and had killed my second — and, I believe, my last — deer. I had it tied behind my saddle when I reached home about nightfall. Colonel Crockett surprised me by coming out and helping genial manner me take the deer down from the horse. He

---

* The settlement of Gay Hill, 12 miles from Brenham, was named for a store owned by Thomas Gay and William Hill. Handbook of Texas.

Col. David Crockett: "He was fond of talking and had a large fund of anecdotes"

inquired in a concerning the circumstances of the hunt and the shooting and complimented me as a young hunter.

In a bantering tone, he challenged me to a shooting match. I accepted, since he offered to shoot "off-hand." My pride swelled and I would not have changed places with the president himself. We tried our skill with the rifle every day he remained with us. My recollection is that we made a drawn match of it. His rifle was ornamented with a silver plate, set into the stock, engraved with the words, "David Crockett." He called it Bessie.

John Milton Swisher from "Swisher's Memoirs"

At the time I saw Colonel Crockett, I judged him to be about 40 years old. He was stout and muscular, about six feet and weighing 180 to 200 pounds. He was of a florid complexion, with intelligent gray eyes, and had small sandy colored side whiskers. Although his early education had been neglected, he had acquired such polish from his contact with society that few men could eclipse him in

conversation. He was fond of talking and had an ease and grace about him,
a strong natural sense, and a large fund of anecdotes. All of which made him irresistible.

During his stay at my father's, it was a rare occurrence for any of us to get to bed before 12 or 1 o'clock, we were so interested in hearing him talk. He talked about himself in the most unaffected manner, without any attempt to display genius or even smartness. He told us a great many anecdotes, which amounted to nothing much in themselves, but his inimitable way of telling them would convulse us with laughter.

He said he never knew why the people of his district elected him to Congress. It was a matter he knew precious little about and had no idea what he would do when he got there. His friends assured him he would soon find out.

Colonel Crockett had not been long in Washington before he found himself famous. Glowing accounts of his great hunting exploits were published and circulated. No less than 20 horses were sold by different dealers, at large prices, upon the assurance that each was the very horse that Davy Crockett had ridden to Washington.

AT THE CONGRESSIONAL ELECTION in 1835, Crockett was a candidate for re-election in his district in Tennessee. Before the election, he addressed his constituents and gave them a full account of his stewardship.

He told them he had served them faithfully and that he was still the same man they had elected the first time, except now he was better qualified to serve them. "If you re-elect me," he told them, "I will serve you to the best of my ability; if you do not re-elect me, you may go to hell and I'll go to Texas." He was defeated and shortly afterward came to Texas.

I shall never forget the day Colonel Crockett left us for San Antonio. We watched him as he rode away, by the side

of his young traveling companion, B. A. M. Thomas —
with feelings of admiration and regret, admiration for the
man and regret that he was leaving us. We little thought
how soon he would perish.

What Texan does not recall, at the mere mention of his
name, the bravery of that great soul at the massacre of the
Alamo? It happened on March 6, 1836, only a few weeks
after he left us.

On that day, a few patriots, surrounded by many
thousands of the enemy, slew ten times their number before
they yielded their own lives. None had even the hope of
escape. Crockett is reported to have been standing calmly,
proudly erect, with his clubbed rifle in hand, dealing death
to the foe with an unerring aim. Indeed.

———————

*JOHN MILTON SWISHER was born on May 31, 1819 in
Franklin, Tenn. He moved to Texas with his family in 1833. In
March 1836, though only 16, he joined Houston's army and
fought at the battle of San Jacinto. He later worked in the
treasury department of the Republic and was clerk of the Ninth
Congress. In the Civil War he served as a Confederate
purchasing agent in Matamoros. Afterwards, he was president of
a stock company for the construction of a street-railway system
in Austin. He married Maria Sims in 1844; she died in 1870. He
married Helen Nickerson in 1873. After she died in 1875, he
married Bella French. Swisher died on March 11, 1891 and was
buried in Oakwood Cemetery in Austin.*

6

FIGHTING AT THE ALAMO

José María Rodríguez
COUNTY JUDGE

My earliest recollection is when I was a boy about six years old. One morning I was going with my father and mother up Soledad Street, where the Kampmann Building is now, and as we got a little further up the street we were stopped by a sentry. There were other soldiers and we saw some breastworks there.

My father told me that General Cos, the Mexican general, was in possession of the town. We went a little further down, where the present corner of Travis and Soledad Street is. We crossed a ditch on a plank and went up Soledad Street to see my uncle, Jose Olivarri, my mother's brother.

I heard a great deal of shooting towards the Plaza and my father told me that General Burleson, of the Texas Army, was trying to capture the city. The next day General Cos capitulated and was allowed to take his arms and leave the city.

Ben Milam was killed at the Veramendi house. The arms the Mexican soldiers had were old English muskets that did not reach over 50 yards. The Texas Army used long-range flintlock rifles. Shortly after that, Colonel Travis was put in command with a small garrison at the Alamo.

Colonel Travis was a fine-looking man of more than ordinary height. I recollect him distinctly from the fact that he used to come up to our house from the Alamo and talk to my father and mother a great deal.

OUR HOUSE WAS the first one after you crossed the river coming from the Alamo. Colonel Travis usually stopped at our house coming and going. He was a very popular man and was well-liked by everyone. My father was always in sympathy with the Texas cause but so far had not taken up arms on either side.

A report came to my father from a reliable source that Santa Anna was starting for San Antonio with 7,000 men, composed of cavalry, infantry, and artillery — a well-organized army.

My father sent for Colonel Travis and he came to our house. My father told him about the coming of Santa Anna and advised him to retire into the interior of Texas and abandon the Alamo. My father told Travis that he could not resist Santa Anna's army with such a small force.

Colonel Travis told my father he could not believe it, that General Cos had been defeated less than three months before and it did not seem possible to him that Santa Anna could have organized such a large army as that in such a short time.

Colonel Travis remained at the Alamo. He told my father, "We have made up our minds to die at the Alamo fighting for Texas." My father urged him again to retire, as General Sam Houston was in the interior organizing an army.

"My father advised Travis to leave the Alamo"

The Mexicans in San Antonio who were in sympathy with the Texas war of independence organized a company under Colonel Juan Seguin. There were 24 in the company, including my father. They joined the command of General Houston. My mother and all of us remained in the city.

One morning early a man named Rivas called at our house and told us he had seen Santa Anna in disguise the night before looking in on a fandango on Soledad Street. My father being away with General Houston's army, my mother undertook to act for us and decided it was best for us to go into the country to avoid being there when General Santa Anna's army came in.

We went to the ranch of Dona Sanchez Ximenez. We left on ox-carts, the wheels of which were made of solid wood. We buried our money — almost $800 — in the house. It took us two days to get to the ranch.

One morning at daybreak, I heard some firing. Pablo Olivarri, who was with us, woke me up and said, "You had better go up on the house. They are fighting at the Alamo." We got up on the house and could see the flash of guns and hear the booming of cannon. The firing lasted for about two hours. The next day we heard that all the Texans had been killed and the Alamo taken.

A few days later, an army of 1,200 men under General Urrea came by from San Antonio on the way to Goliad to attack Fannin. I saw these troops as they passed the ranch.

Not long after Urrea's army passed by, we heard of the massacre of Fannin's army at Goliad. My mother, along with other loyal families, decided to move to East Texas for safety. We started with all our goods and chattels in big ox-carts. The Flores and Seguin families were among those who went with us. Most of us traveled in the carts. Horses were very scarce, the army taking nearly all they could find.

We had gotten as far as the Trinity River on the road to Nacogdoches when we heard that Santa Anna had been defeated. They all returned to San Antonio except for our family. We went to Washington, the Texas capital that was later called Washington-on-the-Brazos, as my father was still in the field with Houston's troops.

———

JOSÉ MARÍA RODRÍGUEZ, the son of Ambrosio Rodríguez and María de Jesús Olivarri, was born on Oct. 29, 1829, in San Antonio. His father left to join Houston's army as part of Juan Seguin's company. As a young boy, he heard the sounds of the storming of the Alamo from a ranch southeast of San Antonio. José María Rodríguez was elected tax assessor and collector for Bexar County and alderman for San Antonio in 1857-58. He moved to Laredo, where he taught school and practiced law. In 1879 he was elected county judge for Webb County, a position he held for 35 years. He married Feliz Benavides and they had two children. He died on Feb. 22, 1913. His book, "Memoirs of Early Texas," was published the year he died.

7

THE RAID ON PARKER'S FORT

James T. DeShields
WRITER

The Parker family moved from Illinois to Texas in the fall of 1833. This family clan settled on the west side of Navasota Creek near the site of the later town of Groesbeck.

The Parker colony consisted of several families: the patriarch of the clan, John Parker, with his wife; his son James Parker, his wife, and four children; another son, Silas Parker, his wife, and four children; another son, unmarried, Benjamin Parker; a daughter, Mrs. Rachel Plummer, her husband L. M. T. Plummer and infant son; another daughter, Mrs. Sarah Nixon, her husband, L. D. Nixon; Mrs. Nixon, the mother of James Parker's wife; Mrs. Elizabeth Kellog, a daughter of Mrs. Nixon; Mrs. Duty; Samuel Frost, wife and two children; G. E. Dwight, wife and two children. A mile away were the homes of old man Lunn, David Faulkenberry and his son Evan, Silas Bates, and Abram Anglin. These families were the advance guard of civilization.

In the spring of 1834, John Parker and his sons and the other colonists put up a wooden palisade for protection against hostile Indians. They called it Parker's Fort.

The struggling colonists tilled the soil and hunted buffalo, deer and turkeys to supply their larders with fresh meat.

On the night of May 18, 1836, all slept at the fort. Next morning, James Parker, L. D. Nixon, and L.M.T. Plummer went to the fields, a mile distant, to work. About nine a.m., the fort was visited by a large force of several hundred Comanche and Kiowa braves.

The Indians halted about 300 yards from the fort, raised a white flag and made signs of friendship. Benjamin Parker went out to them. They pretended to be looking for a place to camp and asked for a beef to eat.

Parker returned to the fort. He said they were hostile and intended to fight, but that he would go back and try to avert it. He went back and was immediately killed. The whole war party charged the fort. Cries and confusion reigned. The bloody tragedy was soon enacted.

Silas Parker fell on the outside of the fort. Mrs. Plummer, fighting gallantly, was knocked down and taken captive. Samuel Frost and his son Robert were killed inside the fort trying to defend the women and children. The elder John Parker, his wife, and Mrs. Kellogg tried to run from the fort to escape. They were driven back and the old man was killed, scalped, and his body mutilated. Mrs. Parker, known as Old Granny, was speared and left for dead; but she was only feigning death. Mrs. Kellogg was captured.

When the attack on the fort commenced, Mrs. Sarah Nixon escaped and ran to warn her husband and the men working in the fields. L. M. T. Plummer mounted a horse and rode to warn the Faulkenberrys, Lunn, Bates and Anglin. James Parker and L, D. Nixon started for the fort, but Parker met his family on the way and carried them five miles down the Navasota and hid them in the river bottoms. Nixon, though unarmed, continued on toward the fort. He met Lucy, the wife of Silas Parker, and her four children. They were soon surrounded by Indians, who compelled Lucy, the mother, to lift up her two older children, Cynthia Ann and John, on to the backs of horses behind two mounted warriors. Indians on foot forced Mrs. Parker, her two youngest children, and Nixon back into the fort.

As the Indians were about to kill Nixon, David Faulkenberry appeared with his rifle. He forced the Indians to fall back. Nixon, after his narrow escape, left in search of his wife. He fell in with Dwight, with his own and Frost's family. Dwight and party overtook James Parker and went with him to the hiding place in the river bottoms.

Mrs. Silas Parker took her two youngest children, carrying the infant and leading the other one, and left the fort with David Faulkenberry. Seeing them leave the fort, the Indians made several feints as if to charge, but Faulkenberry would brandish his rifle and keep them at a distance.

As they were entering the woods, the Indians made another charge. One of them, more daring than the others, dashed up and Mrs. Parker's dog jumped and seized the nose of his horse, and both Indian and horse somersaulted and landed on their backs in a ravine. At that moment, Silas Bates, Abram Anglin and Evan Faulkenberry arrived, causing the Indians to retire.

At twilight, Anglin and Evan Faulkenberry started back to the fort. On their way they saw an apparition in white, which was no ghost but old Granny Parker. She had been speared and undressed, except for her underclothes, and left for dead. She had crawled from the fort.

At the fort they could find no one alive or hear a human sound. The list of those killed included John, Silas and Benjamin Parker; Samuel and Robert Frost. Those seriously wounded included Mrs. John Parker (old Granny) and Mrs. Duty. Those captured included Mrs. Rachel

Plummer and her two-year-old son James; Mrs. Elizabeth Kellogg; and the two oldest children of Silas Parker, Cynthia Ann, nine years old, and her younger brother John, who was six.

Those who had hidden themselves in the Navasota River bottoms were returned to Fort Parker. A burial party from Fort Houston went up and buried the dead.

Of the captives, Mrs. Elizabeth Kellogg soon fell into the hands of the Keechis. She was sold to a party of Delawares who carried her into Nacogdoches and delivered her to the whites. They were paid all they asked, $150.

On the way to Fort Houston, escorted by James Parker and others, they encountered a wounded Indian. Mrs. Kellogg recognized him as the man who had scalped elder John Parker. The Indian was killed on the spot.

Mrs. Rachel Plummer remained a captive for 18 months. Soon after her capture she delivered a baby. Its crying so annoyed the Indians that they brutally killed the infant before her eyes. After this, she was made the personal servant of a cruel Indian woman who continually abused and beat her. One day, the Indian woman tried to hit her with a club and Mrs. Plummer wrenched it from her hand and knocked her down. Indians watching shouted "Bueno! Bueno!" and patted her on the back. She fared better after this and was eventually ransomed, north of Santa Fe, by William Donohue. She was treated like a member of the Donahue family and on a trip to Independence, Mo. with Mr. and Mrs. Donahue she saw her brother-in-law, L. D. Nixon. He escorted her back to Texas.

Mrs. Plummer had not seen her son James since their capture and knew nothing of his fate. She died on Feb. 19, 1839, a year after reaching home. Her son James Pratt Plummer, after six years of captivity, was ransomed and taken to Fort Gibson in 1842. He reached his grandfather's home in 1843 and grew up to be a respected citizen.

Cynthia Ann and her brother John were held by separate bands of Comanches. They soon lost the language, manners and customs of their own people.

John Parker grew up with Comanche boys of his own age. In early manhood, he rode with a raiding party into Mexico. Among the captives taken on the raid was a Mexican girl of great beauty, Dona Juanita. On the trip home, John came down with smallpox and the Indians prepared to leave him behind, in the Llano Estacado, to live or die as fate decreed. The young Mexican beauty refused to leave him and the Indians consented. John was nursed back to health and the two settled down on a ranch across the Rio Grande.

MANY EFFORTS WERE made, without success, to find Cynthia Ann Parker. In 1840, Col. Len Williams, an Indian trader named Stoat, and a Delaware guide named Jack Harry, fell in with Pah'-hah-yo'-ko's band of Comanches on the Canadian River. With this tribe was Cynthia Ann. She was about 14 then and had been a captive for five years.

Col. Williams found the Indian into whose family she had been adopted. He offered to redeem her. The Comanche told him that all the goods he carried would not ransom her. At the same time, Col. Williams said, the fierceness of his look "warned me of the danger of further mention of the subject." But Pah'-hah-yo'-ko prevailed upon him to let them see her. She came and sat down by the root of a tree. They told her of her relatives and asked what message she would send them. She kept quiet and refused to speak.

Some 15 years after her capture, when she would have been 24 or 25, a party of white hunters visited the Comanche encampment on the upper Canadian. They recognized Cynthia Ann and sounded her out about returning to her own people, but she shook her head sadly and pointed, in explanation, to the naked little Comanche children playing at her feet. It was not unexpected, this response of a mother.

On Dec. 18, 1860, Capt. Lawrence Sullivan Ross, better known as Sul Ross, led a command of Texas Rangers and a detachment of Second Cavalry in an attack on a Comanche village on Mule Creek, a tributary of the Pease River.

In the attack, the Comanche chief Peta Nocona, Cynthia Ann's husband, was killed along with many warriors. The attackers captured three Indian women, one of whom, carrying an infant, had blue eyes. Ross told his guide, "Tom, this is a white woman; Indians don't have blue eyes."

Ross suspected she might be the long-sought Cynthia Ann and sent word to her uncle, Col. Isaac Parker, who met them at Fort Cooper. She remembered not one word of English and was dark and thoroughly Indian in gesture and manner. Col. Parker was about to give up and leave when he said, "My niece's name was Cynthia Ann." The sound of the once-familiar name touched a chord and she pointed to herself, saying, "Cynthia Ann! Cynthia Ann!"

She was taken to her uncle's home at Weatherford. Gradually, her mother tongue came back. She was taught to spin, weave, and perform domestic chores. She recognized some people, such as Abram Anglin, who had been a neighbor at Fort Parker. But she yearned to return to her Comanche life and find her two sons, Pecos and Quanah. Her daughter, she knew, had been killed in the raid that killed her husband. She sought every opportunity to escape and had to be closely watched. She died some years after her recapture, preceded in death by her little daughter, "Prairie Flower." Her son Quanah later became the chief of all the Comanches.

––––––––––

JAMES T. DeSHIELDS was born in Louisiana on May 3, 1861. At the end of the Civil War, his parents moved to Texas and settled in Bell County. DeShields collected books relating to Texas history, which led him to write historical articles for newspapers and magazines. He published "Frontier Sketches" in 1883 and "Cynthia Ann Parker" in 1886. He published other books on Texas history in later years, including "Tall Men with Long Rifles." He died in Dallas on Feb. 8, 1948.

8

BACK FROM THE DEAD

Bigfoot Wallace

SOLDIER, TEXAS RANGER

(William Alexander Anderson Wallace — later known as Bigfoot — was a new arrival in Texas in 1837 and "green as a cut-seed watermelon" when he was hired to join a surveying expedition to the wild Palo Pinto country. On the trip, Wallace became separated from the surveying party and was utterly lost, miles from the camp. As he tried to make his way back to the settlements, he was captured by Comanches.)

About daylight I was roused by the furious barking of the dog I called "Comanche." Looking up, I was horrified to see a dozen Indians coming toward me, not more than 40 or 50 yards distant. I seized my gun and sprang behind the tree under which I had been sleeping. As I did so, I saw that I was completely surrounded. There was no chance of making an escape.

I resolved to sell my life as dearly as I could. As the circle of warriors drew closer, I kept dodging from one side of the tree to the other, keeping my gun pointed at those nearest me. Presently one of the Indians — the chief, I suppose — said something in a loud voice. They all halted. He then took a step toward and asked, in the Mexican language, who I was and what was I doing there. I had picked up a smattering of Spanish and by signs and phrases told him I was an American, that I had got lost from my party and was on the way back to the "settlements."

He made signs for me to put down my gun, which I did. As soon as I laid my gun on the ground, the chief took possession of it and others seized my hands and tied them with deer thongs behind my back.

Bitterly did I regret that I had not fought it out. But it was too late to repent and I made up my mind to meet my fate with as much courage as I could "screw up." The dog "Comanche," however, pitched into the whole crowd while they were tying my hands. It was only after they had kicked and beaten him with their spear handles that he gave up the contest and retired to a safe distance in the rear.

The chief ordered one of the Indians to pick up my shot-pouch and other equipment and we all started off at a brisk walk up the river.

We traveled about five miles when the Indians gave some whoops which were answered by similar whoops and we came in sight of the lodges of a large encampment. A crowd of old men, women, and boys came out to meet us. They soon surrounded me, yelling and hooting and, I suppose, calling me all sorts of hard names. I was glad when my guard took me away and escorted me to one of the lodges. They untied my hands and made signs for me to sit down. I took a seat on one of the skins scattered around the floor. I was in no pleasant frame of mind. I was pretty well satisfied that they intended to put me to death.

In a little while an old woman came into the lodge, bringing buffalo meat and a gourd of water, and made signs for me to eat. I had no appetite and took only a sip of water.

Outside the lodge, there was whooping and yelling and running to and fro. Something was up and I was very much afraid it involved me. Things quieted down in an hour or so. My reflections during the night were anything but agreeable, and my sleep was broken and disturbed.

About sunrise the old woman came into the lodge with some provisions, which she placed on the floor. She took one of my hands, rubbed it, patted it, all the while humming in a sort of mournful bumble-bee tone. At length she got up to leave, but before she did so she tried very hard by signs to make me comprehend something. But I couldn't understand what it was.

Not long after she left the lodge, I heard a great "pow-wowing" outside then the most terrible racket commenced that I ever listened to, yelling and whooping and beating of drums and rattling of gourds. After the row began, several warriors came into the lodge. One of them proceeded to blacken my face and hands with a mixture he had in an earthen vessel.

When I was painted in this way, they made signs for me to follow them, which I did unwillingly. I had no doubt they were going to put me to death, attendant with all sorts of tortures.

My guard led me out into a square between the lodges. All the Indians — men, women and children — were assembled. My guards proceeded to bind me hand and foot to a post fixed in the ground. Near me there was a great heap of dry wood and a fire was burning. Twenty or thirty grim warriors stood around, painted and blacked-up in the most fantastic way. With their tomahawks and scalping knives in their hands, I figured they were to act as my executioners.

Bigfoot: "I resolved to sell my life as dearly as I could"

When they fastened me to the stake, the chief who had first captured me made a speech to the crowd. I could understand nothing of what he said, but it seemed to me that he was telling them how the white people had encroached upon them, had stolen their hunting grounds, had driven them far into the wilderness, and that it was a good deed to burn every one of them that fell into their hands.

After he had finished speaking, the painted warriors formed a ring and one of them heaped up the dry wood on all sides of me, as high as my waist. Others danced around me, singing the "death song" and brandishing their tomahawks and knives.

THE PROCEDURES HELD MY UNDIVIDED attention. Sure enough, I thought, my time had come. At this moment the old woman I had seen in the lodge rushed through the crowd and began to throw the wood from around me, all the while talking and gesturing in the wildest manner. One of the warriors grabbed her and by main force put her out of the ring. But she continued to address the crowd and made a regular set speech, and every now and then she would turn and point to me.

She at last, it seemed to me, brought over a majority to her side. After a great deal of jabbering, a number of women rushed in between the warriors and untied me from the stake. I knew that I was saved, brought back from the dead.

I learned afterward that the old woman had lost one of her sons in a fight with some neighboring tribe. She had made a claim to me as a substitute for her loss.

My adopted mother conducted me to her lodge. She patted me on the head and sang another droning bumble-bee ditty over me, to which I made no objection. I was very glad to get off being roasted alive.

The old woman had another son, Lobo-lusti-hadjo, translated as Black Wolf. According to Indian laws he was now my brother, and he proved to be a considerate and kind brother to me as long as I lived with the tribe.

When I had been with the tribe for three months, I longed to be with my own people. I told Black Wolf I was determined to make my escape back to the settlements. Black Wolf cautioned me not to say a word to anyone, and said that he would be sorry to see me go but he would help me all that he could.

One day Black Wolf and I went on a "bear hunt." About 30 miles from the village we camped together that night for the last time. Next morning, Black Wolf traced out on the ground the route I was to follow.

During my stay with the Indians, I had acquired considerable knowledge of the woods and how to steer my course through them, even when the sun was not visible. In eight days after parting from Black Wolf, I arrived safely at the settlements. That ended my first expedition into the wilderness. The dog Comanche lived with me until he died of old age. He left a progeny behind that, for chasing varmints and sucking eggs, could not be beat by any other dogs in the state of Texas.

WILLIAM ALEXANDER ANDERSON WALLACE (Bigfoot) was born in Lexington, Va., on April 3, 1817, the son of Andrew and Jane Ann (Blair) Wallace. In 1836, when he learned that a brother and a cousin had been shot down in the Goliad Massacre, he set out for Texas. In 1840 he moved to Austin then San Antonio. He volunteered for the Mier expedition and was captured and sent to Perote Prison. He later joined Jack Hays' company of Texas Rangers and fought in the Mexican War. He died on Jan. 7, 1899 and his body was later moved to the State Cemetery in Austin.

9

HOG-KILLING WEATHER

Mary Austin Holley
TEACHER, AUTHOR

Jan. 27, 1838, Quintana. Morning too foggy to see the town. Cleared off bright after breakfast. Sun was too hot to walk in. Sat with doors open — went into the warehouse of McKinney & Williams — a spacious place full of goods of every description — New Orleans' prices. Mrs. Thomas F. McKinney's garden is all made — potatoes — peas planted — carrots, cabbages, celery growing.

Had for lunch oysters, very large — even finer than those of Galveston. I love the sea — the open sea — I feel all the time as I sit at the open door and gaze on the perpetual blue and listen to the roar of its breakers.

Three deer were brought in last night. We had venison at breakfast and dinner. Nothing could be finer. One need not complain of fare when tables are loaded with venison, oysters and beef of the finest quality. These meats are exceedingly tender. Smaller game might be had in any quantity, but they do not seem to think it worth the trouble.

They live sumptuously here. All foreign things at command. Strong coffee at rising, breakfast, dinner and supper. London ale and champagne are common drinks. They have a delicious kind of battercake made of equal parts of cornmeal and rice. Breakfast and supper differ very little from dinner.

We crossed over to Velasco, across the mouth of the Brazos from Quintana. Went shopping — they have one store — visited the Archer House, a fine hotel. Large two-story with gallery painted white, looks well. Had a commanding view . . . Looked at the old fort — the work of the Mexicans — Velasco looks quite like a place. The Quintana side is the highest and driest. Crossed the ferry at sunset. It was lovely. A schooner under full sail was crossing the bar. A boat was landing and many people were on the shore. The vast sea all before us — the scene was lovely.

We called at the hotel in Quintana — a spacious good building — and walked on to look at some town lots. Mrs. Perry promised me one. It is her property. There is considerable building and business going on here. Found my satin dress too warm. Took a shawl on our walk which I had to carry on my arm and wished I had left it at home. Met, in our walk, several gentlemen returning from the mouth of the Bernard where they had been all day eating oysters and fish — galloping all the way on the beach — 12 miles.

* * *

FEB. 15, 1838, BOLIVAR ON THE BRAZOS. Had a very cold night with ice. The high grass of the prairie is covered with sleet and looks like a vast field of snow — a sad spectacle here. Has not happened since the winter of 1832.

They are killing hogs today to salt. They always take a cold time to kill hogs and beef so it will keep. They drive

Mary Austin Holley wrote charming letters from Texas

them up and shoot them — having never tasted corn or anything they do not procure themselves, they are invariably fat — fatter than stall-fed.

Feb. 22, 1838, Velasco. Went over to Quintana in the wagon . . . Ball at Velasco this evening — went in a skiff after dark. Returned at midnight — Quite a genteel ball. The first opening of the new house which is in the form of an L — being a long room with wings — one for dancing, the other for supper — at which the ladies, 60 in number, were seated. Supper handsome — dressed cakes and sugar pyramids — other confectionary, oranges brought from New Orleans, much order and taste. The rooms new and painted white, have a neat appearance. The ballroom was brilliantly lighted by rows of sperm candles over the doors, windows and all around. Mirrors were ranged at each end under which were hair sofas. Round the ceiling were flags festooned displaying the Texas Star, which also waved from the center cake on the supper table. Had the music of two violins mingled with the roar of the sea, upon which you look from the gallery of the house.

———————

MARY AUSTIN HOLLEY, born in 1784, married Rev. Horace Holley, a minister at Greenfield, Conn., who died of yellow fever in 1827. They had two children. Mrs. Holley became a governess in Louisiana and visited her brother, Henry Austin, in Texas in 1831 and again in 1835 and 1838. She was a cousin of Stephen F. Austin. Her books based on accounts of her travels give a vivid glimpse of life in Texas in the 1830s. She was called "the first lady ambassador at large" for the Texas Republic. She died of yellow fever on Aug. 2, 1846 and was buried in New Orleans.

10

SNAP JUDGEMENT

John J. Linn
MERCHANT, MAYOR

In the year 1838 Michael Campbell, a native of New York, killed a man in Victoria by the name of Lindsay. Sheriff "Snake" Johnson arrested the murderer. Campbell got a change of venue to Jackson County where, in the absence of a jail, he was chained to the sill of a house.

During the session of the court the jury retired to the shade of a live-oak, which was in close proximity to where Campbell was chained, to consider the evidence and arrive at a verdict in the case. Campbell heard the jurors order a bottle of whisky and saw the sheriff deliver the same. Two of the jurors lay down to sleep and said they would agree to any verdict the others should decide.

Hearing this, Campbell sent for his counsel, Mr. Blow. He instructed him to obtain another change of venue.

He was brought back to Victoria and his trial came on in due course. The prosecuting attorney was John Morris

John J. Linn, mayor and alcalde of Victoria

and Mr. Blow was the counsel for the defense. The jury brought in a verdict of murder in the first degree.

Judge J. W. Robinson proceeded to pass sentence: "Michael Campbell, you have been tried in accordance with
the laws of this country, and the jury has pronounced you guilty of murder in the first degree. Now, therefore, this day, before the setting of the sun, you must die. Mr. Sheriff, take the prisoner and see that this sentence is executed by his being hanged by the neck until dead. May the Lord have mercy on his soul,"

"Judge, you've taken snap judgement of me," said the prisoner.

"No more than you took on poor Lindsay," said the judge.

Old "Snake" Johnson executed the sentence by hanging Campbell from the limb of a post-oak tree on Diamond Hill.

* * *

ONE DAY A TONKAWA Indian known as "Joe" came into my store in Victoria. After a long silence he asked me where I came from. I told him Louisiana. He wanted to know from whom I had purchased my land. When I informed him, he said that the white people were buying and selling the lands of the Indians without any regard to their claim whatever.

God had given this country to the Indians, who originally peopled it, he said. But they would soon be dispossessed of their inheritance. "If I wished to buy something from your store," he said, "I must do so with your consent and pay what you ask. But if a white man's wants a piece of the Indian's land, he goes to another white man and the trade is made."

In essence, in my interpretation, such were the ideas of Tonkawa Joe in regard to the title of property. I confess that when he asked if I thought the course pursued by my countrymen was honest, that I would fain have made some ethical defense, but could only say that I had paid for all I possessed. But to a white man.

―――――

JOHN J. LINN, born in Ireland, moved to Texas in 1829 and settled at Victoria. He built a wharf on Lavaca Bay at a place that came to be called Linnville. He was mayor and alcalde of Victoria. During the revolution, Linn was quartermaster of the

Texas Army and he interviewed the captured Santa Anna, whom he knew. In writing his memoirs, Linn was helped by the expert assistance of historian Victor M. Rose. Linn died on Oct. 28, 1885 when he was 87. He was buried in Evergreen Cemetery, Victoria.

11

A DELIBERATE FALSEHOOD

Z. N. Morrell

PREACHER

In 1838 there were only a few small settlements scattered along the Colorado Valley, 50 miles west of the Brazos. For about 80 miles west of the Colorado, the settlements were smaller and more scattered, as far as Goliad, and beyond this, in a southwesterly direction, there was not a community of civilization east of the Rio Grande. Even Mexicans feared to go through these vast plains, given as they were to various roving tribes of hostile Indians.

A few of us believed that these wild lands would be reclaimed, and, acting under this belief, made preparations to explore the southwest.

I rode 75 miles, alone, to the town of Columbus on the Colorado where I met three gentlemen. It was about the tenth of March. The grass was very fine and we traveled over undulating prairies that lay between us and the Guadalupe River. The largest herds of deer we had ever seen appeared in every direction, as many as one hundred in plain view at a time. We camped near the town of Victoria.

Twenty-fire miles brought us to Goliad. Here stood the breastworks of 1836. The capture and murder of Fannin and his men occurred just two years before. We found at Goliad two or three Mexican families and about as many Irish. I secured use of the old Catholic house of worship and preached to less than a dozen persons. This was the first gospel sermon they had ever heard, and probably the last.

There was no road across the country. The distance to San Patricio was 60 miles. The map of Texas was laid out, the compass was laid on it, and the direction ascertained. The compass chose our path. The land along our route was very rich, but timber and water were scarce.

On the second day after leaving Goliad we saw, for the first time, a herd of antelope. There was no time for a conference over what to do. I had no intention of running my horse after such game, but when my comrades started after them and I saw the elegance with which the antelope moves, the excitement of the chase was contagious. I dropped my baggage and succeeded in cutting off a young one from the main herd. Seeing that it was cut off, it fell down and cried like a lamb. I held the beautiful little animal in my hands and would freely have paid a hundred dollars for the privilege of handing it over to my little daughter at home. We examined it well, and after our curiosity was satisfied, it was released.

It was 60 miles from Goliad to San Patricio, yet, desirous of seeing as much of the country as possible, we traveled to the junction of the Rio Frio and the Nueces. These flow together, both lovely streams, and flow to the gulf under the name of the Nueces.

The junction is about 50 miles from Goliad, and San Patricio is on this river about 50 miles below. We camped at the junction and had the greatest quantity of wild meat at our command. We pushed on to San Patricio to meet a

Rev. Z. N. Morrell, Baptist preacher and Indian-fighter

body of surveyors on their way to this point from Victoria. We arrived in good time and met the surveyors, who numbered eight and there were four in my party.

We examined with interest the village of San Patricio, which was once occupied by Irish settlers. No one had lived there since the campaign of '36, when the Mexican army invaded the country and drove the colonists east.

Corpus Christi was the place where we agreed to pitch our camp. This was simply a name given to a locality on our southwestern coast at the mouth of the Nueces River. We saw no indication of any former settlement at this place. We were informed by an Irishman that it was at this point that the colony of San Patricio received its supplies by ship. We arrived at this point about sunset. In view of the many Indian signs, guards were detailed but little sleeping was done.

The next morning the beginning corner was established, right on the bay, and the surveying work went forward. Every man's gun hung by his side. We were in a country occupied by the most hostile Indians, some of them cannibals, and the nearest assistance, in the event of an attack, was 90 miles away. Each night my party went to some secluded place two or three miles away to camp, while the surveyors camped wherever the work ceased.

Our services not being needed by the surveyors, Uncle Matthew Burnett and I decided to ride eight or 10 miles to the west to examine the country. We traveled leisurely in the direction of a small creek, some six or seven miles, and were suddenly startled by a clear, shrill yell.

LOOKING BACK, we saw 12 Indians on horseback. They halted in full view, spears glistening in sunlight. The nearest timber was four miles off. We, the Indians, and trees each formed one point of a triangle. We knew enough about Indians to know that our safety depended on our reaching the timber. They stood perfectly still, waiting to see which course we would take.

We felt confident we could beat their horses to the timber, except for four, which from a distance looked to be in good condition. If these should get before us, we agreed to fight our way through them to the trees. As we moved off in the direction of the timber, they started for the same point. As I was riding the faster horse, I remained behind Uncle Matthew and we held our horses up for half the distance, determined to put them to full speed at the close of the race.

Every Indian was whipping his pony and every time they yelled, we answered. Before the race was half through, the Indians were scattered. The four good horses out-ran the others by 200 to 400 yards. As we rode up a hill out of the hog-wallow land, the outcome of the race was doubtful. I ran right up by the side of my friend and with my lariat whipped his poor wearied horse with all my might.

The race was close but we passed out a little in advance of the leading Indian and on reaching the timber leaped to the ground and prepared to shoot the leaders. No sooner did we present our guns than shields were thrown up. They leaned over on the opposite side of their horses with only an arm and leg exposed to fire and wheeled out of range. We could have shot one or two but held our fire, knowing that the rest of them would be upon us before we could reload.

They were wary of our guns. They did not come near enough to reach us with their arrows. Every time they made an advance we presented our guns and they fell back. Knowing the Indians could speak Spanish, I addressed them in that language, calling them dogs and cowards. Then I called, in English and Spanish, as if I were addressing a company of men hiding in the woods. They were made to believe that assistance was at hand and they rode away in haste. We were greatly relieved.

The Indians went south. We made our way in the opposite direction back to camp. My mind was not at ease. I had made a willful misrepresentation to the Indians, making them believe other men were at hand. "Lie not one to another" is a plain command and I was plainly guilty of a deliberate falsehood. Our lives were saved, and I hope, in answer to prayer, that God has forgiven me.

Z. N. (WILDCAT) MORRELL was born on Jan. 17, 1803, in South Carolina. He moved his family to Texas in 1836 and farmed at the Falls of the Brazos. Morrell fought in the battle of Plum Creek and rode with Jack Hays. He founded one of the first Baptist churches in Texas and, it was said, never missed an opportunity to preach a sermon. He married Clearacy Hayes and they had four children. She died in 1843. He died in 1883 and was buried at the First Baptist Church of Kyle. In 1946 his body was moved to the State Cemetery in Austin.

12

THE DEATH OF CHIEF BOWLES

John H. Reagan
POLITICIAN, BUREAUCRAT

In June 1839, Mr. Lacy, who was the Indian agent for the Cherokee tribe, which was then occupying the territory now known as Smith and Cherokee counties, was the bearer of a communication to Chief Bowles from Mireabeau Lamar, who had been inaugurated president of the Texas Republic on Dec. 10, 1838. W. G. W. Jowers and I accompanied Mr. Lacy, the agent.

When we reached the residence of Chief Bowles, he invited the agent, the interpreter, Jowers and myself to a fine spring near his house. He and others in his tribe seated themselves on a fallen tree. The president's message was read and interpreted by a half-breed named Cordray.

In his communication, President Lamar cited a number of offensive acts committed by the Cherokees. One was that the Cherokees had assembled a force on the San Antonio Road, east of the Neches River, when the people of Texas were flying to escape Santa Anna's army, for the purposes of attacking the Texans if Santa Anna should be successful. Another indictment was that the Cherokees had massacred a number of white people and stolen the horses of the Texans. It was further recited that Edward Burleson had captured some Mexican officers and Cherokees on their way from Mexico to Chief Bowles, carrying to him a commission as a colonel in the Mexican Army and instructions for his participation in a combined military action against the Texans in the coming spring.

Lamar said Texas could not permit such an enemy to live in the heart of the Republic. He said the Cherokees must relocate north of the Red River, either peaceably or by compulsion.

Chief Bowles, in the conversation that followed, said that he could not make a definite answer as to leaving the country until he could consult his chiefs. It was agreed that he might have 10 days for such a consultation.

At the end of that time, Dr. Jowers and I again accompanied Mr. Lacy and his interpreter to the residence of Bowles. The chief of the Cherokees said his young men were ready for war, that they believed they could whip the whites. He said that all the council was for war, except for himself and Big Mush, one of the chiefs. He said he knew that in the end the whites would win but that "it will cost you a bloody frontier war for 10 years."

Bowles said that while he did not concur in the judgement of his tribe, he had led them many years since separating from the main tribe of the Cherokees, first in Lost Prairie, Ark., and afterwards at the Three Forks of the Trinity, the country now surrounding the city of Dallas. He said that he had tried to hold that country for his tribe but other Indians claimed it as a common hunting ground and in the course of three years they had killed about a third of his warriors. Then, with the consent of Mexico, he had settled near the Spanish fort of Nacogdoches. He declared

Reagan when he was postmaster general of the Confederacy

that Gen. Houston had confirmed the Cherokees' right to that country by treaty.

Chief Bowles asked for time for his people to make and gather their crops, but was informed by Mr. Lacy that he had no authority to act outside of the scope of the letter by President Lamar.

Bowles said that if he fought, the whites would kill him. If he refused to fight, his own people would kill him. He added that to him personally it mattered little, that he was 83 years old and by the laws of nature could live but little longer. But he felt a great interest in the future of his wives (he had three) and his children. His tribe, he said, had always been true to him and though he differed with them in opinion on this particular issue, he would stand by them. The council ended with the understanding that war would follow.

These conferences produced a strong impression on my mind, for two reasons. The first was that neither the agent, Lacy, nor the chief could read or write, and neither spoke the language of the other. The second was the frankness and dignity with which the negotiations were carried out — neither tried to disguise his purpose or mislead the other.

The two armies now began to assemble. General Rusk's regiment of volunteers moved up to within six miles of where the Indians were in camp under Chief Bowles (below today's city of Tyler).

The leaders soon agreed on a neutral line, which was not to be crossed by either side, and that neither party was to move without giving notice to the other.

The Texans were buying time so that Gen. Edward Burleson's regiment of regulars and Landrum's force of Red-Landers might come up. Bowles was also seeking delay to give time for warriors from other tribes to reach the front.

After the arrival of Burleson and Landrum, the question arose as to who would be in command, either Gen. Rusk or Gen. Burleson. The volunteers wanted Rusk and the regulars wanted Burleson. These two men refused to antagonize each other and by common consent it was agreed that Kelsey Douglass, commander of the militia in that region, would assume the responsibility.

AT SUNRISE on the morning of July 15, John Bowles, a son of Chief Bowles, and a half-breed interpreter named Fox Field, rode into camp under a flag of truce. John Bowles notified Gen. Albert Sidney Johnston, Secretary of War of the Republic, who was with us, that he had a message from his father. He told Johnston that the Cherokees would break camp that day and move west of the Neches River. Gen. Johnston thanked him and observed that Chief Bowles had acted honorably in giving notice of his move. Johnston requested him to tell his father that the Texans would give pursuit. Bowles and Field were escorted half a mile beyond our pickets.

Texas forces crossed the Neches and scouts were sent forward with instructions that if they came up with the Indians to open fire at long-range so as to keep the Texans advised of the position of the enemy.

The Indians occupied the bed of a dry creek which ran north to south then turned east. Just above this bend was a prairie bottom half a mile long. Near the lower end of the prairie, parallel with the creek, was a thick growth of hackberry.

When the firing of our scouts was heard, Burleson's regiment crossed the creek below the bend, and moved toward the rear of the line of the Indians, who were posted in the creek bed above the bend. Rusk's regiment, to which I belonged, wheeled to the right and in front of the line of the enemy.

As David Kaufman and I were riding, at the lower end of the thicket, an Indian rose up and fired. Kaufman and I chased him until he jumped into the creek.

We headed our horses between the thicket and the creek and ran the gantlet of fire from the Indians, but neither of us were hurt. As we were coming to the head of the thicket, Dr. Rogers of Nacogdoches was hit by three shots and killed. We lost six men killed and several more wounded in this engagement. The Indian loss was much greater and they retreated. We learned later that only part of the Indian warriors were engaged.

WE CAMPED ON the battlefield and next morning, July 17, we encountered the enemy in full force near the Neches.

Chief Bowles displayed great courage in these battles. In the second engagement on July 17, he remained on the field on horseback, wearing a military hat, a silk vest, and handsome sword and sash which had been presented to him by President Houston. He was a magnificent picture and very conspicuous during the whole battle. He was the last to leave the field when the Indians retreated.

His horse was shot from under him and he dismounted, after having been wounded himself. As he walked away, he was shot in the back and fell. Then, as he sat up, with his face toward us, I started toward him to secure his surrender. At the same time, my captain, Bob Smith, from further down the line, ran toward him with a pistol in his hand.

We reached him at the same instant. Realizing what was imminent, I called, "Captain, don't shoot him." But he fired at once, striking Bowles in the head and killing him instantly. I had been so impressed with the manliness and dignity of Chief Bowles that I did not want to see him killed. I would have saved his life if I could.

JOHN H. REAGAN, born on Oct. 8, 1818, in Sevier County, Tenn., arrived in Nacogdoches in 1838. He became involved in the Cherokee campaign in which Chief Bowles was killed. Reagan worked as surveyor before being elected captain of a militia company in Nacogdoches. In 1846 he was elected county judge of Henderson County and later elected to the state Legislature then to Congress. After secession, Reagan was appointed postmaster general of the Confederacy. He returned to his home at Palestine after the war. In 1875, he was elected to Congress then to the Senate in 1887. He left the Senate to become the first chairman of the Texas Railroad Commission. He was married three times, to Martha Music, who died in 1845; to Edwina Nelms, who died in 1863; and to Molly Taylor, who survived him. When he died on March 6, 1905, the entire Texas Legislature attended his funeral.

13

GEN. LAMAR DID NOT
DANCE WELL

Mary Maverick
DIARIST

President Mirabeau Lamar with a very considerable suite visited San Antonio in May 1841. A grand ball was given in his honor on May 17 in Mrs. Manuel Yturri's long room — (all considerable houses had a long room for receptions). The room was decorated with flags and evergreens; flowers were not much cultivated then.

At the ball, Gen. Lamar wore very wide white pants which at the same time were short enough to show the tops of his shoes. He and Mrs. Juan Seguin, wife of the mayor, opened the ball with a waltz. Mrs. Seguin was so fat that the general had great difficulty in getting a firm hold on her waist, and they cut such a figure that we were forced to smile.

Gen. Lamar was a poet, a polite and brave gentleman,

and a first-rate conversationalist. But he did not dance well.

At the ball, Jack Hays, Mike Chevalier and John Howard had but one dress coat between them, and they had agreed to use the one coat and dance in turn. The two that were not dancing would stand at the hall door, watching the happy one who was enjoying his turn — and they reminded him when it was time for him to step out of that coat. It was great fun watching them and listening to their wit and mischief as they made faces and shook their fists at the dancing one.

Mrs. Yturri had a new silk dress fitting her so tightly that she had to wear corsets for the first time in her life. She was very pretty, waltzed beautifully, and was much sought as a partner. She was several times compelled to escape to her bedroom to take off the corset and "catch her breath" as she said to me who happened to be there with my baby.

DEC. 7, 1844: WE TRAVELED seven miles to Decrow's Point on Matagorda Peninsula, still in a brisk norther, but delighted to arrive at our journey's end and have rest once more. We moved into a house occupied by Judge and General Alex Somervell, of Mier fame. The arrangement was that we should keep house and furnish them board, they to retain a portion of the house.

Gen. Somervell was the collector of revenue for the port. The house was very close to the bay, and every evening Mr. Maverick took me down to bathe in the saltwater.

A few days later I had the pleasure of an introduction to His Highness Prince Carl of Solms-Braunfels, son of the Grand Duke of Braunfels, and who was on his way to the Colony of New Braunfels of which he was the founder. The Prince and his suite spent a day and night with us and the Somervells.

Next evening, he came near to land in his vessel and serenaded us. Gen. Somervell was a noted laugher — he saw the prince's two attendants dress His Highness. That is, they would lift him up into his pants. Gen. Somervell

Mary Maverick and her children

was so overcome by amusement at the sight that he broke into one of his famous fits of laughter, which could be heard all over Decrow's Point. The Prince and suite were all very courteous and polite to us. They wore cock feathers in their hats and did not appear quite fitted to frontier life in Texas.

———————

MARY ANN ADAMS MAVERICK was born on March 16, 1818 on her father's plantation near Tuscaloosa, Ala. On March 4, 1836, she married Samuel Maverick and the couple moved to Texas. They settled at San Antonio, stayed for a time on Matagorda Island, then returned to San Antonio. Mary Maverick kept a diary and used it to write her memoirs. She died on Feb. 24, 1898, and was buried in San Antonio's City Cemetery No. 1.

14

CAPT. DENTON'S GRAVE

Andrew A. Davis
METHODIST MINISTER

In the spring of 1841, the campaign was made in which John B. Denton was killed. The company was made up of General (Edward H.) Tarrant, a lawyer, Colonel Coffey, James Bourland, William Bourland, Mack Bourland, Colonel Porter, Henry Stout, Dick Hopkins, Capt. Denton, Clabe Chisum, J. L. Lovejoy, Colonel Bill Young, and Captain Yeary. These are sufficient. Many of the other names have faded from my memory. I was 14 years old then, a young boy mounted on a mule, at the time of the campaign.

On the day before the taking of the Indian village, a lone Indian was seen and Gen. Tarrant divided the company and ordered the men to cut off the Indian from the timber and to capture him. This was quickly done. The capture of the Indian occurred on the prairie 10 miles west of the village, at a point not far where Fort Worth is located today. Gen.

Tarrant took the company off the prairie and into a secluded place on the river. There we remained all night.

About sunset preparations were made to kill our prisoner. His hands and feet were tied behind to an elm tree. Twelve men with their guns were ordered to take their positions as a firing squad.

THE SCENE WAS an awful one. The men were ordered to present arms and at this moment the alarmed man, looking as apologetic as any Indian could, said something that sounded like, "Oh, man! Oh, man!" While he did not utter those exact words, what he said was more like them than anything else. The meaning was clear.

Gen. Tarrant told Capt. Yeary and an interpreter to see if the Indian would reveal anything. Prior to this, he had been sullen and would not say a word. He was made to understand that if he would tell where the Indian village was located, he would not be hurt. He made a full revelation and said, "We be friends." He was untied but kept under guard. After dark, Tarrant sent 10 men under Henry Stout to reconnoiter the village and to select the best point of attack.

This was done and by daylight we were heading for the village, which we reached about nine o'clock in the morning.

From our position we could see the Indians passing about in every direction. We were ordered to deposit our baggage and get ready to charge in five minutes. When the time was up, Gen. Tarrant said, "Are you ready?" The response was in the affirmative and Tarrant said, "I shall expect every man to fill his place and do his duty."

The command to charge was given. A level prairie, about three hundred yards wide, lay between the company and the first huts. The distance was covered in less time than I am using in telling it. In a moment the gunshots rang out over the cries of the alarmed and terror-stricken inhabitants of that Indian city in the wilderness.

Tarrant, James Bourland and Denton led the charge. Every other man followed with the best speed his horse would make. I was riding a mule given to me by Aunt Gordon, my friend at the orphanage (God bless her memory). That mule was a mule and, true to its kind, was slow and lazy, which made me among the last to reach the enemy.

As I passed the first huts, I saw to my right a number of Indians. I fired into them with the best aim my excited nerves would allow. In a moment, our men came upon them from a different direction and for a short time the work of death was fearful. My lazy mule was shot from under me. I felt like I had lost my best friend.

The air was full of bullets and I took to a tree. In a moment I saw a number of our men on foot, some of them by choice and some of them like me because they could not help it. I left my tree and joined them. In less than an hour the village was cleared of Indians. It seemed like the work of death was done.*

We were covered with dust and dirt, wet with sweat, and famished. Tarrant called the company together at a little spring. On roll call it was found that not a man had been killed. A dozen, perhaps, had been unhorsed. A number were hatless and some eight or 10 men were slightly wounded, but none in a painful manner.

Tarrant told the men to go to the Indian huts and look for dried buffalo meat. My, my, how that buffalo meat was used up by these hungry men. After 15 minutes, Tarrant called the men together and ordered Henry Stout and John B. Denton to take 20 men each and pressure the retreating Indians. A great number of them had fled into the Trinity River bottoms by two paths leading out of the village.

---

* In the battle of Village Creek, fought on May 24, 1841 on a small tributary of the Trinity River, three Indian settlements were destroyed. Most of the battlefield site lies under the waters of Lake Arlington. Handbook of Texas.

I fell into the squad commanded by Capt. Stout, who took one trail and Capt. Denton and his men took the other. About 60 yards from the river, the two trails came together. At this point, Capt. Stout brought us to a halt and said it was too dangerous to take a small squad of men into the cottonwoods by the river. We heard the sound of horses and Capt. Denton and his men rode up.

Denton said, "Captain, why have you stopped?" Stout repeated what he had told the men. Without a word, Denton spurred his horse on into the path. Stout followed and we all moved towards the river.

A well-worn buffalo trail led down into the river. The northern bank of the river was high and covered with brush. Here the Indians were hidden, waiting for us.

WHEN THE COMPANY reached the point opposite, the Indians opened a deadly fire. Capt. Stout was wounded and had his arm broken.

The scene of death was awful to endure. Capt. Yeary shouted, "Why in the hell don't you move your men out to where we can see the enemy? We will all be killed here."

The men began to retreat and Stout recovered enough from his shock to tell the men to do the best they could for themselves.

About this time someone said, "Capt. Denton is killed." The shot was so deadly there was no death struggle. He had balanced himself on his horse, raising his gun to fire, when he was hit and instantly killed. The men took him from his horse and laid him on the ground.

We returned to the command at the Indian village. We feared that after we left that the Indians would scalp and mutilate the body of Capt. Denton. But this was not done. A squad was sent back to the river to retrieve Denton's body. I was one of the volunteers who went.

About 4 or 4:30 p.m., the command moved out from the village with 80 horses and some 15 or 20 head of cattle taken from the village.

We moved up the river to a point not far from where Fort Worth stands today. There we spent the night. Early next morning we crossed the river and traveled in the direction of Bird's Station, aiming for Bonham. At about 11 a.m. we halted on the prairie on the south side of a creek with a high bank on the north side. Here Capt. Denton was buried.

I have never for a moment doubted that I could find the identical spot. The tools with which the grave was dug were brought from the village and were ample for the purpose. If any person has found a shallow grave and is of the impression that it is Capt. Denton's he is mistaken. His grave was dug to a good depth. A thin sheet of rock was cut so as to fit in the bottom of the grave and similar rocks were placed on either side and at the head and feet. Another rock was placed on top of the body and the earth was filled in. We rode away, quiet and thoughtful, after burying one of God's noble men.

ANDREW A. DAVIS was born on March 10, 1827, the son of Nancy (McKelvey) and Daniel Davis, in Red River County. After the battle of Village Creek, in which he participated in 1841, he entered McKenzie College and on Oct. 12, 1844 was licensed to preach in the Methodist Church. In 1847 he married Mariah Samantha Lynn at Clarksville. He served in various circuits in Northeast Texas and at one time was a trustee of Southwestern University. Davis died on Feb. 13, 1906 and was buried in Oakwood Cemetery in Corsicana.

15

A PLACE OF SOME IMPORTANCE

William Bollaert
CHEMIST, TRAVELER

March 23, 1842. I accompanied Capt. Wade and others on the "Washington" to Corpus Christi. The wind blew hard from the southeast. Arrived at 3:30 p.m. It is high bluff land, with muskit (mesquite) timber. Messrs. (Henry) Kinney and (William) Aubrey are the principal traders here. Their log house is fortified and they have a piece of artillery.

We learned that Carnes (Karnes) and his party had been for some time past doing military duty here, but had left for San Patricio where they were surprised and murdered by the Mexicans, with (Ewen) Cameron alone escaping. We found that Cameron went off to join the volunteers. This spot at the present may be looked upon as a good point for trading with Mexico. When the question is settled between the two countries (Texas and Mexico), then Corpus Christi will become a place of some importance.

* * *

Sept. 20, 1843. After visiting the church of San Antonio, towards sundown I accompanied Major John Coffee Hays a few miles from town down the river to his encampment preparatory to starting westward. Here was found Hays' "spy company" busy preparing supper — plenty fine beef, cornbread, coffee, and with the luxurious addition of sugar. Over our pipes a few songs were sung, the blanket was spread, and then to sleep.

* * *

JAN. 2, 1844: I ATTENDED the marriage ceremony of a runaway match at Huntsville. The bride and bridegroom had ridden some 15 miles full tilt, the bride was deposited with a friend, the bridegroom posted off to the deputy county clerk for a license which cost only one dollar.

And now behold them before, or rather by, the bedside of Judge K———, who is almost bedridden. A certificate was handed to the judge by the deputy county clerk, purporting that she was over 18; she took the oath to that effect, when the judge, after examining the marriage license, asked them if they wished to be man and wife, and then after asking them this separately, to which they nodded assent, the judge concluded that, "What God hath joined, let no man put asunder," and they were married. In a few minutes the married, and, I hope, happy pair mounted their horses and off they went to the bridegroom's log cabin.

———————

WILLIAM BOLLAERT, an English visitor, spent two years traveling in Texas, from 1842 into 1844. Bollaert was educated as a chemist but was known as a keen observer. He died in 1876.

16

THE MARCH TO PEROTE

James L. Trueheart
DISTRICT COURT CLERK

(James L. Trueheart was clerk of the district court in San Antonio when those at court was captured by Mexican troops under Gen. Adrian Woll. Trueheart was taken to Mexico with other prisoners and held for two years in Perote Prison, where he kept a diary that chronicled the march from San Antonio to Perote and the hardships endured by the Texas captives. After he was released in 1844, he again became district court clerk in San Antonio.)

Wednesday, Sept. 14, 1842. We were informed that tomorrow we leave for the Rio Grande.

Thursday, Sept. 15. Application was made to Gen. Woll to allow every person to ride his own horse, to which the general consented. I signed a document pledging not to attempt to escape between Bexar and the Rio Grande. I much regretted this later. John Johnson was released, on account of his youth. Antonio Menchaca's release was brought about by his family. We rejoiced about it; his conduct throughout the whole affair has been that of a true Texan.

An hour before sunset we were marched out of our rooms, two and two, each person carrying his baggage on his back.

After a delay of 30 minutes, we were ordered to march. The officer in charge of the march is Capt. Emeterio Pasas. We passed by Gen. Woll's quarters. Many of my companions were compelled to walk, not being provided with horses. We camped the first night two or three miles from town. We were closely watched.

Friday, Sept. 16. Prisoners with their own horses were soon deprived of them and given poor animals in their place. It was provoking to see the Mexican officers riding their fine horses while we were mounted on decrepit mules. We reached the Medina River and camped, after a long day's march.

Saturday, Sept. 17. We made an early start. J. R. Cunningham, sick with fever, fell from his horse. He was placed in one of the carts with wounded Mexican soldiers. We reached the Seco about eight o'clock at night.

Sunday, Sept. 18. A little after dark we got to the Rio Frio and camped. It was here that Cunningham was last seen by his companions.

Monday, Sept. 19. After we had proceeded four or five miles, I remembered having left my money where I had slept. I got permission to return and look for it. I found it under a bunch of grass where I had left it.

We crossed the Nueces and made camp. We passed a very disagreeable night on account of continual rain. Capt. Pasas seems very uneasy about us, fearing we might try to escape. He was up repeatedly during the night to see that everything was all right.

Tuesday, Sept. 20. Several Mexican carts broke down and were left behind. Most of the prisoners were in fine spirits, believing their captivity would be of short duration.

Wednesday, Sept. 21. It rained before daylight. We made an early start on account of the rain. The weather soon cleared and we had a beautiful day. We came within sight of the Rio Grande.

A Mexican soldier trying to catch a rattlesnake was bitten on one of his toes. Dr. Booker scarified the bite. The soldiers have killed many rattlesnakes, among the largest I have ever seen. They are much pleased with the sport.

Thursday, Sept. 22. We reached the Rio Grande del Norte, sometimes called Rio Bravo. We stopped under a large pecan tree, where we rested and cooked something to eat. We were permitted to bathe in the river, a source of much pleasure to us. We commenced crossing the river in dugouts and canoes, each man carrying his own baggage. The horses got across safely, except for two or three which drowned. At sunset we moved to the top of a hill and camped in a sheep pen.

Friday, Sept. 23. We arrived at the Presidio de Rio Grande and were formed up in the square in front of a large crowd of citizens who were anxious to see the Texas prisoners. We were taken to an old dilapidated building on the square. Presidio de Rio Grande is going to decay and appears to be a miserable place. We remained in Presidio several days.

Tuesday, Sept. 27. About eight o'clock we left Presidio, with a great crowd following us along the street. We passed over a beautiful country, with a large cornfield that stretched as far as the eye could see. We reached San Juan de Nava about four o'clock and were quartered in a granary. Houses here were indifferent, made precisely of mud.

Wednesday, Sept. 28. The country we traveled through was beautiful. We crossed a dry creek, called Agua Verde,

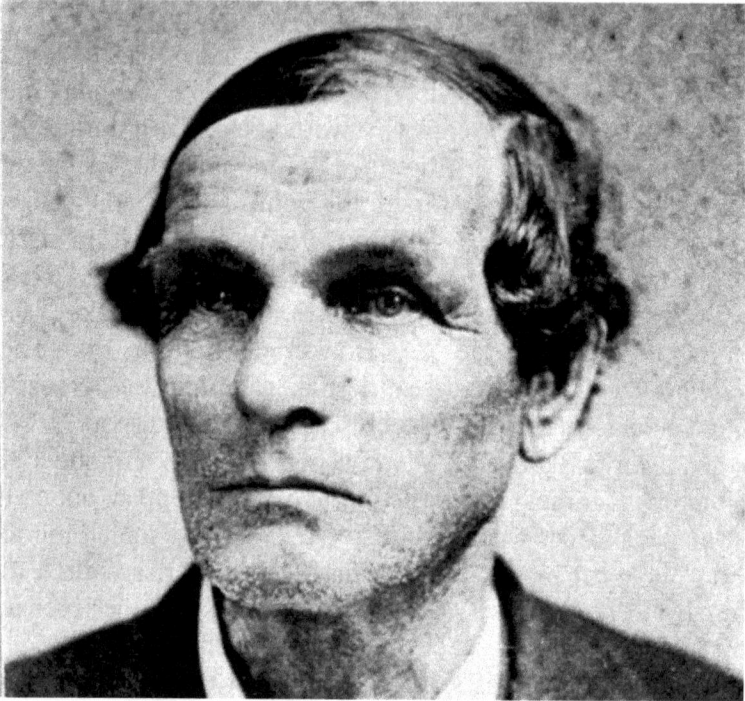

James L. Trueheart: The captives were in fine spirits

by which the town beyond (San Fernando) is also
sometimes known. We were met by a crowd of men and
women. The window as we passed by his quarters.

commanding general of the place peeped at us through his

I had loaned two dollars to one of the officers and by
repeatedly dunning him I got one back. I learned from one
of the soldiers that J. R. Cunningham had died on Sept. 19
and was buried on the west bank of the Leona.

Friday, Oct. 7. After more than a week at San Fernando,
we were ordered to leave our quarters. We marched out of
town the same way we had entered. We passed through
Morelos, in a very fertile country, and finally reached San
Juan de Matas at three o'clock in the afternoon. This
village was in the loveliest valley I had seen since we left

San Antonio. At San Juan de Matas, we saw several Negro fugitives from Texas.

Saturday, Oct. 8. We got up early to prepare to march. A severe norther started to blow at daybreak, with drizzles of rain, making it cold and disagreeable. Our quartermaster gave us a bag of biscuits, which we divided among the men.

On the edge of the valley, we saw a small collection of Negroes working in a cornfield. A very tall Negro man stretched himself to his full height and abused us with taunts. "Oh, white man! You are catching hell now!" There was much force in his remarks. No one replied.

The countryside was beautiful until we reached the mountains. The road consisted of going up and down. The route was rocky and destitute of vegetation.

WE CAME TO Rosita, a dry creek, where we camped. It again commenced to blow and rain and we passed a miserable and disagreeable night. Many prisoners remained awake, trying to amuse themselves, which was believed by Capt. Pasas to mean that we were planning an escape. It made him very uneasy. He stayed up all night, watching and reconnoitering the camp. As to our treatment on the march, we had nothing to complain of regarding the officers, but the soldiers were of the most insolent and villainous character and used every opportunity to mistreat us.

Sunday, Oct. 9. We were blessed with a fine day. By the middle of the day we were clear of the mountains and in sight of the Sabinas River. We reached a small stone ranch house about sunset, where we camped. One of the prisoners amused the residents of the place by hooting like an owl, for which he received bread and other gifts.

Monday, Oct. 10. We moved up the Sabinas and crossed the same way we crossed the Rio Grande.

Tuesday, Oct. 11. We traveled down the river 10 or 12 miles. I was quite indisposed, with my nose frequently

Perote Castle was used to incarcerate Texans and other miscreants

bleeding. In whatever direction the eye turned could be seen mountains. About five o'clock we reached a hacienda on the Salado, in a beautiful and fertile country.

Wednesday, Oct. 12. We crossed the Salado, having in view the next hacienda where we were to stop. The hacienda was called Las Animas. I was very much struck with the beauty of this hacienda. Capt. Pasas had sent ahead to have a beef butchered by the time we arrived. The beef had not been brought up and butchered. Capt. Pasas sent for the alcalde and there was a lengthy and loud altercation that afforded us with some amusement.

Thursday, Oct. 13. We started early and soon reached the pass in the mountains. We crossed a small stream filled with sulphur water, which was quite warm, making it disagreeable to drink. By the middle of the day we reached a hacienda and were conducted to a large yard surrounded by a rock wall. This was a sheep ranch, having on the place, we were told, 200,000 head.

While at the hacienda one of the prisoners and a Mexican commenced dancing to see who could out-dance the other. A crowd of Americans and Mexicans gathered to see the contest. Both dancers exerted themselves to the intense enjoyment of the spectators. The American, finding that he was about to be beaten, stopped dancing, clapped his hands, and crowed like a rooster. The way the Mexican dancer outdid one of us afforded great mirth to the bystanders.

Saturday, Oct. 15. We reached Monclova today at 3 p.m. The streets were filled with spectators. You could hear them, as we marched along, making observations about us. We stayed in Monclova two days to rest. Monclova is badly built, the houses being generally of mud. The town was, for a long time, the capital of Coahuila and Texas.

Tuesday, Oct. 18. We were on the march before dawn. We met some 15 carts returning from the fair at Saltillo. At length we came in sight of where we intended to pass the night. On arrival we were placed in a cow pen. The weather threatened and we passed a cold and disagreeable night.

* * *

THURSDAY, NOV. 12. WE ARRIVED today at the hacienda Represada, a very ordinary hacienda, where the lady who attended a store entertained us by playing her guitar. One of our party presented those present with a bottle of liquor. As soon as that was drunk, Capt. Pasas got another one in order to keep the party going. We spent an agreeable time for three or four hours.

Tuesday, Dec. 6. We arrived at Tula, where we received very bad quarters, criminals being put in the same room with us. We objected but to no effect, the alcalde telling us that if we were not satisfied that we could go to the calaboose. We have heard that we are to go to Perote Castle and not to Mexico City, as we had been assured all along. This became a matter of lengthy conversation among the prisoners.

Tuesday, Dec. 13. We changed our direction, leaving the main road to Mexico City and taking a turn to the left.

Thursday, Dec. 22. At three o'clock we reached Perote and were formed up in the square, in the presence of the governor, and delivered to his charge. We were marched to two large rooms and locked up. After an hour, we were given leave to go purchase provisions. There was a small store in the castle. San Carlos de Perote was off the road leading from Mexico City to Veracruz, halfway in between. There was a village near the castle. The castle was surrounded by a large ditch. According to my estimate, the castle covered about 26 acres and could house 8,000 to 10,000 men.

Monday, Dec. 26. We were told we had to be chained and to select our companions. Fortunately, along with the interpreters, I was permitted to have a single chain. For all things, being chained to another person is most unpleasant. There were many long faces while the fetters were rivetted on above the ankles.

———

JAMES L. TRUEHEART was born on Aug. 12, 1815, in Virginia. He moved to Texas in 1838 and settled at San Antonio, where he became clerk of the district court. When members of the court were captured in September 1842 by Gen. Adrian Woll, Trueheart was taken to Mexico with other prisoners and incarcerated for two years in the prison at Perote Castle. He was released in March 1844 and returned to San Antonio, where he again became a court clerk. In 1848 became county clerk, a post he held until 1850. He married Petra Margarita de la Garza on Feb. 15, 1848. He died in San Antonio on Nov. 30, 1882. His diary account of the capture and imprisonment of Texans following the Woll invasion was published in 1934.

17

THE PIGS OF GALVESTON

Mrs. Houstoun

TRAVEL WRITER, NOVELIST

Dec. 18, 1843, Galveston. There exists a spirit of goodwill and mutual helpfulness in Texas that was very pleasant to me. I believe this to be the case in new settlements, before refinement begets selfishness and the indulgence of luxuries hardens the heart.

I have reason to speak gratefully of the courtesy of Texans. During our stay, I experienced repeated instances of goodwill, one in particular. The pier where our yacht, the Dolphin, was anchored extends a considerable distance into the sea. The landing was at all times difficult, especially at low water. To a lady, the clambering ascent, for there were no steps previous to my arrival, was almost impracticable.

The morning after our yacht arrived, I prepared to go on shore in the gig, really dreading the difficulties which I was to encounter. What was my surprise and satisfaction to find, when the boat touched the wharf, that a most convenient flight of steps, with a hand balustrade, had been erected during the night. This was done without any regard for expense and solely for my accommodation. The person to whom I was indebted for this useful service neither expected, nor would receive, any remuneration. He was an ale-house keeper on the wharf, and a very well-educated man, for any station of life.

There is one large flourishing hotel at Galveston, besides several smaller ones. Fashionable persons assemble in the Tremont House. The dinner-hour is two and after the quarter of an hour, which is the time an American allows himself for this meal, they are to be seen reading the newspapers on the veranda of the hotel, in every variety of bodily contortion.

I believe it is not in the nature of an American to sit still or sit straight. They are always rocking or balancing themselves in their chairs or, with legs stretched over the railing of the veranda, spitting streams of tobacco juice into the garden.

THERE ARE MANY large stores in Galveston. Under this denomination come warehouses and what in England we call shops. Three newspapers are printed at Galveston; their contents are amusing enough. The advertisements likewise are not deficient in entertainment. The most numerous are those of medical men, of whom Galveston boasts a large supply. It is quite a treat to a stranger, at least it was to me, to drive through this very original city and see the different amusements, callings and trades. There are plenty of attorneys' offices; law is decidedly popular, even in this new country. I noticed no small sprinkling of grog-shops.

Some of the most frequented stores are those selling drugs and chemicals. Every ship that comes in is announced as containing leeches by the thousands, quinine by the hogsheads, and calomel by lots; not to mention demi-johns of castor oil. Doctoring must answer here, if anything does.

The designation of "dry store" is appended to the largest number of business houses in Galveston. Till I made enquiries, I could not imagine what these stores contained. The very name was an anomaly, for said dry stores almost all stood in water, or in mud and mire, which to English feet seemed scarcely fordable.

But such trifles are totally disregarded by the hardy settlers. Their wives and families seem equally disposed to make light of difficulties, and there is something very praiseworthy in this undaunted spirit of enterprise.

Now that I am on the subject of mud and mire, the numerous pigs of Galveston are the only living creatures that benefit from this oozy environment. The pigs themselves are frightful. Their long tails are destitute of curl, even when they retain their original number of joints, which, however, is seldom the case. The dogs, both wild and tame, are inveterate pig-hunters, being often hungry themselves. It was a rare sight to meet one of these pigs with ears or tail.

The pigs of Galveston seem to occupy as important a position in society as the pigs in Ireland. They are not, however, clean feeders. Nothing seemed to come amiss to the Galveston swine. I watched as they disputed carrion remains with the disgusting turkey-buzzards. When I observed this, I carefully stayed away from pork for the rest of my stay in Galveston.

MATILDA CHARLOTTE JESSE was born Aug. 16, 1811, at West Bromwich, Staffordshire, the daughter of Edward Jesse. She married Rev. Lionel Fraser, who died very young, then married Capt. Houstoun of the 10th Hussars. Mrs. Houstoun's "Texas and the Gulf of Mexico, or Yachting in the New World" was published in 1845. She was a keen observer, if sometimes condescending. She published 30 novels and several narrative works before she died at her home in June 1892.

18

RIDING MATCH

<u>J. W. Wilbarger</u>

MINISTER, AUTHOR

Among the many original characters who have figured in Texas none perhaps deserves a more conspicuous place than Col. Henry L. Kinney. He emigrated to Texas when quite a young man and in 1839 settled on Corpus Christi Bay, where the thriving city of Corpus Christi now stands. He established a trading house there, long known as Kinney's Ranch.

As he was a man of energy and enterprise, he accumulated means enough to enable him to control most of the trade from Mexico and the important towns along the Rio Grande.

In a country where horsemanship was almost a universal accomplishment, Col. Kinney was noted for his equestrian abilities. He always kept on hand for his own use a number of the best blooded horses that could be bought in Texas. In his frequent journeys over the state, it was well known that

Henry Kinney was famed for his skill on horseback

it was no unusual thing for him to ride 100 miles in less than 24 hours without dismounting.

In 1844, a great riding match came off in San Antonio. It was between Col. Jack Hays' Texas Rangers, 50 Comanches, and some Mexican rancheros. The performances took place on what was then a smooth open prairie west of San Pedro Creek. All the officers of the garrison with their families and all the citizens of San Antonio assembled at the appointed time to witness it.

I had seen what I thought to be many astonishing equestrian performances in the ring, but none of them could compare with those I witnessed that day on the prairie near San Antonio.

The Comanches were famous riders. So were the Mexican rancheros. And some of Hays' Rangers were fully equal, if not superior, to them. Judges were appointed to rule upon the merits of the performances and quite a number of valuable prizes were distributed. The first prize for horsemanship was awarded to John McMullen, one of Hays' Rangers. The second prize went to H. L. Kinney, who was a competitor. The third, I think, was awarded to a Comanche rider.

* * *

FOR SEVERAL YEARS, Kinney's Ranch on Corpus Christi Bay was the extreme settlement in the southwest. As such, it was exposed to frequent raids by Indians. Col. Kinney and the men he employed to protect the settlement had many contests with them. Kinney was one of those cool and fearless men who are especially fitted by nature for a life of wild adventure. His many exploits among the Indians would afford material for a most interesting narrative. We give one instance of a fair sample of others.

The Comanche Indians were one of the most warlike tribes on the American continent. They were feared by Americans, Mexicans, and other Indians. Not long after the riding contest in San Antonio, 17 of these warlike savages, under one of their chiefs, attacked some homes near

Kinney's Ranch. After killing or driving off the inmates, they hastily retreated.

Col. Kinney and 11 other men, mounted on their fastest horses, gave immediate chase. After going a few miles, they overtook the Indians on an open prairie.

Both parties dismounted and began the fight at a distance less than 50 yards. Each individual on both sides singled out his particular target and did his best to kill him. After the fight had continued for some time in this way, the Indian chief dashed to the front and, holding up his buffalo shield before him, ran along the line of his antagonists. The whites all fired at him, but their balls only rattled off his tough rawhide shield.

The object of this maneuver was soon apparent. The chief having drawn the fire of the whites, the Indians rushed upon their foes before they had time to reload. Col. Kinney alone succeeded in mounting his horse before the Indians, with spears and tomahawks, were upon them.

ONE OF KINNEY'S men was instantly killed. Another was speared and wounded in several places by arrows. A young Mexican, a clerk of Kinney's, was speared and had his horse killed under him, which he had finally managed to mount. The Colonel dragged the young Mexican up behind him on his own horse.

At this juncture, an Indian threw a spear into the Mexican's body with such force that the blade went completely through the young Mexican and wounded Kinney in the back. At the same moment, a second Indian aimed a blow at the Colonel which missed him, but went through the sleeves of his buckskin hunting shirt. While he was trying to free himself from this spear, a third Indian rushed upon them and drove his spear through the bowels of the young Mexican, who relaxed his hold and fell dead from the horse. Colonel Kinney turned upon his assailant, pulled a pistol from his holster, and shot the man dead on the spot.

Similar desperate fights were going on between other Indians and Kinney's men. At length, finding this hand-to-hand battle was a losing game for them, the Indians withdrew, leaving seven warriors dead on the ground. There is little doubt that the remaining 10 warriors were all, more or less, severely wounded. Of the 11 white men in the fight, three were killed and all the rest were wounded.

The great error of Col. Kinney and his men was in firing simultaneously at the chief, protected as he was by his tough rawhide shield, which was impenetrable by the round balls that were in use at that time. Many Texans have lost their lives by wasting their shots on such shields. Later on, with the introduction of improved firearms and the conical ball, the Indians generally put aside those shields as useless encumbrances.

The fight outside Corpus Christi, taking into consideration the small number of both parties, was one of the hardest and most obstinately contested engagements that took place between the whites and Indians on the Texas frontier.

––––––––––

JOHN WESLEY WILBARGER was born in 1806, the son of John Wilbarger and Ann (Pugh) Wilbarger. Wilbarger moved from Kentucky to Texas in 1837; his brother Josiah was living near Bastrop. Josiah had been scalped by Indians in 1833 and left for dead; he survived and lived for another 11 years. John Wesley served as a Methodist minister and surveyor. He began collecting the material for "Indian Depredations in Texas" in the 1870s. The book was published in 1889. J. Frank Dobie said his classic work has "for generations been a household heritage among Texas families who fought for their land." Wilbarger died in 1892 and was buried in Round Rock Cemetery.

19

THE FIRST WINE

Henry Castro

EMPRESARIO

July 20—24, 1844, San Antonio. I received many visitors, explained my plans to my colonists, and made preparations to visit the colony lands.

July 25. Left San Antonio with five men of Captain Hays' company of rangers. Our party consisted of seven, making in all 12 men, and well-armed. Camped first night on Medio Creek, 12 miles west.

July 26. Mr. John James, who accompanied us, killed three bears on a creek and saw many horses. James Dunn, one of the rangers, chased them and killed a fine stallion. Crossed the Medina River and killed two deer and one alligator and caught some trout. Camped on the Medina.

July 27. Re-crossed the Medina. At seven o'clock we had an alarm. One of the rangers reported having seen some mounted men, and not being able to make out who they were, six men left our camp to reconnoiter. They returned without any result. My grant begins four miles west of the Medina. The first thing I saw on my grant was a bee tree full of honey. Reached Quihi Lake 10 miles from the Medina. This point has water, timber, hills and prairie. Camped on the Hondo Creek, which is a good place for a settlement.

July 28. Reached the Rio Seco, 12 miles west of Hondo Creek, still on my grant. Caught trout and killed two deer. Ascended the Seco and camped at a waterhole.

July 29. Rode across the country and again reached the Hondo, where we gathered some persimmons and wild grapes. Camped three miles from Quihi Lake.

July 30. Followed the banks of the Quihi Lake. The valley possesses all the advantages for a colony. Procured honey and fish in abundance. Camped on the Medina.

July 31. Returned to San Antonio. Two of our rangers were taken sick with a fever. I have, during this excursion of seven days, seen 160 miles of country, which can only be compared to an English park. With coffee, sugar and flour, we have lived well with the products of our hunting and fishing and always had plenty of honey.

August 25, San Antonio. Some of my colonists who had left Galveston in the early part of July will not reach this place as soon as it was expected on account of sickness. At a ranch 40 miles below San Antonio, the Indians attacked a cart which unfortunately had been left behind the convoy. A young colonist, aged 19, named Z. Rhin, was killed. The driver, who was an American, escaped. The Indians burned the cart and its contents. The driver remained in the woods. One of the hands of poor Rhin was nailed to a tree.

August 28—31. These few days were employed in preparations for our expedition. On Aug. 31, all the colonists who were to form part of the expedition, with their families and many of my American friends, were invited to a farewell dinner. It went off exceedingly pleasant and, owing to the number of toasts drunk, became enthusiastic.

Sept. 1. At four a.m., I had gathered 22 carts. The farming utensils, baggage, and provisions were ready to be loaded. My employees told me that malicious rumors had been circulated that we would not start on that day. I sent 10 men on horseback in all directions to contradict such rumors, assuring everyone that nothing but death would prevent me from starting. Although I made every effort, my colonists came in slowly, making excuses and various pretenses.

IT WAS TWO O'CLOCK in the afternoon and rain was falling by torrents, as if to create more embarrassments for me. I had made guarantees that we would have at least 50 men at the time of our departure. It became necessary to supply the number of colonists missing with Mexicans paid by me. Although it was still raining hard at four p.m., it appeared to be a proper time to call the roll of the colonists. Only 27 were there. But with my paid Mexicans we were 50. The train of carts being loaded, I ordered it to start.

September 2, on the Medina River. Started with a party to reconnoiter the point where we were to form our settlements. We only returned to camp at midnight.

September 3. Crossed the Medina at about 8 a.m. The actual crossing place (now opposite Castroville) is a beautiful location. Our camp was shaded by large pecan trees, at the foot of a beautiful stream with plenty of game and fish. The improvised kitchen of my French colonists was soon filled with dishes which, aided by the drink I contributed, soon put everybody in good humor and the evening was spent in a gay manner.

September 4. Built a shed in which to place our commissary. Deputy Surveyor John James arrived.

September 5. A dispute arose between the French and German colonists, which I fortunately settled amicably.

September 6. Labor more regularly organized.

September 7. Dr. Cupples and Charles de Montel leave for San Antonio to bring Bishop Odin.

September 8. Storm during the night. It surprised us and gave us a good ducking. Drank twice a little brandy during the night and smoked a pipe, contrary to my habit.

September 9. Arrival of three colonists. One of my men reported having seen a trail of 50 Comanches. The information was sent to Capt. Hays and precautions were taken against a surprise from the Indians. Built a guardhouse.

September 10. Cut timber to construct a large shed to shelter everyone temporarily. Discovered the kind of grass that is proper for roofing. Arrival of Bishop Odin, Rev. Oge, Capt. Hays, and Chevalier.

September 11. Today my table was set on the banks of the Medina, under the rich foliage of the pecan and walnut trees. Besides my customary guests, we had the bishop and Rev. Oge, whom I did my best to please. Amongst the novelties we had for our fare, we had several bottles of wine made from the mustang grape by one of the colonists from the Rhenish province. Without doubt it was the first wine produced on the Medina. It was considered very fair.

––––––––––

HENRY CASTRO was born in France in July 1786. In 1813 he married a wealthy widow, Amelia Mathias. After the fall of Napoleon, he immigrated to the U.S. and became a naturalized citizen. He returned to France and became a partner in a banking house. In 1843 Castro entered into a contract with the Texas government to settle a colony in southwest Texas on the Medina River. Between 1843 and 1847 he brought almost 1,000 families and single men to Texas and established Castroville in 1844, the village of Quihi and Vandenburg in 1845, both near Hondo, and D'Hanis in 1847. He died at Monterrey, Mexico, on Nov. 31, 1865. He was buried in Monterrey at the foot of the Sierra Madre.

20

LETTER TO ROASTING EAR

Thomas G. Western
INDIAN AGENT

To Roasting Ear, Chief of the Delawares, Jan. 25, 1845:

I have read your talk with great pleasure and am glad that you are so strong for peace with the Comanche and all other tribes. I wish to see peace with all red men and all in my power shall be done to effect it. You will hear from me and my chiefs and captains no lies. We speak the truth in the presence of the Great Spirit who hears our words and knows our thoughts.

I like to see old men take hold of peace. Experience and wisdom generally accompany gray hairs. I have great confidence in you and your people, in your words, and their words generally. Talk to Pah'-hah-yo'-ko and impress upon him the advantages and blessings of peace.

Much trouble has lately been caused at the settlement of Corpus Christi; it is supposed by some of the Comanche young men. Young men, white and red, will act foolish.

Tell Pah'-hah-yo'-ko of this and he will talk to his young men. Tell him that all the country this side of the Rio Grande belongs to Texas. Tell him that they are at peace with Texas. The Great Spirit will not be pleased to see them doing bad.

I am satisfied that the Comanche chiefs are honest and good men, but you know their young men are thoughtless. Your influence can be of much good. I have sent a good talk to Pah'-hah-yo'-ko and the other Comanche chiefs who are now at the Trading House on the Brazos. I trust you will talk to them. I have great confidence in you and the Delaware. Be firm and industrious and we will have a strong peace with all the wild tribes of the prairies. Peace be with you. May you live long and be happy.

TO ROASTING EAR, Jan. 26, 1845: My brother, information has just been received that some Delaware are within the Settlements in violation of the law and disturbing the peace of the inhabitants. They find some bad white men to sell them whisky; they get drunk and alarm the women and children. It must be stopped. It is your duty as their captain to prevent it. The Delaware are good people, and we are friends and brothers. But when these young men drink whisky they act foolish.

––––––––––

THOMAS GEHOT WESTERN was born in England on June 21, 1789. The family emigrated to the U.S. in 1794. Western moved to Texas and was operating a store at Goliad at the beginning of the Revolution. He served as commissary of the Texas army and delivered the eulogy at the burial of the remains of the Alamo defenders. He was appointed superintendent of Indian affairs of Texas in 1841, and held that position until Texas was annexed by the United States. He died in Houston on May 2, 1848.

21

ARMY LANDS ON NORTH BEACH

Ethan Allen Hitchcock

COLONEL, THIRD INFANTRY

The Third Infantry under my command left Fort Jesup on Monday, July 7, 1845. We camped that night at Nine Mile Spring, nine miles from Natchitoches, 16 miles from Fort Jesup. Next morning we marched to Grande Cove and boarded two steamboats and arrived in New Orleans on July 10. We were given quarters in the Lower Cotton Press and are tolerably well-sheltered from sun and rain.

On July 23, 1845, eight companies of the Third Infantry boarded the steamer "Alabama" on our way to plant the flag of the U.S. in Texas. Gen. Zachary Taylor is on board in command of the army. Three days later, we arrived within a few miles of the entrance of Aransas Bay and anchored. Next morning we came down and anchored off the entrance to the bay. The ship lay very still, all of us looking on the shoreline and watching two or three sailboats beyond the island. After breakfast some will go on shore in a small boat.

Gen. Zachary Taylor in command at Corpus Christi

Gen. Taylor is anxious to get the men on shore (on St. Joseph's Island) but our lighters are not here and we do not know when they will be here. I sent Lt. Chandler on shore to examine the land for water. He planted a small flag of the U.S. on a sand hill, the first Stars and Stripes to fly over Texas soil.

Chandler returned and reported it next to impossible to obtain water but, as he landed near the western or southern extremity of the island, we saw that people were living higher up the island and we saw cattle besides. We sent a company off to shore. With great difficulty, three companies of men were landed with their mess chests.

On July 27, I came from the steamer with the last of the Third Infantry to board the lighter "Undine." We slept on board. This morning we went ashore and rode among the encampments of the regiment. Lt. Henry with K Company found good water and has supplied his company with fish and oysters. I rode down last evening and again this morning and ate with him.

Companies G & E are three miles from the south end of the island on the sea side, tolerably well-supplied with water. The remaining five companies (two having been left in New Orleans) came on shore yesterday and landed on the bay side. They are not well supplied with water. We can dig down about the depth of a barrel and find water, but it is brackish. The eight companies of the Third are all ashore on St. Joseph's. There are two or three families living on the island.

On the morning of July 29, Gen. Taylor determined to take two companies on board the "Undine" and attempt to pass up Aransas Bay to Corpus Christi Bay, although the boat drew several inches over four feet and four feet was the deepest water reported over the flats separating the two bays. The general changed his mind two or three times about the movement. Finally, two companies went on board the lighter and went five miles then ran aground. There was three and a half feet of water there and we were still three or four miles from the flats. We remained aground all day and the following night.

To lighten the load on the vessel we landed by raft a quantity of provisions in barrels. We continued to land freight until, with constant labor, the boat was floated off. The general sent the captain of the "Undine" to examine the flats in person. He returned to report a depth of water of two feet and 11 inches.

The general then ordered everything out of the vessel. The captain assured him he could bring her down to three feet six inches and it was hoped she might be forced through the mud and then, when she returned, a sort of channel might be made. The unloading proceeded until nightfall.

Col. Ethan Allen Hitchcock commanded the 3ʳᵈ Infantry

The unloading finally brought the boat to the mark of three feet and seven inches. The general and the captain saw no reason for abandoning the original plan of trying to force the
boat over the flats. Early on July 31, she was put under steam and went over to within a few yards of the flats and there halted, hard aground. The captain, named Brice, was again sent on the flats with the small boat but returned and reported what he ought to have known perfectly well the day before, that the flats could not be crossed.

We dropped back a few miles to where the freight lay scattered on shore. By this time, several small fishing boats gathered around us. The general directed the quartermaster to make arrangements and ordered two companies to board them. Gen. Taylor was beside himself from anxiety, fatigue, and passion. I undertook to tell him that in my opinion the troops could be very comfortable at St. Joseph's for a few days until the water should rise over the flats, which occurs with winds from the southeast. But he would not listen and was impatient to get the companies off.

Two companies were finally on board six small boats. My adjutant and myself, along with a Col. Cook, a citizen of Texas, took a seventh boat. We left about 11 a.m. We had no difficulty, as the day turned out, but landed about an hour before sundown. It was July 31.

All accounts agree that our safe arrival is little short of a miracle and is attributable to the mere accident of the bay being tolerably calm. I am now ashore, however, with two companies (K and G) of the Third Infantry, the first troops to occupy the soil of Texas. Corpus Christi is a very small rancho, or village, at the head of the bay of the same name. The next morning, Aug. 1, several citizens called and expressed their gratification at our arrival.

––––––––––

ETHAN ALLEN HITCHCOCK was the grandson of Revolutionary War hero Ethan Allen. He was the commander of the Third Infantry and considered Gen. Zachary Taylor's most capable senior officer. Companies of Hitchcock's Third Infantry were the first to arrive at Corpus Christi on Aug. 1, 1845 and they were the first to leave for the border on March 8, 1846. Hitchcock was ill when the regiment left; he traveled on a makeshift bed on boxes of ammunition in a wagon pulled by oxen. In the coming war with Mexico, Hitchcock served as an adviser to Gen. Winfield Scott and was put in charge of covert operations. He resigned from the army in 1855 but returned to active duty in the Civil War and acted as a military adviser to Abraham Lincoln. He died in Sparta, Ga., on Aug. 4, 1870.

22

TRADERS FROM CAMARGO

N. S. Jarvis

ARMY SURGEON

A caravan of Mexican traders arrived today (Aug. 10, 1845) from Camargo. Bodies of these are constantly arriving and a contraband trade of large amount is carried on between them and the merchants of Corpus Christi. They bring horses, mules, specie, bullion, and Mexican blankets. They buy tobacco, powder, prints and domestic cloths. All this they smuggle across the border.

The horses they bring are mostly wild horses, immense herds of which roam the prairie. The prices they sell these for vary from five to 10 dollars. They are generally small and shaggy, wild and unbroken, but hardy and enduring.

Col. Kinney, the owner of Corpus Christi, arrived from Austin, bringing with him two Lipan Indians. I was amused by a conversation I had with one of the Lipans. On alluding to their possible connection or relation to Comanches, he probably understood because he immediately and warmly asserted in Spanish, which they both talk, to convince us that no such connection between the tribes existed, he said he had killed a Comanche warrior, two women, and ate a baby. Under the impression that we had misunderstood him, as to that last particular, we asked him again and he repeated the fact that it tasted good.

Gen. Taylor arrived with his staff. Lt. Dobbins and three men left for San Patricio to meet the Second Dragoons.

We had a most terrific thunderstorm. Lightning struck our camp, killing a black servant owned by Lt. Braxton Bragg and wounding another servant. The man who was killed was sitting in his tent with his head leaning against the tent pole, the top of which was hit by lightning.

The Dragoons coming from San Patricio were about 30 miles away and hearing the thunder mistook it for Mexican artillery and thought our encampment was under attack. They began a forced march to come to our assistance.

A few miles away they met Gen. Taylor, who undeceived them. They said the thunder exactly resembled the booming sound of artillery fired at regular intervals.

Gen. Taylor and party returned today (Aug. 25). They described the country between here and the Nueces as most beautiful, abounding in herds of wild horses, deer and turkeys. One of the general's party shot a tiger, but did not kill him. The Drags are expected here day after tomorrow.

A PARTY OF OFFICERS went out on a hunt a few days ago. They returned, having killed a number of deer and other game. Lt. Dobbins shot a panther seven-foot long that leaped at him and missed him and was about to take another leap when the lieutenant shot him in the head.

A Mexican was apprehended today (Sept. 3) in the Dragoons camp charged with an attempt to decoy away slaves, the servants of some of the officers. He was immediately put in irons.

Lt. Scarritt of the engineers was ordered (Nov. 18) to take a party and cut a passageway through the reef that bars the entrance of the Nueces Bay from Corpus Christi Bay so as to admit boats up the Nueces River.*

The cold weather continues (Dec. 3, 1845). The thermometer dropped as low as 23 degrees. It was so severe as to freeze the fish in the bay. Cartloads of fish were gathered along the reef; they were completely frozen in their attempts to reach the waters of the Nueces River.

The regiments have been engaged in surrounding their camps with chaparral bushes to shelter them from the piercing effects of the norther. The cold has never been felt so severely here, on the recollection of the oldest residents of the place.

———————

NATHAN S. JARVIS, a surgeon in the U.S. Army, was originally from New York. He served in the Seminole Wars in Florida and in the Mexican War. Dr. Jarvis was in charge of the army's general hospital at Corpus Christi during the encampment of Zachary Taylor's army, from August 1845 to March 1846. He died during the Civil War while he was the medical director of the Department of Maryland.

---

* Lt. Scarritt's cut was made on the south end near the Corpus Christi shore. Afterwards, when the reef became an underwater road across the bay, at high tide horses would have to swim across that gap in the reef.

23

GRANT CAST AS DESDEMONA

James Longstreet
LIEUTENANT, U.S. ARMY

In March 1845 I was assigned as lieutenant in the Eighth
Regiment, and joined my company at St. Augustine, Fla. At
the time, the new republic of Texas was seeking annexation
with the United States, which would endanger the peace
between Texas and the republic of Mexico.

Annexation became the big question of the day. James
Polk was the nominee of the Democratic Party in 1844.
Henry Clay was on the other side as the Whig nominee.
Polk was elected and his party prepared to signalize its
triumph by annexing Texas as soon as it came into power.
But in the last days of President Tyler's administration,
joint resolutions of annexation were passed by both houses
of Congress. When the resolution was passed, diplomatic
relations between the governments of Mexico and the U.S.
ceased. On July 4, 1845, the Texas Congress ratified
annexation and Texas was a State of the Union.

Gen. Zachary Taylor's little army of observation was ordered to Corpus Christi and became "The Army of Occupation." All other available forces were ordered to join him, including Gen. Worth and his forces in Florida.

At the time there were in the line of the army eight regiments of infantry, four of artillery, and two of dragoons. By the middle of October 1845, there were 3,860 men of all arms concentrated at Corpus Christi. Seven companies of the Second Dragoons marched from Fort Jessup to San Patricio on the Nueces River, about 28 miles up from Corpus Christi; the other three companies were halted at San Antonio.

Near our camps at Corpus Christi were extensive plains well adapted to military maneuvers, which were put to prompt use for drill and professional instruction. There were
many advantages in the way of amusement, as well. Game on the wild prairies and fish in the broad gulf were plentiful, and there was the salt water for bathing.

On one occasion during the winter of 1845 a violent north wind forced the waters over the beach, in some places far enough to disturb our camps, and when they receded, quantities of fish were found in the puddles left behind, and turtles more than enough to supply the army.

THE OFFICERS BUILT a theater, depending upon their own efforts to reimburse them. As there was no one outside the army except two rancheros within a hundred miles, our dramatic company was organized from among the officers, who took both male and female characters.

In comedy and farce we did well enough and soon collected funds to pay for the building. The house was filled every night. Gen. Worth always encouraged us, Gen. Taylor sometimes, and Gen. Twiggs occasionally.

We found ourselves in funds sufficient to send over to New Orleans for costumes and concluded to try tragedy.

Lt. Grant was cast to play the role of Desdemona

The "Moor of Venice" was chosen. Lt. Theoderic Porter was selected to be the Moor and Lt. U. S. Grant was to play Desdemona, the daughter of Brabantio. After rehearsal, Porter protested that male heroines could not support the character or give sentiment to the part, so we sent to New Orleans and secured Mrs. Hart to play the role of Desdemona. Then all went well and life through the winter at Corpus Christi was gay.

JAMES LONGSTREET JR. was born on Jan. 8, 1821 in South Carolina, though his family was from northern Georgia. He graduated from West Point in 1842 and served in the Mexican War; he was wounded at Chapultepec. As a lieutenant general, he commanded the First Corps in Robert E. Lee's Army of Northern Virginia. He died on Jan. 2, 1904, at the age of 82, and was buried in Gainesville, Ga.

24

BREAKING WILD MULES

Ulysses S. Grant

LIEUTENANT, FOURTH INFANTRY

The preparations at Corpus Christi for the army's advance to the Rio Grande processed rapidly. The principal business consisted of securing mules and getting them broken to harness. The process was slow but amusing.

The animals sold to the government were all young and unbroken, even to the saddle, and were quite as wild as the wild horses of the prairie. When they were brought in, the mules were first driven into a stockade, called a corral, which included an acre or more of ground.

The Mexicans, who were all experienced in throwing the lasso, would go into the corral on horseback with their lassos attached to the pommels of their saddles. Soldiers detailed as teamsters and blacksmiths would also enter the corral, the former with ropes to serve as halters, and the latter with branding irons and a fire to keep the irons heated.

A lasso was then thrown over the neck of a mule, when he would immediately go to the length of the tether, first one end and then the other. While he was plunging and gyrating, another lasso would be thrown by another Mexican, catching the animal by a forefoot. This would bring the mule to the ground. Then he was seized and held by the teamsters while the blacksmith impressed upon him with hot irons, "U.S."

Ropes were then put about the neck, with a slip-noose which would tighten around the throat if pulled. With a man on each side holding these ropes, the mule was released from his other bindings and allowed to rise. With more or less difficulty, he would be led to a picket rope outside and fastened there. The delivery of that mule was then complete. The same process was gone through with every mule and wild horse with the army of occupation.

The method of breaking them was less cruel and more amusing. It is a well-known fact that when domestic animals are used for specific purposes, from generation to generation, their descendants are easily, as a rule, subdued to the same uses. At that time in northern Mexico, the mule — or his ancestors, the horse and ass — was seldom used except for the saddle or the pack.

At all events, the Corpus Christi mule resisted the new use, pulling wagons, to which he was being put. The treatment he was subjected to in order to overcome his prejudice was summary and effective.

FIVE MULES WERE allotted to each wagon. A teamster would select at the picket rope five animals of nearly the same color and general appearance for his team.

With a full corps of assistants, he would then proceed to get his mules together. In twos, the men would approach each animal selected, avoiding as far as possible its heels. The ropes would be put about the neck of each animal, with a slip noose, so that he could be choked if he was too unruly.

They were then led out, harnessed by force and hitched to the wagon in the position they had to keep ever after.

Two men remained on either side of the leader, with the lassos about his neck, and one man retained the same restraining influence over each of the others.

All being ready, the hold would be slackened and the team started. The first motion was generally five mules in the air at one time, backs bowed, hind feet extended to the rear.

After repeating this movement a few times, the mules would start to run. This would bring the breeching tight against the mules at the wheels which these last seemed to regard as a most unwarranted attempt at coercion.

They would resist by taking a seat, sometimes going as far as to lie down. In time, all were broken in to do their duty submissively if not cheerfully. But there never was a time during the war when it was safe to let a Mexican mule get entirely loose.

————

ULYSSES SIMPSON GRANT was born on April 27, 1822. His father was Jesse Grant and his mother Hannah Simpson Grant. He graduated from West Point and was commissioned a second lieutenant in the 4th Infantry. In 1845, he was stationed at Corpus Christi with Zachary Taylor's army and served throughout the Mexican War. In the Civil War, he rose from brigadier general to become commanding general of all the Union armies. He was elected president in 1868. He died of throat cancer on July 23, 1885. His widow, Julia Dent Grant, died in 1902.

25

LEAVING FOR THE BORDER

Daniel P. Whiting

CAPTAIN, SEVENTH INFANTRY

On Aug. 24, 1845, orders were received for our movement to Corpus Christi. We left in the steamer "Creole" for that destination. My wife and family took a schooner to New Orleans and from thence to Jefferson Barracks, Mo.

On Aug. 28, we landed at St. Joseph's Island and took the transport steamer "Dayton" — an old and unsafe boat which a few days afterward blew up, killing several officers. We reached Corpus Christi on Aug. 31 and encamped with other troops already there under Gen. Zachary Taylor.

On clearing the ground for our camp, which was covered with brush and scrub, we found the place infested with rattlesnakes. Many were killed. I was awakened one night by the rattle of one in my tent, close to where I was lying. I

Daniel P. Whiting: "I was almost broken down"

called some men and sprang out. When the snake was killed, I found it to be about six feet in length. The called some men and sprang out. When the snake was killed, I found it to be about six feet in length. The encampment was a fine esplanade, after it was thoroughly cleared.

After all the forces arrived, the camp was two miles in extent, parallel to the shore, extending from the village of Corpus Christi to the point of land made by the junction of the Nueces Bay with Corpus Christi Bay. Here were located the artillery, the Third, Fourth and our own Seventh regiments of infantry. Our regiment was commanded by Col. Hoffman who was taken sick and died Nov. 26. The command passed to Maj. Jacob Brown. I made a sketch of the camp about this time, which was afterwards published in my "Army Portfolio."

We had much good music in the camp, with several fine regimental bands. I used to have frequent musical soirees at

The camp of Zachary Taylor's army of occupation at Corpus Christi, by Capt. Daniel P. Whiting

my own tent with various amateur and professional performers. Such recreations as billiards, bowling alleys and a theater comprised our amusements while regimental brigade drills made up our official occupation.

When winter "northers" set in, our camp was defended by hedges and embankments. Our tents sprouted chimneys made of casks of different sizes diminishing towards the top.

I had a mess conducted by the wife of one of my sergeants. She was called "The Great Western" from being a gigantic woman of great strength and hardihood who afterwards became quite famous. One day I was attracted by hearing a noise in my campground and looking out I saw her pick up a man who had offended her and, as if he were a child, set him down in her wash tub.

A terrific norther visited the camp one night, raising the tide of the bay to unusual height, the waters overflowing the flats beyond the upper end of the plain. After it subsided, vast numbers of fish of the best species of the

111

Gulf were found stranded in a frozen, numbed state. Many wagonloads of fish were distributed throughout the camp.

About the first of March, 1846, the Third, Fourth, Fifth, Seventh and Eighth regiments of infantry maneuvered on the plain as an army in the field, giving some conception of the grandeur of display attending the movements of as many thousands as we numbered hundreds.

One prominent feature of our concentration was the opportunity for fraternity and association between officers of different corps. All regional sectionality and jealousy of feeling was overcome at Corpus Christi. A general harmony and mutual consideration were acquired and cultivated. This contributed to a unity of feeling and esprit de corps that prevailed throughout the war.

Our little army began its movement for the Rio Grande on March 8. Brigades left on successive days. Our own was among the first to depart. Leading off on foot at the head of my company, I was sorely fatigued on the first day's march. In fact, I was almost broken down by the time we reached Twelve-Mile Motts, where we camped. The next day I was less so but very sorry I was only a captain of foot.

On the second day we marched 16 miles to Agua Dulce. By the third day, I began to believe I could succeed if I continued judiciously. We marched 14 miles to San Gertrudis Creek. On the fourth day, I arrived at camp quite efficient and afterwards, and throughout the war, I continued to travel afoot, never mounted, without fatigue or weariness. Many a stout man succumbed where I never faltered.

———————

DANIEL POWERS WHITING graduated from West Point in 1832 and was ordered to Fort Gibson in Indian Territory. He was transferred to Newport Barracks in Kentucky where he married Indiana Sandford; she later died during childbirth.

Whiting's regiment in Florida was ordered to Texas to prepare for an expected conflict with Mexico. Whiting was at the bombardment of Fort Brown and in the battle of Cerro Gordo. He died on Aug. 2, 1892.

26

LOST IN A BLIZZARD

James Buckner Barry
TEXAS RANGER

When I returned to the falls of the Brazos in late 1845, I joined the little army of the Republic of Texas, commanded by Major Jack Hays. I was placed in Capt. Thomas J. Smith's company, which was assigned to the protection of that portion of the frontier between the Brazos and Trinity rivers, a day's ride above the settlements.

There were only 30 men in Smith's company and he divided the company into three squads. One squad of 10 men had its headquarters near the Brazos River on Tehuacana Creek. This was 10 miles below the Waco village where the city of Waco is now located.

One squad of 10 men had its headquarters on the Trinity River about halfway between where Dallas and Fort Worth have grown up today. The squad I was with had its rendezvous point on the head of Richland's Creek. This squad was commanded by Sgt. James Sanford.

During the time of my service with Capt. Smith's company, Texas and the United States invited all the Indians — friendly and hostile — to meet in a great peace council on Tehuacana Creek, 10 miles below the Waco village. Treaties with such warlike tribes as the Comanches, Kiowas, and Wichitas would secure peace on the frontier pending the expected war with Mexico.

After many delays, a great treaty council was held with eight or 10 tribes. There were about that many thousands for the whole of the tribes attended. The Indians did not believe in representative government; they wanted the voice of the whole tribe on questions involving tribal interests. The United States sent two commissioners, Gen. P. M. Butler and G. M. Lewis, to make the treaty with the Texas Indians.

THE TRIBE OF LIPANS, which had befriended Texas in all its struggles, was there. The tribe had no sins to atone for, with one recent exception. Two young Lipan warriors had come across two German settlers getting timber on the Medina River. As they could not talk English, Spanish or any Indian language, the Lipans took them to be intruders and killed them. Gen. Butler told the Lipan chief to bring these young warriors in, that they would have to stand trial for murder.

The Lipan chief balked. He told Gen. Butler that these Germans were not good Texans. He said they could not talk like good Texans, their clothing was not like that of good Texans, and they wore wooden shoes, not boots like good Texans. That night, the whole tribe decamped and ran away to Mexico. There were but five of us rangers and we made no attempt to follow them.

Another tribe present, the Wacos, said they had some captives and stolen horses which they would release. But a part of their tribe resisted, especially some of the older women who had raised the captives from childhood and had become attached to them. It was decided that we had better send a showing of soldiers to intimidate the Wacos.

Two days after the treaty council was over, Capt. Smith started 16 of us to the Waco village with a Delaware scout, Jack Harry, to act as interpreter. We followed the trail up on the east side of the Brazos River for perhaps 100 miles and crossed the divide on to the Trinity, near where the city of Weatherford now stands.

A blizzard struck us, together with a snowstorm. It was bitterly cold, with a cutting north wind, and some of the boys became faint-hearted and talked of going back. But Jack Harry, our Delaware scout, counseled no. In the absence of our experienced captain (Smith), our guide had become our acting captain, assisted by Sgt. Sanford. Jack Harry declared that the snow would help us find them, that the Indians would not travel with their women and children in a snowstorm, and that we would overtake them.

THE SNOW COVERED THEIR TRAIL but Jack Harry thought it made no difference. We could keep the course we were following and if we missed them we would eventually find their horse tracks. He said the Indians would turn their horses loose to forage whatever they could in the blizzard and, after it quit snowing, there would be lots of horse tracks as they gathered in their herds.

In the white face of winter, we kept our course as best we could. There was nothing to guide us but the north wind and drifting snow. But so well did our Delaware keep his course that we rode right into their camp. The snow was falling so thick that it hid the smoke and their wigwams were covered with snow, looking like the surrounding hills and rocks.

The first I knew of being in their camp was when I saw little naked children running from one of their snow hills (wigwams) to the other, giving the alarm of our approach.

While our interpreter was talking to the chief, we rolled some logs into a ravine and started a fire. The chief was the only Indian who showed himself, at that time. I suppose the warriors were inside their tents preparing their weapons.

We stayed right among them for two nights. They could neither move their women and children nor find their ponies while it snowed. We were in but little better fix. The grass was covered with snow and there was nothing but brush for our horses to eat. They were tired and hungry.

Next day, some of their young warriors came out and advanced toward us. They were warpainted and their bows were ready. Our interpreter told them to go back or they would get into a fight.

They laughed and asked where his men were who were going to fight. Sgt. Sanford told him to tell them that we had come after their captives and horses and were not going back without them. If they did not have the captives and horses there when the sun rose next morning, there would be a battle, and we could kill two of them to their one of us, and we would also kill their women and children.

NEXT MORNING AT sunrise they brought up one prisoner and five head of horses. We did not ask any more questions. We well knew we would all have left our hair among them if the weather had allowed them to remove their women and children to a place of safety. We also knew that they had some 60 or 70 warriors at this camp and the Wichitas, their good friends, had about that many at their camp nearby.

We left with our horses and prisoner and rode away. That evening Jack Harry killed a deer. We agreed not to eat it until morning, when the 18 of us devoured it, even to the soft bones.

The cause of our being so hungry was that the thousands of Indians who had come down for the treaty conference, and returned the same way, had driven off all the buffalo from that section of the country. Then the extreme cold weather had driven the smaller game into the timber and we had no time to stop and hunt. The grass was still covered with snow and our horses were growing weak for want of feed.

Such conditions led to a falling-out among ourselves and our little squad divided into two groups. Seven of us contended that the nearest settlements were on the Trinity. The others thought the falls of the Brazos would be the nearest. We separated without a goodbye.

Late in the evening one of us, Caps, killed a wild goose and next morning one of the boys killed a hawk. We divided this food into seven portions and after each man had hidden his share in his stomach, we resumed our course. The snow had commenced melting as we went through the Cross Timbers near the headwaters of Mountain Creek.

In the edge of the timber, we saw an Indian butchering a buffalo. Sgt. Sanford ordered us to form a V on him, which we did. He mounted his pony and tried to make his escape, but we ran him down.

He made us to understand that he was a Choctaw, that a good many Choctaws had come across the Red River to hunt buffalo and were camped on the Trinity River.

We turned him loose and went back to his buffalo and got plenty of meat. We found a place in the timber where the snow had melted, built a fire, roasted the meat, and filled the vacuum within us.

WE PURSUED OUR COURSE AND came upon a camp of buffalo hunters. They were directly across the Trinity River opposite where the city of Dallas now stands. We lay over two or three days while our horses filled up on the winter grass in Trinity bottom.

We then struck out for the falls of the Brazos. There was no road and only one settlement of four families between this point on the Trinity and the Brazos, near where I think is now Ash Creek in Hill County.

A dry blizzard hit us, but we found enough brush on the creek to keep us from freezing. To keep warm next morning we walked and led our horses.

When we were within six or eight miles of the settlement on the Brazos, we saw a horse standing still with a saddle on. We steered toward the horse and found his rider frozen to death with the bridle reins tied around one wrist. As it was too cold for an inquest, we rode on to the settlement and reported the scene.

A party of men started out to bring the man in. When they found him, the horse had also frozen. In arriving at this settlement, we learned that our captain had orders to muster out the company.

JAMES BUCKNER (BUCK) BARRY was born in North Carolina on Dec. 16, 1821. He immigrated to Texas in 1845 and soon joined the Texas Rangers as a member of Capt. Thomas J. Smith's company. Barry then worked surveying headrights in the Robertson Colony. In 1846 he served in Hays' Texas Mounted Riflemen in the Mexican War. In 1847, he married Sarah Matticks and they eventually had six children. In 1849 he was elected sheriff of Navarro County and moved to Corsicana. In 1855 he moved his family to Bosque County. In the Civil War, Barry led rangers in frontier protection, from the Red River to the Rio Grande. He rose to the rank of lieutenant colonel. He was elected in 1883 to the Texas Legislature and presented with "the finest gun that could be bought" for his service in protecting the frontier. Barry died on his birthday day, Dec. 16, in 1906. He was buried in the Barry Cemetery in Bosque County.

27

MUSTANG COUNTRY

Thomas A. Dwyer

MUSTANGER, RANCHER

I well remember when I first came to Texas in 1848. You could see thousands and tens of thousands of wild horses, mustangs, running in immense herds all over the western country, as far as the eye or telescope could sweep the horizon. The whole country seemed to be in motion.

I have had my gentle-led pack mules "cut off" from my party by mustangs circling and circling around us, and gradually closing in, until by a sudden rush they cut off my animals and darted away with them.

On such occasions, even the wearied and slow-gaited pack mules seemed as if "the speed of thought was in their limbs" in their struggle for liberty. I have lost them, along with the goods on their backs more than once.

In traveling, time and again, I have had to send out my best mounted men to gallop off and act as "videttes" and "flankers" to scare away the immense masses of mustangs that were charging around and threatening to rush over us.

After yelling and firing at them, they would wheel and go thundering away.

At that time many of the Hispanic citizens, whose families lived at Corpus Christi, Goliad and San Antonio, and also at towns along the lower Rio Grande, supported themselves chiefly by "running," that is, catching wild cattle, and by "mustanging," that is, hunting wild horses.

The supply of wild cattle and horses seemed so abundant as to be inexhaustible. The horned cattle were never found in droves, but the horses almost universally ran together in large herds.

In the course of a few years, say by 1857, very few herds of mustangs were to be met, and almost no wild cattle. They had been persistently hunted down and caught or killed. The grown cattle were hunted for their hides, which were sold at half a dollar apiece, or the young cattle were caught and gentled and sold at a dollar a head.

The mustang hunters — "mustangers" — were formed into regularly organized companies, with a "capitan" at the head, who directed all their movements. Concert of plan and action insured success.

The companies sometimes numbered as many as 200 men. Each man had one or more gentle running horses, generally kept in the best condition.

AFTER HAVING AGREED on a point of meeting, the mustangers provided themselves with a few necessaries, such as coffee, if they could afford it (the greatest of luxuries in the field); "dulce," the small cones of hard brown sugar; a bag of "pinole," parched corn ground on a metate; or wheat flour for tortillas; some lariats, ropes made of rawhide, twisted and greased and very pliable; tin cups, butcher knives, blankets, and arms and ammunition.

In those days, Indians were very numerous and very dangerous. They had not yet been beaten back by

hundreds of miles. And they were particularly fond of mustangers' animals and their scalps. It was a great matter for the mustangers to travel in strong parties and to be well and bravely led.

Parties of mustangers would remain in the field for months, winter and summer. Sometimes they erected little shelters for themselves, generally limited to a few branches of trees with a strip or two of an old blanket overhead and on the north side.

They had fresh meat in the greatest abundance; the

country in those years was literally overrun with wild cattle, deer, antelopes, wild hogs, turkeys, hares, prairie fowl and quail.

To see mustangers in full chase was to behold one of the most exciting scenes presented on the Texas frontier. I have witnessed these mustang chases innumerable times, and reveled in their excitement.

The days of mustanging were over by 1859 and I turned to raising horses and mules. I do not wonder that I took to frontier life for many years, with all its dangers and roughness. I had grown tired of city life, with its routine occupations and pleasures. Eleven years at law in London and Dublin, with few briefs, and just 40 guineas in fees (equal to $200 in American money) had given me a big disgust, not only of law but of civilization at its overcrowded centers, fenced in by restrictions, conventionalities, etiquette, artificiality and red tape. I left it all behind and came to South Texas to start a new life.

———————

THOMAS A. DWYER, an attorney in Dublin and London, gave up the practice of law and moved to South Texas. He arrived in Corpus Christi on Dec. 2, 1848. He commanded a company of mustangers for a decade before he started his own ranch where he specialized in breeding horses and mules for sale. Dwyer for a time leased James Durst's old Diezmero Ranch along the Nueces River below the village of San Patricio. The 8,000-acre ranch was later sold to James Bryden.

28

GOING WEST

John H. Peoples
JOURNALIST

(The Mazatlan Rangers with John H. Peoples departed for the California goldfields in February 1849. They struck out from a camp at Twelve-Mile Motts up the river from Corpus Christi and took a line of march for the Rio Grande. The trip across South Texas took 33 days, three times longer than expected. Peoples, in a letter to the Corpus Christi Star, was disgusted with his fellow travelers.)

March 10, 1849, Presidio Rio Grande: I arrived at this place five days ago, in company with 25 of the best men who left Corpus Christi under the name of the Mazatlan Rangers. We are preparing provisions and supplies for a regular start for the Pacific.

It is unnecessary to give you a description of the country over which we passed, as it would be folly to run a road to this point over the trail we took, which measures 231 miles. A better route could be obtained in less than 170 miles over an open and level country with plenty of grass and water.

I did not intend to write anything for publication until my arrival at El Paso del Norte. But a gentleman from Laredo informed me that accounts of our great suffering had reached that place. These accounts originated with the men who came up with us as far as the Laredo road and turned off on that road to Laredo. I am induced, therefore, to make a statement of facts about this trip. There is not a man of truth or character in that party who will corroborate such a silly statement, as regards to our "great suffering."

YOU KNOW HOW we started from Corpus Christi. The wagons were loaded with trunks and other things unnecessary for such a march, and were pulled by three yoke of oxen, which were in poor condition when they started and for the first few days grew even worse by neglect.

A large number of the men in the party were unfit to go to California by any route, and will be unfit to stay there if they ever arrive, unless they can get some situation in the shade, next to a cologne lake. These are men who know nothing of life beyond the measuring of tape and handing out of needles and thread, and such occupations that real men scorn.

Such men, after paying their $150 at New Orleans to join the company, deemed it out of character to do any actual labor in facilitating their progress. The result was that we moved along very slowly, for the good and willing men of the command were too much disgusted to labor not only for themselves but for the others as well.

When every means had failed to get along harmoniously, it was decided to dissolve the company and force each man to work his way through. This was accomplished before our arrival at the Laredo road. Except for 25 of us, the rest all started off south, though their course was north of west, in order to travel on a smooth road. If they suffered one hour after leaving Corpus Christi, then it was on that road. Unless they should include in their bill of suffering such things as sunburned hands, torn pants, and pricks from nopal leaves.

They were never without water, except for one day, when they would not travel 16 miles to reach it. Provisions were plenty and the country abounded in game, yet they complain of "suffering." How many of such men do you think will ever reach the Pacific shore?

The smaller party of 25 men who came up with me to the Presidio Rio Grande are the best of men. They might complain of a want of water for a short time, but this was caused by the loss of our Mexican guide and our inability to find the first water-hole. Our mules and oxen went without water but by feeding on nopal they stood it well.

I am convinced that had the Mazatlan Rangers started from Corpus Christi traveling over a smooth and even road, with their wagons loaded as they were, and with that same don't-care attitude, it still would have taken 25 to 30 days to travel what should take nine or ten days. Of the 33 days it took us to reach this point, since we left Corpus Christi, on 12 of those days we did not travel at all, and on some of the traveling days we made less than six miles. This mode of leisurely travel will give you some idea of the character of the men who started out from Corpus Christi.

JOHN H. PEOPLES, a newspaperman from Louisiana, was one of the country's first war correspondents in the Mexican War. He published the American Flag in Matamoros in 1847, the Vera Cruz Eagle, and the American Star in Jalapa, Puebla, and Mexico City. After the war, he returned to Corpus Christi to edit the Corpus Christi Star. He sold the Star and left Corpus Christi with the Mazatlan Rangers in February 1849. He was drowned while trying to cross the Gulf of California.

29

NO BELLS TOLLED

Emmanuel Domenech

MISSIONARY PRIEST

In May of 1849, at San Antonio as at Castroville, the cholera epidemic made dreadful ravages. My day was spent running from one bed to another, and from the church to the graveyard.

I saw nothing but agony, death and burials. I hardly had time to take my meals. Calls were incessant. I was constantly employed in dispensing remedies, as well as in consoling and praying for the dying. As the epidemic was doing its work of destruction, I performed the duties of nurse-tender; executed the prescriptions of the doctor; administered potions; and in short was occupied with the body and soul at the same time.

I was not always successful in curing the body but it frequently happened that a dying man was pacified by my words and even in the midst of convulsions, would seize my hand in a sign of gratitude and resignation. Then I conveyed him to the graveyard, as horrifying a spectacle to behold as the cholera itself. Wolves and foxes, attracted by the odor of dead bodies, tore into the tombs.

One day I decided to pay a short visit to the cholera patients of San Antonio. Next morning, I was awakened at an early hour by a severe pain in my throat. My whole neck was swollen. Two tiny black spots led me to suppose I had been stung by a venomous insect. This was confirmed by the presence of a large tarantula on the ground.

I washed the bites with liquid ammoniac. Still, when I mounted my horse, half my body was paralyzed. Charles, a young French gentleman, would not hear of my proceeding alone on my journey to San Antonio so he accompanied me.

WHEN WE ARRIVED at San Antonio, I was unable to move a limb. Having no money to pay a surgeon's fee, I begged Charles to make incisions in my neck with his penknife. This gave me great relief. I repeated it and continued to cauterize the bite wounds with ammoniac until I was cured.

San Antonio, which a few days before was so gay, so crowded with people, so full of life, was silent as the grave. The streets were deserted. The church bells no longer tolled for the dead; if they had they done so, the tolling would have been continuous night and day.

The parish priest could find no time even to say mass. One third of the population had fled, and were camped in the woods, along the rivers and streams. Another part shut themselves up in cabins, from which you could hear cries, wailings and supplications. A third part of the population were in the throes and agonies of death.

We met no one in the streets, save for those who were carrying the dead. Coffins were scarce and the dead were in many instances strapped to dried ox-hides and were dragged along, all livid and purple, to their graves. It happened not infrequently that one of those who dragged them along was suddenly struck by the scourge, and after writhing an instant or two, expired by the side of the corpse.

In a short time, the malady pursued the fugitives to the banks of the rivers, or into the depths of the woods, and those silent retreats were made witnesses of heart-rending scenes and horrifying spectacles of men dying alone and unaided in the midst of the wilderness.

FOR SIX WEEKS THE EPIDEMIC raged with undiminished intensity. The preservation of the parish priest's life during all that time was something wonderful, if not miraculous. By what means did he succeed in maintaining life for six weeks, without sleep, without a sufficiency of food, and in the midst of continual fatigue?

The population exclaimed, "It is God alone that sustains him." And they spoke the truth. It was his reward and recompence. Of all the ministers of the various sects then in San Antonio, the good priest was the only one who braved danger to succor his suffering people.

———————

EMMANUEL HENRI DIEUDONNÉ DOMENECH was born at or near Lyons, France, on Nov. 6, 1825. Emmanuel was recruited as a missionary by Bishop Jean Marie Odin and traveled to America in 1846 with Claude M. Dubuis. Domenech was ordained in San Antonio on Oct. 1, 1848 and stationed at Castroville and later at Eagle Pass. He returned to France in 1852. A journal of his experiences was published in Paris in 1857 and translated into English as "Missionary Adventures in Texas and Mexico." He died at Lyons, France, on Sept. 9, 1903.

30

DINNER AT EBERLY HOUSE

Jane Cazneau
WRITER

The steamer "Palmetto" cast its swarm of seasick passengers ashore at Indianola. It was the fourth day out from Galveston, early in March 1850. Everybody was disappointed in Indianola. It was not much to look at and was so different from their ideas, though nobody found room for serious complaint.

A belt of white sand separated the ocean of green prairies from the ocean of blue water. Along the belt was arranged a line of wooden buildings, unrelieved by trees or enclosures. They looked like oversized packing boxes set out on the beach to dry. The people were in such a hurry to commence business that they deferred adornments for a season or two. Lavaca, Indianola's neighbor and rival, looks much the same. Yet, when these forlorn undraped villages plant trees and robe themselves in verdure, as Galveston has done, they will be charming places.

Looking west on Main Street, Indianola

Lounging, good-natured, indifferent "boys," as they call their black male servants, whether from nine to 90, took charge of the baggage of a dozen or so passengers. They marshalled us up to "our house" and in a short time all were disposed of somewhere.

THE HOTEL, EBERLY HOUSE, was brim-full. However, in Texas a single gentleman belongs to an unprivileged class and a gallant colonel was ejected from his snuggery and I was installed in the very midst of his books, boxes, and newspapers, not to mention firearms of every size and description. The gentleman himself was most active in putting things in order for a lady stranger.

When I pressed my regret at the inconvenience of taking possession of his private sanctum, the colonel refused to think of it in any other light than a thing of natural course.

The dinner bell, with its sharp impatient clang, called the party to their first meal on Texas ground. It was abundant and excellent. One of our party thought the venison and wild turkey could have been improved on in the cooking process, but I thought them excellently done.

Our English passenger was delighted with the fine oysters and astonished to meet roast beef so juicy and tender and turtle so perfectly delicious, in this out-of-the-way corner of the world.

But fish, oysters and turtle abound along the Texas coast. They may be had for the taking. The prairies swarm with fine cattle, and beeves may be had for seven or eight dollars a head. Whatever other privations might be before them, the settlers in Texas need not be afraid of dying of famine.

As the sun went down, the sea breeze came up from the bay and we gathered on the balcony to admire the gorgeous canopy of crimson and gold.

One day was given to Lavaca and the next we took up our line of march to San Antonio in a stagecoach chartered for our own private service.

———

JANE McMANUS STORM CAZNEAU studied law with her father, a member of Congress from Troy, N.Y., and married Allen Storm and had a son. Jane Storm moved to Texas, bought land at Matagorda, and married William Cazneau in 1849. Cazneau, from Boston, was a business partner of Henry Kinney of Corpus Christi. Jane Cazneau wrote for northern newspapers under the pen name of Cora Montgomery; she was credited with first using the term "manifest destiny." She died in a shipwreck in 1878.

31

LETTERS FROM THE BORDER

Henry Redmond

TRADER

(Extracts of letters in March and April 1852 from Henry Redmond at a settlement called Bellville on the Rio Grande to his business partner, William Mann, in Corpus Christi.)

March 17, 1852 . . . The troops stationed here leave in the morning for Leona. We shall be left without any protection, which I regret exceedingly. The Indians have been very troublesome since you left.

Gen. Harney sent us word that he recommended a permanent post be established at this place. The general will be at Corpus Christi in three or four weeks. You will have to urge the necessity of having troops stationed here.

I am afraid the ranch (their business outpost) will be deserted before we can get protection. The Indians have been at the Capitania Ranch, three miles above this place, three times during the last month. And they have stolen horses from here in the night. In fact, they have put everybody afoot.

Lieutenants Tyler and Stewart have been out but could not catch them. Tyler followed them below Rio Grande City, where they were followed by a new company beyond Laredo.

April 5 . . . I have seen nothing in the way of business — cash taken in will not amount to fifty dollars. I have no hopes of it getting better unless we get some troops stationed here for protection. For the last 18 days, Indians have been passing up or down daily, killing and destroying everything in their route.

The Indians have a large encampment 40 miles from here between Salado and Rio Grande. The people who were induced to return to their ranches on this side of the river have left, or they are about to leave.

THE FORMER ALCADE of Guerrero, Fernando Cuellar, passed here today on the way to Guerrero. The Mexicans have been talking of raising some 300 men from Camargo, Mier, and other places to break up this party of Indians. Yet nothing has been done and I expect the Indians will be permitted to pass the summer here.

April 16 . . . Some 50 Comanches, with Tecumseh as chief, came through two days ago looking to give Lt. Tyler a fight, but the troops had left, which I think the Indians were always aware of.

They killed a horse at Isidro Bela's and the captive (the one who came in before you left) recognized the horses as belonging to the party which attacked the Capitania Ranch a few weeks before. The inhabitants of the ranch lost every horse they had, together with two American horses belonging to Fernando Cuellar.

If you would send me an ambulance or some other conveyance, I would come in and bring two or three more of our friends who would like to make the trip but have not

134

the means of getting there. If I should not come over, be particular to impress on Gen. Harney how defenseless we are.

Without some protection, we cannot exist here much longer. Not a day passes but the Indians are about, stealing and killing everyone they encounter.

April 28 . . . As regards Kinney's fair (the Lone Star Fair), I will come if absolutely necessary, but you have to send me a conveyance. I have nothing but my mule left. I am afraid to venture outside this country badly mounted.

––––––––––

HENRY W. REDMOND, from England, arrived in Texas in the 1830s. He was at Victoria, engaged in the Mexican trade, then moved to Corpus Christi not long after it was founded in 1839. He became a business partner of William Mann and married Louisa Bowie Baskin, the sister of Esther Baskin Mann, William Mann's wife. Louisa died in 1849. In 1850, he moved to the Rio Grande Valley and established a trading post called Bellville, or Redmond Ranch, across from Guerrero. Redmond married Refugio Diaz in 1853 and they had four children, one of whom, Henry Redmond, became a physician associated with Dr. Spohn in Corpus Christi. Henry W. Redmond Sr. died in 1870.

32

A FAIR CELEBRATION

J. Williamson Moses
SURVEYOR, RANGER, MUSTANGER, JUDGE

Henry L Kinney, "empesario" or founder of Corpus Christi, was one of the most public-spirited men who ever lived west of the Nueces River. He conceived the idea of having a grand fair or exposition in the City by the Sea that would begin on May 1, 1852.

Corpus Christi was then known as Kinney's Ranch, as by its more high-sounding name. Col. Kinney determined to bring the young and growing place into notice by having this fair: and was assisted by John Schatzel, a warm friend of the colonel's, along with Frederick Belden, Henry Gilpin, George Noessel, Henry Berry, and several other of the old timers, whose names are still gratefully remembered.

The colonel made preparations on a grand scale and spared no expense in providing for accommodation of the large concourse of visitors who were invited from far and near, from the Mississippi to the interior of Mexico, and many, yes, very many, came.

As if by magic, Corpus Christi grew into a big city, for the time at least. The town presented the novel and picturesque appearance of an immense camp and village in one. Tents, large and small, were pitched everywhere. Lots that had been vacant were occupied by canvas houses; soda-water fountains, ice-cream stands, confectioneries and restaurants were found conveniently located, and a gay and lively scene met the eye all over the place.

The bright colors and fancy dresses, the beautiful "rebosos" and graceful "tapalos" of the Mexican senoritas and senoras, the broad-brimmed and richly ornamented sombreros of their male companions, their silver trimmed "pantaloneros" and "chivaros," their gorgeous saddles and bridles, heavy with silver, all presented a wonderful sight to many who had come over from the older states, and had never seen anything like it before.

Indeed, a Mexican caballero in those days, mounted on a prancing pony, was quite a novelty to many, and with their jingling spurs and silver-chained bridle reins, made music wherever they went, and attracted a great deal of attention. They were themselves much taken with the many things displayed by the people from New Orleans and other cities which had never been seen in this portion of Texas before.

THERE WAS A GAY and lively time in Corpus Christi, such as I do not think has ever been equaled since. There was a race track prepared with great care in the Rincon (North Beach), close to where General Zachary Taylor's camp had been. Fast horses were brought from different parts of the state to contend for prizes.

Capt. "Legs" Lewis, Capt. Richard King, Gen. Hugh McLeod, Texas Ranger Andy Walker, and many other notables were there and took prominent parts in the sports and festivities. It was a gala time in Corpus Christi.

Amongst other amusements there was a circus, with

J. Williamson Moses recalled Kinney's Lone Star Fair

the finest horses and the best performers that have ever been seen in the region of the Nueces River.

A short time before the fair, Col. Kinney requested me, as I was out running mustangs a great deal at that time, to catch if I could a fine-looking paint stallion for him, or procure one or two from some of the other mustangers on the range. He wanted to present them to the manager of the circus, who would have them trained to perform.

I was lucky enough to lasso a beautiful paint roan and Don Cecelio Balerio, a very successful mustanger, secured

138

a very fine dun paint, both of which animals were turned over to Col. Kinney, and by him presented to the manager of the circus. I had the pleasure of seeing the wild steed of the prairie a short time afterwards enter the ring and behave as well as other horses that had been probably years in training. I heard that the roan paint had been afterwards trained to trot in single harness and made quite a reputation as a fast goer in New Orleans. He could have been disposed of for as many dollars as he would have brought cents if sold here soon after he was caught.

Horses around Corpus Christi were very cheap in those days, particularly mustangs, which could be found in thousands on the range and could be had for the roping or penning. The highest price for an unbroken mustang then was about five dollars.

J. WILLIAMSON MOSES was born on his father's plantation in South Carolina in 1825. He came to Texas in 1846. He knew Sam Houston, Edward Burleson and David Burnet. He worked with James Giddings as a surveyor in the Pedernales region before he joined John Sutton's company of Texas Rangers. In the 1850s, Moses was captain of a crew of mustangers working out of Corpus Christi. He later opened a store at Banquete. During the Civil War, he served in John Rabb's Confederate company on the border. After the war, he joined other Confederate emigres in Mexico. He moved back to Texas, passed the bar exam and was elected county judge of Aransas County. He moved to San Diego where he died on April 28, 1893. His obituary said, "Another old Texas landmark is gone, lamented by all."

33

COMANCHE HORSE RACE

Richard Irving Dodge
COLONEL, U.S. ARMY

In good weather, nearly half an Indian male's waking hours are passed in the saddle. Riding is second nature to him. He was strapped astride a horse before he scarcely learned to walk and could not, as a man, remember a time when he could not ride.

I have never seen the riding of Arabs and Cossacks and other famous horsemen, so I cannot say how the Indian compares, but I am satisfied that he could hardly be surpassed by any of them.

When traveling from place to place, under ordinary circumstances, a more unromantic or less dangerous-looking specimen could not be found than an Indian warrior. His seat and carriage on horseback are particularly ungraceful. The short stirrups force him to sit almost on the small of his back, and the back itself is rounded into an unseemly curve. His left hand holds the reins. His right is armed with a short stick with lengths of rawhide, and a light blow of this marks every step of the horse. The rider scarcely ever turns his head or moves his body, and even when he is most watchful, he appears to see nothing.

The Indian on horseback looks stiff, constrained, and uncomfortable. And yet this uncouth object can perform incredible feats of horsemanship. With his horse galloping at full speed, he will pick up from the ground a small coin. He will throw himself on the side of his horse, in such a position that only a small portion of an arm and leg can be seen from the other side.

One method of Indian racing is to start from a line, and rush full-speed at a tree. The one who first reaches it is the winner. Another is to rush at a heavy pole placed horizontally six feet from the ground, resting on forks firmly set. If the rider stops his horse an instant too soon, he fails to touch the pole, and if an instant too late, the horse passes under the pole, leaving the rider dangling on the pole or thrown to the ground.

The training of the ponies has quite as much to do with the success of an Indian race as his speed or the actions of the rider. Great pains are taken in training, and a pony thoroughly up to his tricks is highly prized.

As a jockey, the Indian rider understands all the tricks of professional horse-racing, but the Indian rarely comes into sporting competition with whites. It is exceedingly difficult to hit on a fair distance between the Indian and American horse. The start being always from a halt, the small quick pony is almost sure to win at from 100 to 300 yards. The long stride of the American horse is equally sure of carrying him to victory from 600 yards to two miles.

A tribe of Comanches under Chief Mu-la-que-top was camped around Fort Chadbourne near San Angelo. Some of the officers of the fort at this time were "horsey" fellows and owned blooded horses, the speed of each being known, by repeated trials, almost to a foot.

141

Chief Mu-la-que-top was bantered for a race and after several days of negotiating a contest was set against the third-best horse of the garrison, for a distance of 400 yards. The Indians bet robes and items of various kind, to the value of 60 or 70 dollars against money, flour, sugar, to a like amount.

At the appointed time, all the Indians and most of the garrison were assembled at the track. The Indians brought out this miserable pony that looked like a sheep with a three-inch coat of rough and matted hair stuck out all over his body. His general expression of neglect, helplessness, and patient suffering struck pity in the hearts of all beholders.

THE INDIAN RIDER was a stalwart man of about 170 pounds who looked big and strong enough to carry the poor beast on his shoulders. The rider was armed with a huge club, with which, after the word was given, he belabored the miserable animal from start to finish. To the astonishment of all the whites, the Indians won by a neck.

Another race was proposed by the officers and, after much dickering, accepted by the Indians, against the next-best horse of the garrison. The bets were doubled. And in less than an hour after the first race, the second race was run by the same miserable pony, with the same apparent exertion and the same result.

The officers were thoroughly disgusted. They proposed a third race and brought to the ground a magnificent Kentucky mare, of the true Lexington blood, and known to beat the best of the others by 40 yards in 400.

The Indians accepted the race, and not only doubled the bets, as before, but piled up everything they could raise, seemingly crazed with the excitement of their previous success.

The riders mounted. The word was given. Throwing away his club, the Indian rider gave a whoop, at which the sheep-like pony pricked up his ears and ran like the wind, gaining almost two feet to one of the Kentucky mare's. The last 50 yards of the course was run by the pony with the Indian sitting facing his tail and beckoning to the rider on the mare to hurry up and come on.

It later transpired that the sheep-like pony was famous for his speed celebrated among all the tribes of the south, and that Chief Mu-la-que-top had just returned from a trip to the Indian nation, where he had run the horse and easily cleaned the Kickapoos out of many ponies.

RICHARD IRVING DODGE was born on May 19, 1827, in Huntsville, N. C. He graduated from West Point in 1848 and was assigned duty with the 8th U.S. Infantry. He was stationed at Fort Chadbourne in Texas from June through September 1853. As a career officer stationed on the Western frontier, he studied the habits and customs of the native tribes and in 1882 wrote "Our Wild Indians," which Gen. Sherman called "the best description extant . . . of the American Indian as he is now." Dodge died June 16, 1895 at Sackets Harbor, N.Y., and was buried in Arlington National Cemetery. His widow, Julia Rhinelander Paulding Dodge, died in 1926 and was buried at Arlington.

34

KOWEAKA'S CHOICE

Rupert Norval Richardson
EDUCATOR, HISTORIAN

In the 1850s new forts was built in the very heart of the
Comanche range, especially Forts Phantom Hill and
Chadbourne. The Indians did not like them but could not
openly resist them.

Chief Sanaco and his understudy Yellow Wolf called at
Fort Belknap to express friendship. Buffalo Hump was the
arrogant one. In the days of the Republic, he had sent word
to President Houston to wait for him, to have everything
ready, and he would come for a talk when he was ready.

The Buffalo Hump who came to Fort Phantom Hill was
older and less brash but still a man of insolent bearing. The
great chief of the Comanches, in the company of two pretty
young wives, expressed friendship with the troops, and ate
of the sugar, hard bread and beef that the fort commissary
provided.

At Forts McKavett and Terrett, 200 miles south of Fort Belknap, the Comanches were equally at home. Officers came to know Sanaco, Yellow Wolf, Buffalo Hump and another chief named Ke-tem-i-see, which the whites shortened to Katumse.

Although the line of forts cut through Comanche country, the Indians could still stay on the outside and carry on their accustomed way of life. But the growing pressure of the settlers and soldiers caused a large number of Texas Indians to migrate into Indian Territory. Of these, the most troublesome were the Wacos and Wichitas, who persisted in returning from time to time to steal horses and engage in all sorts of skullduggery.

FEDERAL RELATIONS WITH THE INDIANS on the Brazos during the early 1850s were in the hands of Jesse Stem, an Ohio lawyer who had joined the U. S. Indian Service and came to Texas in 1851.

In February 1852, at Fort Graham, far down the Brazos, Jesse Stem delivered presents and powwowed with Buffalo Hump and Yellow Wolf, of the Southern Comanches, and Pah'-hah-yo'-ko, chief of the northern Comanche bands that visited the Brazos country. Stem also had a good audience with the lesser tribes, the Wacos, Keechis, Caddoes, and others.

Stem, a few months later, moved to the Crossing of the Clear Fork of the Brazos, halfway between Forts Belknap and Phantom Hill. He was not armed and troops were more than 30 miles away. The Ohioan stated candidly that along with looking after the Indians he expected to make some money. He decided to locate some land, both for speculation and for a corn farm. He began farming and raising livestock and called the establishment he set up the Agency for the Indians of Texas.

The Comanches understood that Stem's agency was there to serve them and "nobody shoots Santa Claus." The Comanche chiefs — Sanaco, Katumse, Buffalo Hump and

Pah'-hah-yo'-ko — called on him, received his presents, and consumed his beef.

The good agent did not just preside over the agency, hold "talks" with the chiefs, and hand out presents. He also felt responsible for the conduct of his wards. Once word came that a party of Wacos were making way with stolen horses. Stem armed his employees, called on Chief Sanaco for help, and the little force of white men and Comanches (strange allies) set out and captured the Wacos and their stolen horses.

Stem soon made the acquaintance of Koweaka, a Wichita chief who had come down from Indian Territory with 22 men in order, he said, to fight the Lipan Apaches. The agent ordered them to return to Indian Territory, stating that their real purpose was to steal horses.

The agent, for the chief's benefit, reviewed the thefts of the Wichitas in recent months, extending as far away as Fort Croghan, 50 miles above Austin (near today's Burnet). The chief agreed to talk to his people and help stop horse-stealing.

A MONTH LATER Koweaka returned to the agency with eight men and several women and children. They were driving 14 horses to be given up. So enthusiastic had the chief become on the subject of restoring stolen property that he had stolen four horses from the Caddoes and brought them to the agency to give them up. The other horses in the bunch were of little value, except for two that had been stolen at Fort Croghan.

Only recently, on a dark and rainy night, Indians had crept to the stable lot at Fort Croghan and made away with some of the finest horses the dragoons had.

The commander at Fort Croghan at that time was Major Henry H. Sibley (later a Confederate general). When Sibley discovered the loss of nine horses, he took a squad of 17 men and headed to Stem's Indian Agency at the Clear Fork of the Brazos. Everyone he talked to assured him that the theft was the work of the Wichitas.

While Sibley was at the agency Koweaka brought in the 14 horses. There in the herd were two dragoon horses; not of the recent nine that had been stolen, but two which had been taken some weeks before that.

"I was not to be trifled with in this matter," Sibley wrote later. He added that Stem, the Indian agent, had also lost patience with Koweaka and his crowd. The two men decided to make the chief and his party prisoners, take them to Fort Belknap, release two of the men as messengers to bring in the other horses, and hold the party captive until the animals were delivered.

STEM AND SIBLEY ANNOUNCED their intent to the Indians. Chief Koweaka asked for a private talk with Sibley and explained his difficulty in restraining the young men and urged that he be permitted to return to his tribe. Sibley said no, he was adamant, and the Indian was forced to accept his decision.

The Wichitas were disarmed and allowed to retire to their tents. Sentries were posted to see that none escaped.

Koweaka went to his lodge with his wife and seven-year-old son. He pulled off his moccasins and placed them near the head of their pallet, a token that he would not need them again.

At midnight, as a guard made his rounds, an Indian charged toward him. He fired and killed the Indian. The whole camp was aroused. Koweaka rushed out, threw himself on the guard, and stabbed him to death before he himself was shot down. Most of the other Wichitas escaped.

After the melee was over, an examination of the lodges revealed Koweaka's wife and son lying side by side, as if in deep sleep, but stabbed to the heart. From two old Wichita women who had not attempted to escape, it was learned that the wife had assented to her fate. "She seemed to have received the fatal blow without a struggle," Sibley wrote his wife. "Both bodies were carefully covered up, the child lying in his mother's arms. The chief's moccasins were near their heads."

On the banks of the Clear Fork of the Brazos on a March night in 1853, Koweaka, the Wichita chief, and his loyal wife had to choose between a white man's iron cage and death. They chose death.

RUPERT NORVAL RICHARDSON was born on April 28, 1891 near Caddo. In 1915 he married Pauline Mays and Richardson served as principal of Cisco High School then Sweetwater High School before becoming a professor of history at Simmons College in 1917. He was associated with Hardin-Simmons University until his death, serving as dean of students, vice president, and president. Among his many scholarly publications was "The Frontier of Northwest Texas." He died in Abilene on April 14, 1988.

35

IT TAKES ALL SORTS

Frederick Law Olmsted
TRAVELER IN TEXAS

Dec. 24, 1853. San Augustine. Late on Christmas Eve we were invited to the window by our landlady to see the pleasant local custom of the Christmas Serenade.

A band of pleasant spirits started from the square, blowing tin horns, and beating tin pans, and visited in succession every house in the village, kicking in doors, and pulling down fences, until every male member of the family had appeared, with appropriate instruments, and joined the merry party. They marched to the square, and ended the ceremony with a centupled tin row. In this touching commemoration, as strangers, we were not urged to participate.

Feb. 23, 1854, near Gonzales. We passed cotton fields and wagons loaded with cotton. One carrying eight bales, drawn by 10 very lean oxen, was from San Marcos bound for the coast.

Engraving of Frederick Law Olmsted in 1893

Across the wet hogwallow prairie in the latter part of the day, the road was very heavy. In the creek, near which we made our camp, a cotton team was stalled, and it was late at night before the whipping and swearing came to an end.

While we were at breakfast in the morning, the teamster came to ask our assistance. He had cut trees for fulcrum and lever, and thought with our help he should be able to get out. We worked for an hour under his guidance, covering ourselves with mire but accomplishing nothing.

A man appeared on horseback, who added his exertions. After perceiving that our combined efforts would not suffice to raise the wheel, the man on horseback said,

"Stranger, I'll give you my advice. I'm sick and not able to help you much. I'm going now to see a doctor. But your wagon isn't very badly stalled, sir. The mire is not deep here. That wheel is on the gravel now. I'll tell you what's the matter; your cattle are too weak. Now you take them all out, and give them a feed, and turn them out to graze till another team comes up, and they'll have to help you, because there isn't room to get by." With that he mounted and rode on.

We did the same, the teamster offering us no thanks, but shouting after us, "What'll you take for that mule?"

FEB. 27, 1854, SOUTH OF GONZALES. "Which way did you come?" asked someone of the old man.

"From ———."

"See anything of a runaway nigger over there, anywhere?"

"No, sir. What kind of a nigger was it?"

"A small, black, screwed-up-faced nigger."

"How long has he been out?"

"Nigh onto two weeks."

"Whose is he?"

"Belongs to Judge ——— up here. And he cut the judge right bad. Like to have killed the judge. Cut his young master, too."

"Reckon if they caught him, it would go hard with him."

"Reckon it would. We caught him once but he got away from us again. We were tying his feet together and he give me a kick in the face and broke. I had my six-shooter handy, and tried to shoot him, but every barrel missed fire. If he's got across the river, he'll get to the Mexicans in two days and there he'll be safe. The Mexicans will take care of him."

"What made him run?"

"The judge gave him a week off at Christmas and he made a good deal of money and when the week was up, I guess he didn't want to work again. He got unruly and they were going to whip him. The judge treats his niggers too kind. If he was stricter with them, they would have more respect for him and be more contented, too. Never do to be too slack with niggers."

MARCH 1, 1854, GUADALUPE RIVER. We crossed the Guadalupe on a ferryboat, the bridge having been long ago carried away in a freshet. The ferryman informed us that a steamboat of light draft used to ply the river to Victoria.

Two men overtook us and made offers of horse-trading. On learning we were from New York, one said, "From New York! You're a long way from your native home, ain't you? I expect you seem to think the country here tolerable curious. Folks from up north always think people here are awful rough. We ain't so smart down south as you are up north. We don't fix up so much, I reckon, do we? Reckon you see some people that are right curiosities, don't you? Well, folks down south like to live rough. It takes all sorts to make a world."

We passed a man engaged in firing the prairie. He drew a handful of long burning grass along the dry grass tops, at a run. Before the high gale it kindled furiously, and in 15 minutes had progressed a mile to leeward, jumping, with a flash, many feet at a time. In a moderate wind we had once noted the progress of prairie flame, to windward, at about one foot per minute.

FREDERICK LAW OLMSTED was born in Hartford, Conn., on April 26, 1822. He was commissioned to write articles for the New York Times and traveled with his brother in late 1853 and 1854 from Natchitoches through the German settlements to San Antonio and on to Victoria, Port Lavaca and Indianola. The result was "A Journey Through Texas" published in 1857. J. Frank Dobie wrote that Olmsted traveled "in order to see; he saw." He died in 1903.

36

GONE FOR A SOLDIER

Lydia Spencer Lane
SOLDIER'S WIFE

November 1854 . . . Our voyage on the "Josephine" was not a long one, which we did not regret. While walking about on the boat and looking around, I noticed on the lower deck a much-coiled speckled mass. I called the captain and pointed it out, asking what it was. His answer was a cry of horror as he yelled for "Tom, Jim, John!" to come with spades, axes, shovels to kill the moccasin. It was one of the most poisonous snakes of the region and its presence there was unaccountable.

From the "Josephine" we were taken on to a "lighter," a small schooner, which was to carry us to Corpus Christi. There was only room on it for a few of the officers, Col. Sidney Burbank and family, Lt. Lane and myself. Other transportation was provided for the soldiers and the baggage and supplies.

We passed the night on the lighter. I cannot say we slept. The accommodations were of the most contracted description. There was scarcely room to stand upright in the hold, where Mrs. Burbank, children, nurse, and myself were stowed away.

We improved our time by fighting roaches and other things down below while the officers spent the night on the deck.

We made the best of the situation. We had a very funny time, astonishing our friends above us with many a hearty laugh. They wondered what we had found down in the depths to amuse us so much.

Our breakfast next morning was not luxurious — bread, very good, without butter, fried bacon, and coffee, but no milk. We were hungry and accepted the fare thankfully.

WE WERE TO REACH Corpus Christi before noon that day. By some means we heard, before we landed, that people were dying on every side from yellow fever. We were going right into the midst of a raging epidemic.

It was dreadful news to us. There was no escape, no running away from it, nothing to do but land, take the risk, and trust in Providence. Well, I had "gone for a soldier"* and soldier I would be.

We found our camp ready for us. It was right on the beach at Corpus Christi — tents pitched for officers and men. They were selected according to rank. By the time the young officers' turn came to secure one, it was Hobson's choice — take what was left or nothing.

I heard afterwards that a spacious wall-tent had been floored and pitched for us especially, as relative newlyweds, but we only saw the outside of it. An unmarried officer, who was senior in rank to Lt. Lane, with an eye to his own comfort, appropriated it immediately.

---

* The phrase "go for a soldier" meant to enlist in the army. By marrying a soldier, she had also enlisted.

We were put into a large hospital tent with an opening at each end, which could be closed when necessary. We had no board-floor in it, only the sands of the sea for carpeting.

I went into the tent with heavy heart. I expected nothing less than an outbreak of yellow fever in the camp. The situation was grave enough to alarm anyone. But the very first night we spent ashore a violent norther struck the coast and it became very cold. A heavy frost was the result and not another case of fever was reported in the town.

We were very happy, having escaped the awful disease. We began cheerfully to make preparations for the march we had before us to Fort Inge where Lt. Lane had been assigned.

One night during the norther, the wind blew a hurricane and our tent was torn open at both ends. Between the pounding of the waves on the beach, the shrieking of the wind, and the flapping of the loose canvas, the noise was fearful. I expected to be blown bodily out to sea.

With the assistance of some soldiers, after a violent struggle, the tent was made secure and we managed to live in our uncomfortable quarters until we left Corpus Christi for Fort Inge.*

* * *

IN FEBRUARY 1855, MY HUSBAND was granted a short leave and we made a visit to San Antonio, and Austin, where Dr. R. N. Lane, my brother-in-law, was practicing medicine, and well known to many army people.

We left Fort Inge in an ambulance, with no escort. Mr. Lane and the driver were supposed to be sufficient guard through a country where there were settlements and a house to sleep in every night.

---

* Fort Inge was a mile below today's Uvalde on the east bank of the Leona River. Handbook of Texas.

155

Commerce Street in San Antonio, about 1855

At the end of the first day's ride we found D'hanis, a small German settlement, where one Mr. Finger kept a house for wayfarers. The furniture in our room consisted of a bed, washstand, some extremely uncomfortable chairs, and a small table on which our meals were served. With a fire of dry logs we felt quite content after being in the cold wind all day. But in all my wanderings, I have never come across another bed such as that. It was shaped just like an egg. We had to cling like bats to stay in it at all, and had very little rest. I am sure Mr. Finger would have been surprised had we told him the bed was uncomfortable.

The next stop we made was at Castroville. We found quite a nice house kept by a quaint old Frenchwoman —

Madame Tardee. Her place was well patronized by army people at the time. The house was clean and the fare better than one would expect. The bedrooms, upstairs, were divided by canvas partitions. We had to whisper if we did not want to be heard all over the house. Later on we found that canvas played a conspicuous part in the building of Texas houses. Sometimes one whole side would be made of it, the occupants intending "some day" to replace it with more substantial material.

On the third day we drove into San Antonio. We stopped at the Plaza House, then the best hotel in town. It was on the Main Plaza not far from the cathedral. San Antonio's foreign style of architecture interested me very much, and also the gardens, filled as they were with tropical trees and unfamiliar plants and flowers.

After resting at San Antonio, we drove to Austin, taking three or four days to make the distance. We found some very pleasant, cultivated people at Austin, among them Miss Annie Swisher, whom Dr. Lane eventually married. A brighter woman I never met anywhere.

In two weeks our leave was up and we left for the western frontier. We were happy to reach Fort Inge and home. We made no more expeditions until we left for Fort Clark.

———————

LYDIA SPENCER BLANEY LANE was born Nov. 28, 1834. She married Lt. William Bartlett Lane on May 18, 1854 and left with his army detachment when he was assigned to Fort Inge in Texas. The Lanes had two daughters. Lydia Lane's memoir "I Married a Soldier" was originally published in 1893. She died on June 28, 1914 and was buried in Arlington National Cemetery.

37

PINE KNOTS

August Santleben
FREIGHTER

My first visit to San Antonio was made with my father in 1854 when I was nine. On this occasion I was made happy by all the wonderful things I saw in the city, which filled my childish mind with astonishment. The business portion of the town was confined to the two plazas, and most of the improvements were in that vicinity. I suppose the population then was not more than 8,000.

My next trip away from home was when I went with my father to Fort Inge on the Leona River. We rode on his wagon which was loaded with corn he had sold to the government. It was part of a quantity he contracted to deliver, at 40 cents and 50 cents a bushel, as forage for a company of dragoons stationed at the fort, which was four miles below where the town of Uvalde was later built.

Another detachment of dragoons was at Fort Ewell, on the Laredo Road.

All the men in these companies were splendidly mounted on the best horses Missouri could furnish. Their saddles were the old government pattern with solid brass stirrups that weighed two pounds. All the mountings were also of solid brass.

Every soldier was armed with two holster pistols and a Mississippi rifle, called a Yager, which had the same caliber as the pistols so they used the same fixed cartridges loaded with a ball and three buckshot.

I was nine years old then but I took notice of everything. These were the first soldiers I had ever seen. At Fort Inge I ate my first hardtack and saw my first playing cards.

While my father was unloading the corn, I gathered the cards that were scattered around the camp. That was the first time I had seen painted pictures of any kind and I thought the cards were the prettiest things I had ever seen.

I OFTEN WENT WITH MY FATHER on his trips away from home. I am inclined to think that he took me with him to cut down on my mischief-making.

He made frequent trips to Port Lavaca with his ox-wagon, when his team was not needed on the farm, and he received fair compensation for hauling freight both ways, from San Antonio to Port Lavaca and back. I was not only his traveling companion but made myself useful by driving the oxen.

My father contracted with a party in San Antonio to haul a load of pine lumber from a mill at Bastrop, on the Colorado River. I went with him.

Bastrop was a small village with a scattering of houses. The night we camped in the town a public meeting was held in the open air, which I attended. I have no recollection of what the meeting was about, although it was the first political speech I ever heard. I do remember that the place was lit up by torches made of pine knots and they made the most beautiful light I had ever seen.

When I learned that I could get pine knots for the trouble of gathering them, I lost no time in collecting all I wanted, though the task was not as easy as I expected.

On the way home I illuminated our camp every night and still had some left with which I lit up the premises to please my friends. They were delighted because they had never seen anything so brilliant before. The exhibition was brought to a sudden close when I barely missed setting the corn crib on fire.

The light we had been accustomed to was made by wrapping a rag around a stick and saturating it with lard. The lower end was stuck in a tin coffee cup half full of sand. The cup was filled with rendered lard or melted tallow. It made a very dim light. It was the best we could do until candle molds were introduced. Then came sperm candles of northern manufacture. The first I ever saw was in Castroville in 1855 when three of them sold for 25 cents. They were too high-priced for common use and more than the poorer people could afford to pay.

AUGUST MARCUS SANTLEBEN was born Feb. 28, 1845 in Germany, the son of Christian and Sophie (Haas) Santleben. In 1845 they came to Texas and settled at Castro's Corner, north of Castroville. During the Civil War, Santleben freighted cotton to the Mexican border. He later enlisted as a scout for Union cavalry in the lower Rio Grande Valley. After the war, he formed a partnership to establish a stagecoach line from San Antonio to Monterrey, which was expanded to include freighting. Santleben married Mary Anna Obert of Boerne on Dec. 30, 1870. They had seven children and adopted two. Santleben died on Sept. 18, 1911. He was buried in the Odd Fellows Cemetery in San Antonio.

38

MY OLD TURNIP

Nelson Lee

TEXAS RANGER, INDIAN CAPTIVE

In 1855, William Aikens, an intelligent and enterprising man who had been a resident of Bastrop, conceived the project of purchasing a drove of mules in Mexico for the California market. A company was formed with a capital of $7,000. We made our headquarters at San Patricio on the Nueces, 30 miles above Corpus Christi, and hired 19 assistants to accompany us on the trip to California.

We left San Patricio and set out for Matamoros. Our plan was to travel up from this point and buy and collect our drove as we advanced along the Mexican river towns. At San Fernando our drove had increased to 395. We pushed on in the direction of Paso del Norte.

The second of April was remarkably fine, the air delicious and balmy. It was my turn to stand watch that night till 12 o'clock and at last, in the dead hours of the night, I dropped off to sleep.

Was it a dream or was it real, that scream that split the air?

It was as real as you can get. The camp was under attack and filled with painted and yelling savages. I grabbed my rifle but in an instant a rope was thrown over my head and half a dozen Indians sprang upon me. My feet and hands were tied with stout buffalo thongs.

Following the massacre, the only members of the party still alive were Thomas Martin of San Patricio, John Stewart, a Scotchman from San Antonio, Aikens and myself. The others were all slaughtered. The Indians stripped us of every particle of our clothing and gave us leggings and a hunting shirt made of buckskin to wear.

While they were stripping me, one of them discovered my old repeater watch. As he regarded it, the minute hand ticked round to half-past three and the alarm went off. The Indian was utterly astonished. He showed the watch to others and pointed to me. They untied my hands, pointing to the watch. They wanted me to cause it to repeat the alarm.

I wound it up and set it so that in a few minutes off it went again. This was repeated frequently until the leader of the war party wrapped it carefully in a deerskin pouch.

The scene at our camp was awful. The corpses of our butchered comrades had been cut up and hacked about in the most brutal and wanton manner.

Deerskin sacks were thrown over our heads and tied tight, blindfolding and almost suffocating us. We each were mounted on a mule, our hands tied behind us, our feet tied close together under the body of the mount. Unable to see, I was in perpetual suspense.

We halted for the night and the deerskin bags were taken off. One or two horses were killed and the meat brought in for supper. That night we were made to lie on our backs, arms and feet extended. Wooden stakes were driven into the ground to which our hands and feet were tied. Two stakes were driven close to either side of the neck and a strong strip of buffalo hide tied from one to the other, across the throat. We lay on our backs, unable to move hand, foot or head.

On the second day we reached a wide river, which I learned later was the upper Rio Grande. We crossed the river and, on the fourth day the warriors raised a loud whoop, answered by another whoop, and we soon found ourselves in the midst of a great number of tents. We were surrounded by 500 or 600 men, all pushing forward to get a sight of us.

At length the crowd parted to form a passage through which advanced the leader of the war party and an aged chief and squaw. The watch, my "old turnip" as I called it, was produced and handed to me, with signs indicating they wished me to "make it go."

I put on a show. I held it up to my ear, listened to the tick tick tick, and presently it sounded the alarm. The Indians looked enquiringly into each other's faces, as much as if to say, "Well, I never; did you ever?"

The watch was taken by the old chief, whom I later learned was called Osolo, which translated to Big Wolf, and he presented it to his favorite wife, whom I learned was called Moko.

After four days, a strong guard escorted me to a point a quarter-mile from the village. There were Aikens, Martin and Stewart, stripped naked and bound to high posts. I was stripped of my Indian garb and placed next to Aikens. There we stood in tormenting suspense, waiting to learn what diabolical fate was in store for us.

The war chief was at the head of a procession of some 200 warriors. They all moved slowly in single file at a pace that was peculiar — half walk, half shuffle, a nervous spasmodic motion like figures in a puppet show. As the procession approached, two of the youngest members broke from the line and quickly scalped Stewart and Martin. The blood flowed down their faces and into their beards, but the wounds were by no means fatal.

They passed Aikens and myself without molestation.

The strange circuitous march was continued. When they reached Stewart and Martin the second time, they cut them with sharp flint arrowheads, causing the blood to ooze in great crimson gouts. They left Aikens and myself unharmed.

As their tortures continued, Stewart uttered not a word, only grunts of pain, while Martin's pitiful prayers and cries were unceasing. I hung down my head and closed my eyes.

At the end of perhaps two hours came the last act of this fearful tragedy. The warriors halted on their last round. Two of them moved out and, dancing before the victims, drew their hatchets and sent the bright blades crashing through their skulls.

The horribly cut-up bodies were taken down and thrown on the ground. Aikens and myself were unbound, given our hunting shirts to wear, and sent towards the camp. As we moved off, I turned to take a last look at my dead companions. The village dogs were gathered around their corpses, licking at the blood from their innumerable wounds.

Several days later, Aikens was brought to my tent, surrounded by a formidable guard. He was permitted to sit down beside me and an hour's time was granted. He was more familiar with Indian life and customs than I was. He understood their signs and language better.

He had experienced more severe treatment than I had been subjected to. He had learned that he was about to be carried to some distant tribe and that he was sure he was doomed to die by torture, probably like that of Stewart and Martin.

Aikens encouraged me to do everything I could to ingratiate myself in their favor until some opportunity presented itself to escape. And if I should manage to escape, he wanted me to tell of his fate to his friend, Antonio Fernandez of Corpus Christi. He bade me a sorrowful farewell and passed out of the tent. I never saw him again.

I had confidence in his shrewdness and judgement and resolved to follow his advice to the letter. I did everything to make myself agreeable.

It was not long before the chief's squaw, Moko, came with a new group of faces and presented me with the watch with signs to "make it go." I put on my act and fell into a deep mysterious mood. Winding it up and setting the alarm a minute or two ahead, I bowed my face before it, held it at arm's length, and regarded it with an intensity of expression, like that of a tragedian on the stage. I turned my eyes to the heaven and let it whiz.

THE EFFECT WAS most satisfactory. I felt I had made a big hit. As Aikens had predicted, their vigilance over time was relaxed, so much so that I was permitted to wander through the village but not beyond it. They called me "Chemakacho," meaning "good white man." I now enjoyed comparative freedom.

We were visited by the chiefs and warriors of surrounding tribes. There was one visitor in particular, a stout and surly chief, who became fascinated by the watch. He never grew weary of listening to the alarm. I learned that he was known as Spotted Leopard.

About November, after the season of buffalo hunting had arrived, I was ordered one morning to mount a mule. We rode forth with Big Wolf and half a dozen of his warriors. On the journey I was neither tied nor blindfolded. After several days traveling we came in sight of a large Indian village. When we reached the square, the same surly chief who was so fascinated by the watch came forward. We were in the camp of Spotted Leopard.

Next morning, a large number of horses were driven in from the pasture by the women. Piles of buffalo, deer and beaver skins were brought out from the tents and packed on mules. I was then brought out by Big Wolf, who informed me I had been sold. Big Wolf and his warriors departed. In the transaction, I learned, my purchase price was 120 horses and as many skins as three pack mules could carry.

After four days, Big Wolf returned, attended by his four wives and a number of warriors. The wives of the two chiefs, myself, and several old men, gathered for a ceremony with a dance and lighted pipe. Moko came forward with the watch. She kissed it and presented it to me, then turned about, crying, and went into a tent.

I caused it to sound the alarm, perhaps a dozen times. Spotted Leopard approached me with one of his wives, who I found was called Kianceta, the weasel. She was tall and slim with long hair blacker than the feathers of a crow. She was lovely to look upon. Kianceta treated me with all the kindness I had previously received at the hands of Moko. Into her possession was given my old turnip, that weird mysterious thing through which the Great Spirit spoke in a strange voice.

I was at the tribe of Spotted Leopard between two and three years. A frequent visitor to our camp was a chief whose named translated into Rolling Thunder. He was an agreeable man, a compound of sedate solemnity and benign dignity.

Chief Rolling Thunder would fall into a profound reverie when Kianceta, the weasel, presented me with the watch with signs to "make it talk." His discussions with Spotted Leopard became so long and earnest that I had no doubt I was about to be sold again. My surmises proved correct and I was soon conveyed to Rolling Thunder's village.

Time passed. I had no apprehension in regard to my safety so long as I remained an obedient captive. But any attempt to escape would be followed by the severest penalties. It became necessary for me to devise some plan in case the opportunity offered to make my getaway.

While indulging in these speculations, Rolling Thunder ordered me to saddle my mule and accompany him on a long journey. His destination was a village three days' ride to the north. At this place a general convention had been called of all the chiefs of the different tribes.

We traveled leisurely but steadily. On the second day, about one o'clock in the afternoon, we reached the bottom of a deep hollow, where we found water oozing from the base of a precipice and trickling down in a little muddy channel.

He told me to fill the horn. I attempted to obey, but the stream was so shallow that every dip that I made the contents came up more mud than water. He leaped down from his horse, ordered me to hold the bridle, threw his rifle on the ground, and lay down to drink from the little stream.

I saw the hatchet hanging from the pommel of the saddle. I snatched it and leaped upon him and buried the dull edge of the blade into his brain. I took the rifle from underneath him, got his long knife, mounted his horse and rode away on an unknown path toward freedom.

NELSON LEE was born in Brownsville, Jefferson County, New York, in 1807, the son of Parmer Lee. He came to Texas in 1840 and served in the Texas Rangers with Jack Hays, Ben McCulloch and Samuel H. Walker. He served in Hays' regiment during the Mexican War. In March 1855, Lee and five other men formed a joint stock company to drive horses to California. The party was attacked by Comanches and all were killed or captured. Three years later, Lee escaped and made his way to El Paso and eventually to New York. The story of his adventures and captivity was published in 1859. Whether the narrative is true in all or part has been debated. Walter Prescott Webb wrote that Lee, like Cabeza de Vaca, made a hard journey and returned to tell about it. Lee died on Nov. 30, 1870. The Daily Times, Watertown, N.Y., said the "adventurer, author and lecturer" was found very sick near Hammond Corners, where he alighted from the stage. He died soon afterwards. His place of burial is unknown.

39

HARD LICKS

Robert Adams

RANCHER

When I was eight years old, in 1856, my father made an arrangement that I would live in the home of Mr. Samuel Colon* and work for him for food and clothing. He was a freighter and shipped goods out of Corpus Christi by ox-cart to all parts of the country. He was living in Corpus Christi then, but later, in 1860, he moved to Nuecestown and I went with him.

Colon gave me six months schooling while we were at Nuecestown, recompense for all the hard work I did. That was all the schooling that I ever had. My teacher was Horace Taylor, a large man who came from the North and lived with his mother.

---

* Robert Adams disguised the name as Samuel Colon, but census records show the freighter's name actually was Samuel Couling.

168

One day Colon broke my leg. He would have broken my neck if George Reynolds hadn't stepped in and stopped him. It happened on George Reynolds' porch at Nuecestown. There were five or six yoke of oxen hitched to the wagon and some of them were not very gentle. Colon told me to unhitch them and I didn't move to do it fast enough to suit him. He picked me up and threw me down on the floor so hard it broke my leg. I crawled away under the porch. The oxen went off with the wagon and were gone all night, hitched to the wagon, but they were found next morning.

Colon was drunk and angry when he treated me the way he did. They didn't set my leg, just bandaged it up. After a while I walked with one crutch and a cane, but my leg would break time and again. It would wobble at the broken place when I tried to walk and sometimes the splintered bone in my flesh would hurt. It was six months healing.

WHEN I WAS living with Colon in Nuecestown, I used to help gather salt in the lagoons of Laguna Madre or sometimes in the Oso. When water came in high, it filled all the shallow lakes and when it receded the salt could be gathered. It was in small grains about the size of peas and you had to take it up out of the water, which was about two inches deep.

We would pile the salt on the bank and let it drain, and then put it into sacks or buckets and take it to the wagons. But it wasn't dry even then and the salty water would ooze out of the bags of wet salt carried across my shoulders, so that most of the time I was dripping with salty water. In addition to this coarse salt, there was a finer quality, like table salt, that was formed when the wind would blow up the small rivulets bordering the lagoons, leaving the salt on the shores.

The wagons used for hauling the salt were drawn by six yoke of oxen. We would go up the old salt road, which ran from the lakes by Laureles and on to Nuecestown. Here it was stored in a small house to be sold. Most of it was exchanged, though, not sold.

Quite a bit of Colon's freight went to San Patricio and to Robert Love's Rancho Grande, which was on this side of the river opposite San Patricio. About a half mile this side of Rancho Grande, on the main traveled road, old lady Daughtrey had a store and Colon used to haul her provisions.

After six years, I left Samuel Colon in 1862. I worked for Mr. and Mrs. Holthaus, bakers in Corpus Christi, during the winter and spring of 1862 and 1863. I went to Victoria and got a hogshead of yellow sugar for the bakery, to use to make cakes and cookies. A hogshead was an enormous barrel and held hundreds of pounds of sugar.

We had two large ox-carts for the trip. I drove one and a man named Long drove the other. The road wasn't very good and we had to ford all the rivers. One of these was the Guadalupe at Victoria. It was all I could do to keep on my feet, the current was so swift.

It was hard for Mrs. Holthaus to get anyone to work for her, she was so demanding, but I worked for her for six months and got along with her all right. I wasn't fired, either. That was the only time in my life I worked for a salary.

ROBERT ADAMS (JR.) was born in Norfolk, England on March 9, 1847, the son of Robert Adams and Maria Sarah (Anderson) Adams. He arrived in Corpus Christi in 1852 with his parents and brother William. Robert and his brother became sheepmen and later successful cattle ranchers. Robert married Eliza Lorena McWhorter on Aug. 9, 1867 and established the Tecolote Ranch near Alice. He died on Aug. 26, 1944 and was buried in the Alice Cemetery.

40

HUNTING A PANTHER

Thomas Noakes

RANCHER, STOREKEEPER

I went to meet most of the Motts* folks for a panther
hunt. After a good deal of trouble mustering about half a
dozen of them and a neighbor's hounds, we started by
moonlight for some trees on a prairie a few miles off. This
was where a person the day before found the fresh remains
of a calf which the panther had killed and buried in the
grass for a future meal.

As soon as we came to the trees, we found the calf had
been moved and more had been eaten from it and at the
same moment the hounds started at full cry on some trail.
From the direction it led we were afraid they were
running on the heel scent but we could not call them off

* Noakes and his neighbors usually referred to Nuecestown as "The Motts" or
Twelve-Mile Motts. The settlement was 12 miles up the Nueces River from
Corpus Christi. Nuecestown was founded in the early 1850s by Henry Kinney.

Thomas J. Noakes, a self-portrait

and so kept after them as hard as we could across a rough prairie.

We came to a dense jungle of thorny bushes with now and then a tree standing in the midst. Into this thicket the hounds ran him. By this time, we had little doubt that they were running him, hot on the scent. After making it a little too warm for his earthly comfort, the dogs treed him. The thing
now was to get through the bushes to within a sure shot of the tree, which four of us started to do.

We had to crawl on our bellies at the expense of our clothes, pieces of which we were continually leaving behind. We came to within easy shot and poked our heads clear of the bushes to take aim. Before we could do so, we saw the panther spring down and lose himself in the heavy thicket.

We were standing almost immovably in the thorny mass, without being able to see more than a yard or two in any direction. The only way to get out was on our bellies which, snake-like, we proceeded to do. This mode of locomotion might have been pleasant enough in some situations, but not so much with a panther running about.

Before we reached the outside the dogs treed him again. One of the men on the outside fired a long shot and wounded him. We all fired at him, but found that we had to go into the thicket again to get a good shot at him. We went back in and when within 20 yards another man and I fired together, both balls taking effect and he came tumbling down.

We could hear from the cries of the dogs that a tooth-and-nail fight was being carried on and we scrambled to the scene of the action. Before we could get there, the panther's combative organs were stilled in death. We found that it was a female and her cubs were likely not far off. She had been hit by four balls, one of which had only grazed the skin. We dragged her to the outside of the thicket after a while.

We put her on one of the horses and carried her to the first neighbors, where we skinned her. We drew straws for the skin, which was not my lot to win, and then went home.

———————

THOMAS JOHN NOAKES, born in Sussex, England in 1829 came to Texas about 1848. He moved to Nuecestown, where he worked to establish a homestead and ranch. He married Mary (Marie) Ludwig in 1860. After the Civil War, Noakes opened a store at Nuecestown, which was plundered and burned in the Nuecestown Raid in 1875. Noakes kept a diary of the events in his life from 1858 through 1868. He died on March 7, 1877.

41

GROWING UP AT BANQUETE

Eli T. Merriman
NEWSMAN

During the long winter nights, people up in years lying in bed often think of the days when they were children. They recall happenings in the long ago. Before the Civil War, in the 1850s, my father, Dr. Eli T. Merriman, lived on the Agua Dulce. Our place was a mile from the Banquete settlement. My father was engaged in stock-raising and, in addition, practicing medicine. His practice extended as far west as San Diego, east to Corpus Christi, north to San Patricio and Live Oak County, and south to the King Ranch on the Santa Gertrudis.

When I was six years old, in 1858, my mother sent me and my brother John, who was five years old, over to Aunt Mary's to school. Aunt Mary, before she married my uncle, Marcus Fusselman, was Miss Mary Ashton. After his death, years later, she married James Hunter, who owned a livery stable in Corpus Christi.

Aunt Mary had only us two boys to teach. The Fusselman house was about 200 yards from our house; but there were no other houses around. Aunt Mary taught us to recite poems. The one I had to learn and recite was:

"Twinkle, twinkle, little star;
how I wonder what you are;
Up above the world so high;
Like a diamond in the sky;
When the blazing sun is set;
And the grass with dew is wet;
Then you show your little light;
Twinkle, twinkle, all the night."

My brother John's was:

"How I like to see a little dog;
And pat him on the head;
So prettily he wags his tail;
Whenever he is fed."

In those days in Banquete, quilting parties were common, and the ladies at these get-togethers gossiped almost as bad as the men. Some of the ladies dipped snuff, a practice that was common even among the best at that time.

I distinctly remember being sent down to the creek to get hackberry roots to make the snuff brushes for the quilters. There were so many ladies around the frame that I had to crawl beneath the quilt to distribute the brushes.

A few years later I went to a school taught by an old crippled gentleman by the name of Myers. He had a school a mile east of where we lived. It was where the Banquete Creek runs into the Agua Dulce. The Alejandro Ranch was there and Capt. John Rabb, the big cattleman, had his home and ranch headquarters a mile further down the creek.

Eli Merriman's neighbor at Banquete was Sally Skull

Sally Skull, well-known to old-timers, lived for a time at the Alejandro Ranch. She was talked about by everybody around for riding astride, which in Sally's time was thought very unladylike. It was shocking. Women who were considered respectable always rode side-saddle with long skirts almost reaching the ground.

Sally Skull was in the horse-trading business and often went to the Rio Grande. She carried two pistols, one on either side of her saddle horn, and woe to any man who talked about her. She wouldn't hesitate to take a shot at him. She commanded respect. She had the eye of a hawk, with staring eyes.

It was said that people along the border, and in Mexico, were scared of her, galloping all over the country, carrying guns and wearing rawhide leggings and spurs.

While she may have had her faults she was jolly and joking with her friends. She came to our house and brought us some of the finest butter ever made, large yellow balls of butter packed in a stone jar. I saw her and her last husband, "Horse Trough," I think he was called. When visiting at our house, Sally threatened, in fun, to steal my brother John because she said he was such a pretty boy with dimples in his cheeks. Too bad that she had to have such a tragic death, shot and killed by somebody, it was said, over by Goliad.

In 1862, when I was 10, my father sent me to school over on the north side of Banquete Creek, two miles away. The building was one story. There were about 20 boys and girls attending the school. Most of them came to school on horseback.

THE TEACHER had no bell to call us in from recess. He would shout, "Books! Books!" and we went rushing into the schoolhouse. George Eghart and I were hot from running and jumping and we went over to the water bucket for a cool drink. We dropped the dipper and spilled water on the floor. This angered the teacher, who gave us a good thrashing with a big switch. It hurt like the dickens.

When I got home and told my father about it, he sent John to school in my place and sent me up on the Agua Dulce Creek, six miles away, where he had a horse camp. I had not been there long when John came to tell me that the schoolhouse had burned up, or down, it amounted to the same thing. That ended the school on the Banquete.

During the five years of the Civil War, Banquete was the center of Nueces County. Most of the people lived on the north side of Agua Dulce Creek. These included the Rabbs, Myers, Fusselmans, Ingledows, Merrimans, Moses's, Wrights, Ashtons and Moores.

The main business of the place was done on Banquete Creek. This caused rivalry over the location of the post office, which was moved a time or two from one creek to the other. There was no meat market for the folks living on Agua Dulce Creek. First one neighbor and then another would kill a beef and divide the meat among the neighbors.

One day my half-brother James, who was a member of Ware's Confederate company that was camped at the Puerto Ranch, came down to see how I was getting along. When he saw eight ducks on the lake, he said, "I am going to get them. All I need is some caps, as I have powder and shot. Bring me some fire on a stick from the camp house."

This I did. He was stretched out on the bank with the shotgun pointed toward the ducks. I slipped up behind him and handed him the stick with fire on it. He placed it on the tube of the gun and off it went, killing seven of the ducks. Only one managed to fly away. The shot was home-made from slugs cut up into very small pieces and rolled between stove lids. Ammunition was hard to get at that time.

ELI TODD MERRIMAN JR. was born on May 16, 1852. His father was Dr. Eli Todd Merriman Sr. and his mother was Elizabeth Fusselman Merriman. His father moved the family from the Valley to Banquete to raise horses and practice medicine. Among their neighbors was John Rabb and Sally Skull. Dr. Merriman died in the yellow fever epidemic of 1867. Eli Jr. worked as a printer, shop foreman, reporter and editor. He was one of the founders of the Corpus Christi Caller. He married Ellen Robinson in 1880; her father also died in the 1867 epidemic. Ellen Merriman died in 1934 and Eli T. Merriman Jr. died in 1940. Both were buried in Old Bayview Cemetery.

42

LAW AND ORDER IN EL PASO

William W. Mills

CLERK, CUSTOMS COLLECTOR

When I arrived in El Paso in December 1858, there were several large ash and cottonwood trees at the head of El Paso Street, near the little plaza where the main acequia (irrigation ditch) ran. To one of these trees some enterprising citizen nailed a plank which for years served as a bulletin board where people would tack up signed manuscripts giving their opinions of each other's character and conduct.

Mrs. Gillock, who kept a boarding house, notified the "Publick" when her boarders didn't pay their bills. I saw my brother Anson nail up the information that three certain citizens were bald-faced liars. Ten years later, I put up the same notice regarding B. F. Williams. Foolish? Perhaps.

On the second night after my arrival in El Paso, I had my first experience of the manner of settling difficulties. A man named Samuel Schutz and one Tom Massie had a

A grievance board was nailed to a tree on El Paso Street

misunderstanding about the rent of a house. My brother and I went across the river that afternoon and on the way over we met Garver, a half-witted fellow known around town as "Clown." He advised us to return early because there would be some fun that night. I asked what fun and he said, "Oh, killing a Dutchman."

In front of the post office that night I heard Massie tell a friend, "I have taken half a dozen drinks of straight brandy,

180

but damn me if I can get drunk." I went into the post office and found an unusual crowd of men talking in low tones. Mr. Schutz was in his shirtsleeves, playing billiards with a friend.

Presently Massie entered and said — "Mr. Schutz, you told a damn lie!" He raised a cocked pistol and there was no mistaking his intent.

Mr. Schutz made a sound I never heard before, or since. It was not a shriek or an outcry but more like a prolonged sorrowful wail. He grabbed the barrel of Massie's pistol and forced it upwards and they struggled to gain possession of the weapon. Both were powerful men in their prime.

Massie was trying to bring his cocked pistol to bear on Schutz while Schutz was striving to turn it in the other direction.

I was shocked. I stepped forward — "Gentlemen, would you see this man murdered?" Not a man among the passive spectators in the crowd stirred to intervene.

Massie finally let go of the pistol and drew a knife and plunged it into Schutz's shoulder. Schutz ran. Massie recovered his pistol and fired two shots at him as he ran out the door. It was dark outside. Immediately after the shots, Schutz stumbled over a water barrel and lay still. Massie, thinking him dead, fled across the river to Mexico.

Schutz was not hit by the bullets and the knife wound was not serious. The next day "Uncle Ben" Dowell gave me some advice — "My young friend, when you see anything of that kind going on in El Paso, don't attempt to interfere. It is not considered good manners."

IT WAS NOT LONG AFTER the Massie-Schutz affair that I saw a gambler shooting at another member of the same profession in this same post office and a stray bullet killed an inoffensive bystander. The coroner's jury exonerated the killer on the grounds that the killing was clearly "accidental."

There was some sympathy for the innocent dead man but most of it appeared to go to the gambler who had been so "unfortunate" as to kill the wrong man.

Of the Americans then at El Paso, some of them had left crimes or other misdeeds behind them in "the States" and had not come to the frontier of Texas to teach Sunday school. Their ideas of right and wrong were peculiar, but they had such ideas nevertheless.

There occurred an incident which illustrates their views of law and order in El Paso in those days.

A certain desperado been getting drunk and riding his horse into stores and saloons and firing his pistol at random in the streets. Finally, he took a snap shot at the popular member of the Legislature, Mr. Jeff Hill, on main street. This was too much.

In a few moments, 15 or 20 "good citizens" were chasing him over town with shotguns, rifles and pistols. The desperado was brought to earth in the corral of the old Central Hotel. There he was shot and his body pierced by many missiles.

There began an animated dispute among the "good citizens" as to who fired the fatal shot. One claimed to have done the work with his shotgun. Another said such small ammunition at long range would not kill a man, but that it was his rifle shot in the neck that did it. A third said he had dispatched the deceased with three body shots from his six-shooter, and so on.

At last "Uncle Ben" Dowell said, "Gentlemen, some judge or other may come along someday and hold court and some of us may have trouble over this business."

With this in mind, they organized a coroner's jury, composed of the very same men who did the shooting, and they agreed on a verdict to the effect that, "Deceased came to his death by gunshot wounds from the hands of parties unknown." Then, in a judicious mood, they adjourned to get a drink.

About this time the same merchant whom Tom Massie tried to kill, Samuel Schutz, had another rough experience with a crowd of American toughs, most of them gamblers.

Some of the fraternity were broke and had pawned their pistols with Mr. Schutz for ready cash. One day one of the boys reported back that Mr. Schutz had refused to make any more loans on pistols.

"How did you approach him?" asked 'Snap' Mitchell.

"Why, I presented the handle of my pistol and asked him to loan me $25 on it."

"Idiot," said 'Snap.' "You don't know how to soak a pistol. Watch me."

'Snap' went to the store and presented the muzzle of the pistol and got a loan. He not only got the loan but went away with the pistol also.

IN 1850 THE SAN ANTONIO Mail Company had its headquarters on the lot where the Sheldon building later stood. They had in the old adobe house a large stock of merchandise. Two clerks slept in the store each night. One was Mr. Atkins, known as "Old Dad," and the other was a young German named Fred.

Atkins was absent one night and young Fred was sleeping in the store alone. The next morning a window was found to have been dug out of the wall and poor Fred was lying dead with 14 knife wounds in his body.

A large amount of money was taken (there were no safes or banks in El Paso then) along with quantities of valuable goods. This was thought to be the work of robbers from across the river.

After this murder, Mr. Atkins declined to sleep in the store alone. At that time, I was clerking for St. Vrain and Company, merchants, in the old Central Hotel building. As we had plenty of people to protect the St. Vrain store, it was agreed that I should go over each night and sleep in the store that had been robbed. Soon the scare was over and Atkins, saying that "lightning never strikes twice in the same place," left me alone for one night. I had a shotgun and pistol and a good watchdog.

The merchants had employed a Mr. Cullimore, called "Bones," to patrol the town at night. That night about two a.m. I heard the report of both barrels of Bones' shotgun and he yelled, "Look out, Mills."

Probably the same party of robbers had begun to dig out the same window and were half-finished when Bones fired on them. They fled, leaving behind a hat and a handkerchief as remembrances. It was a long time before anyone would sleep in that store alone.

––––––––––

WILLIAM WALLACE MILLS was born in Thorntown, Indiana, on Feb. 10, 1836. In December 1858 he came to Texas following his brother Anson, a surveyor, and settled in El Paso. In 1861 Mills, a fierce Unionist, spoke out against secession. He was imprisoned at Fort Bliss but later escaped and served as a volunteer with Union forces in New Mexico. He married Mary Hamilton on Feb. 8, 1869; she was the daughter of A. J. Hamilton, who was appointed provisional governor of Texas after the Civil War. In 1897, Mills was named American Consul at Chihuahua, a post he held until 1907. He wrote his memoirs entitled "Forty Years at El Paso." He died on Feb. 10, 1913, on the anniversary of his birth. He was buried in Oakwood Cemetery in Austin.

43

WIZARD OIL TIMES

Andrew Anderson
BAY PILOT

When I was a boy I would carry my father's dinner to him when he was building Colonel Moore's dredge boat up on the beach in Corpus Christi. There was a big shell bank along the beach and I used to walk on it. One day I accidentally stepped off and fell down to the beach below and spilled part of father's lunch. This was before the war, in 1860, when I was nine years old.

This shell bank was washed away in one of the storms. We had storms in 1871, 1874, and in 1880, a bad storm which came in the middle of August. Then in 1919 we had the big hurricane. Alfred Vetters' home in the 1700 block of Chaparral was one of the houses that washed away.

I remember ox-carts going down Chaparral Street to the stores and how they would bog down in front of the corner at Peoples Street. They often used five or six yokes of oxen. To improve the sidewalks the city hauled shell and built walks about two feet wide, but they were too narrow.

The mud was so bad that when Clark Pease came and opened his bank, he built a walk from his corner at Chaparral and Peoples south across the street. He tried to get others interested but couldn't, so he just built it himself. The mayor was so angry he made Pease pull it up. I guess it was because Pease built it without permission from the city.

Ox-carts hauling wool to the warehouses could find the place they should go to by looking for the big signs on the tops of the buildings. John Woessner used the horse; Edey & Kirsten used the sheep; Norwick Gussett, the rooster; David Hirsch, the diamond.

I REMEMBER old Judge Russell. One day the boys were forming a fire company and the talk was that they would be exempt from jury duty. I was called and I went up to the courthouse. When court opened, Judge Russell asked if any there thought they had good reasons to be excused. I held up my hand and the judge called me up.

"You think you ought to be excused," he said. "What's your reason?"

"I'm in the fire company," I said.

"That's no excuse," he said. "If there's a fire, we'll all go."

I remember that Judge Russell got tired of the noise made from matches being struck in his court. Those old long matches popped good and loud, which is why they were called pistol matches. He issued an order that no matches could be struck in his courtroom.

The boys called Judge Russell "old duck shooter" because he liked hunting so well. He used to wear a big beaver hat. Some of the boys stretched a wire across the street as a prank and it just so happened that the judge was the first person to come along and it knocked off his hat. He was provoked, but he didn't know who did it.

It wasn't all devilment. I had to go to school. One of my teachers was Mrs. Priour. Her school was in the building

Capt. Andrew Anderson recalled "The Yankee in Texas"

that old lady Hart built on Water Street. It was only a story and a half high; you could barely stand up in the upper story.

The Carpenter school in the Chapman house on the bluff was another that I attended. Another schoolteacher here was Mrs. Marsh, who taught in a building south of the Hart building. Mrs. Marsh would whip us with a little red cowhide quirt. I stole it and pushed it down a hole in the floor. She never found it, or knew who did it, but she got another one.

Living on the beach, I roamed up and down the waterfront. There were a number of wharves then. Three of

Market Hall was the venue for early-day entertainment

the early wharves were Mann's, Rigg's, and Ohler's. It was
at Ohler's that the Yankees landed with a flag of truce
before the town was bombarded. There was the Central
Wharf, but before that Staples had a wharf. Later, Sidbury's
Wharf was important. Sidbury had a lumberyard on the
south beach. His
wharf had a track on which mules pulled flatcars.

Our house had an oyster saloon in front. We served fried
and stewed and raw oysters, fried fish, but no liquor.
Theodore Lawrence, a painter, painted a great big sign for
our oyster saloon. My neighbor, Mr. Gold, would take me
with him to the reef when he went after oysters; we would
drive out with a cart and horse. He would bring back a
great load of oysters to his house, where he would open
them; there was a great pile of shells in the yard.

August Ricklefsen was a butcher in those days. He
would grind his sausage meat by means of a treadmill
operated by a horse. The mill was off to one side of the
wheel turned by the horse. The chopper was of iron and it
cut the meat very fine. The mill was in Ricklefsen's yard at
his home in the 1400 block of Chaparral.

Upstairs over Market Hall was an auditorium where entertainments were held. Sometimes we had regular shows here. Alma Stutz played Mary, the little girl in "East Lynne." Fay Templeton was a favorite. Two of the most popular plays were "Ten Nights in a Bar Room," a temperance play, and "The Yankee in Texas." Another one we liked was "Rip Van Winkle." The actors wore stovepipe hats.

We had medicine shows, too. I remember how they would sell Hamlin's Wizard Oil from a wagon. Four fellows would sing beautifully and the whole street would be full of people listening to their songs. Someone arranged for them to give an entertainment at Market Hall. You paid 25 cents to hear them sing; they had a full house every night for a week, and they sold lots of Wizard Oil.

———————

ANDREW (ANDY) ANDERSON was born in New Orleans in 1852. His father was John Anderson, a ship captain, who moved the family to Corpus Christi in 1853, when Andrew was a year old. Like his father, Andrew became a ship captain, bay pilot and shipbuilder. Andrew worked for Mifflin Kenedy for 20 years, transporting supplies to the Laureles and then La Parra ranches. He met Mary Grant, the daughter of Capt. and Mrs. James Grant, at the Aransas Pass Lighthouse; they were married on Mustang Island in 1890. Mary Grant Anderson died in 1915 and Capt. Andrew died on Oct. 10, 1949, three years short of his 100th birthday. He was buried in Rose Hill Cemetery.

44

HOUSTON FEARED
NO MOBS IN TEXAS

Thomas North
CLERK

Gen. Sam Houston forcefully and forthrightly opposed secession. He spoke his mind freely anywhere, even in the face of threats, denunciations and mobs. We remember the interest and excitement that was manifest a few days before the vote on secession was taken. The "old man eloquent" came down to Galveston from Houston to address the people on the subject of the day.

The rumor spread through the city that Houston had come and would speak the next day at 11 a.m. from the second-floor gallery of the Tremont House. There was a deep undercurrent of excitement, with a glassy calmness on the surface, as in "still waters run deep." There was an unsearchable depth in each man's eye, like the calm that precedes a storm.

In the morning of the day when Houston was to speak a self-constituted committee of several leading citizens visited the general in his quarters and warned him not to attempt making a speech that day. They feared that a serious disturbance might erupt and result in personal harm to Houston. They said, "We are opposed to your views on secession, but we don't want to see you harmed."

The general thanked them and said he had survived stormy times in Texas before and that he intended to make his speech as planned.

One of the parties to this interview came into our office and reported what had passed. I had never seen Gen. Houston and felt a strong desire to go and hear the old warhorse.

But I decided not to go, being a stranger in the country and not wishing to be caught in the presence of a mob. Eleven o'clock came, then 12, and someone came in and said, "Houston has been speaking for an hour or more and all is quiet."

I WENT AND heard the balance of his speech. After seeing and hearing him a few minutes, I did not wonder that he was not disturbed by a mob. There he stood, an old man of 70 years, on the Tremont balcony 10 feet above the heads of the thousands assembled to hear him.

Every eye could scan his magnificent form, six feet and three inches high, straight as an arrow, with deep set and penetrating eyes, looking from under heavy eyebrows, a high open forehead, with something of the infinite intellectual shadowed there, crowned with thick white locks.

His voice had a deep basso tone, which shook and commanded the soul of the hearer. Adding to all this was a powerful manner, made of deliberation, self-possession, and restrained majesty of action. This left the impression that more of his power was hidden than revealed.

Houston warned of dire consequences.

Thus appeared Sam Houston on this momentous occasion. He was equal or superior to it, as he had been to every other challenge he had faced. The mobocrat was tamed by his personal presence. It was morally impossible for Gen. Houston to be mobbed in Texas. The drift of Houston's speech was about the inexpediency and bad policy of secession. He told them they could secure, without secession, what they proposed to secure by it, and would certainly lose through it. He appealed to them, asking if he had not generally been right in the past history of Texas when any great issue was at stake.

He told them he made Texas, and they knew it. He told them that the history of Sam Houston was the history of Texas, and they knew it. Told them that he organized and established the Republic of Texas, and they knew it. That he had wrested Texas from the despotic sway of Santa Anna, and they knew it. That he commanded at San Jacinto, where the Mexican leader was whipped and captured, and they knew it.

"I am an old man now," he continued. "I knew you in infancy, took you and dawdled you on my knee, nursed you through all your baby ailments, and with great care and solicitude watched and aided your elevation to political and commercial manhood. Will you now reject the counsels of your political father, and squander your political patrimony in riotous adventure? I now tell you that this (secession) will land you in fire and rivers of blood.

"Some of you laugh and scorn the idea of bloodshed as a result of secession, and jocularly propose to drink all the blood that will flow in consequence of it. But let me tell you what is coming on the heels of secession.

"THE TIME WILL COME when your fathers and husbands, your sons and brothers, will be herded together like sheep and cattle at the point of a bayonet. Your mothers and wives, sisters and daughters, will ask, 'Where are they?'

"You may," he said, "after the sacrifice of countless millions of treasure and hundreds of thousands of precious lives, as a bare possibility, win Southern independence, if God be not against you. But I doubt it.

"I tell you that, while I believe with you in the doctrine of state rights, the North is determined to preserve the Union. They are not a fiery and impulsive people, as you are, for they live in cooler climes. But when they begin to move in a given direction where great interests are involved, they move with the steady momentum and perseverance of a mighty avalanche. What I fear is that they will overwhelm the South with ignoble defeat.

"I would say amen to the suffering and defeat I have pictured, if the present difficulties could find no other solution, by peaceable means. But I believe they can. Otherwise, I would say, 'Better to die as free men than live as slaves.'

"Whatever course my state shall determine to pursue, my faith in state supremacy and state rights will carry my sympathies with her. As Henry Clay, my political opponent on annexation, when asked why he allowed his son to go into the Mexican War, said, 'My country, right or wrong.' So I say, 'My state, right or wrong.' "

Several times during his speech I noticed that the same men who were applauding were those who had, that very morning, opposed the speaker's political position and warned him not to make the speech. But the power of Gen. Houston over a Texas audience was magical, and doubtless it was well understood by himself. Hence, he feared no mobs in Texas.

––––––––––

THOMAS NORTH, a devout Christian who was a deputy circuit clerk in Stephenson County, Illinois, traveled to Texas just before the Civil War began and stayed five years. He spent time in Galveston, San Antonio, New Braunfels, Matamoros, and points in between. North's book, "Five Years in Texas, or What Did You Not Hear During the War" offers the point of view of religious Yankee in Confederate Texas. It was published in 1871. Other biographical details of North's life and death were not found.

45

SOME OF THE BOYS
NEVER CAME BACK

W. F. Cude

SOLDIER, COWBOY

In 1861, when I was 17, I joined a company of Texas
Rangers. John Donaldson was my captain, under the
command of Col. John Salmon (Rip) Ford. When we
arrived at Brownsville we camped in the old fort. There
were 20 men in our bunch; my brother Jack (A. J. Cude)
recruited for the company.

When I heard my first bugle call, I asked Jack what it
was and he told me it was the rations call. He went to get
the rations and returned with some sacks of grub. He told
me there was some soap in one of the sacks and as I wanted
to wash out some of my clothes, I took what I supposed to
be a cake of soap, went down to the river and used it. When
I got back I complained to Jack that the soap was no good.
He laughed and told me the "soap" I used was piloncillo,
that hard brown Mexican sugar.

We remained on the border for a year, guarding the Rio Grande from its mouth to Rio Grande City. In June 1862 we left the border service and joined the Second Texas Cavalry, part of Sibley's Brigade. We were ordered to the coast, near the mouth of the Brazos, then moved to Houston.

About the middle of December, the Yankees captured Galveston and a call was made for volunteers to go on the steamboats to chase them off. Gen. John Bankhead Magruder recaptured Galveston after a battle that lasted less than an hour. The battle was fought on the first day of January 1863. We captured one warship and two transports, sank one warship and captured about 500 prisoners. One of our boats was sunk, but it was in shallow water and no one drowned.

After this I was in a number of desperate engagements and was captured and taken to Jackson, Miss. on parole. After we reached Jackson, four of us left one night and walked to Beaumont. It took us 16 days. My shoes were worn out and when I got to Houston I went to a store and got a new pair. I told the clerk to charge them to Jeff Davis.

OUR REGIMENT WAS stationed on Galveston Island in 1864 and remained there until the end of the war. We had an easy time on the island. Our duty was to ride the beach five miles and back every two hours and keep watch on a signal station day and night.

In the summer of 1864 yellow fever broke out in Galveston and 14 of our company died. We were camped on the west end of the island at the end of the war.

After the war, in the fall of 1865, I went to school at Moulton, in Lavaca County, and in 1866 I went to Live Oak County where I secured a wagon and ox-team and began hauling freight from Indianola to San Antonio. That fall, I hired to a man named H. Williams who lived on Lagarto Creek, 30 miles from Oakville.

A family named Weaver, with two grown girls, lived a mile from the Williams' place. These girls would help their father in hunting down cattle and carried their pistols with them wherever they went. They had a pack of hounds and hunted with them.

One day they found where a panther had killed a colt of their father's. They went to the Williams' ranch and got two of the Williams' girls to help run down and kill the panther. Mr. Williams sent me to help and gave me an old Enfield rifle to use.

We reached the place and found the Weaver girls had the panther treed. I dismounted and took a shot at him; the ball passed through his foot, causing him to jump out of the tree and make straight for me. I could not run, but those four girls were all looking at me to do something. Luckily, one of the dogs got hold of the panther and things got interesting when the other dogs took a hand in the fight. The panther whipped them all, fearfully mangling some of them. I rushed in and killed it by beating it over the head with my gun.

I made my first trip up the trail to Kansas in 1868. The trail herd was composed of 600 steers gathered in Bastrop County. There were eight hands besides the owners and the cook. After we passed Dallas, lightning struck the camp, killing one of the boys and three others were so badly burned that one of them quit. We had only six hands the rest of the way to Kansas.

There were few settlements on the way, after we passed Dallas, until we reached Kansas. We passed through many prairie-dog towns and rattlesnake dens and lost only one horse to rattlesnake bite.

In the fall of 1869, I drove a herd to Shreveport. We made some money, but the buffalo flies were so bad we never went back to Shreveport. In the fall of 1870, I gathered another herd in Gonzales County and went to New Orleans. We had many rivers and bayous to cross and ferrymen wanted from $5 to $10 for their services. I also drove a herd that year to Natchez, Miss., and made some money on this venture.

In the fall of 1871, I saddled up my favorite horse, "Old Ball" and rode to Kansas. When we reached north Texas I found that the Chisholm Trail had been abandoned (grassed-out) and took the herd far to the west to cross the Red River.

The last herd I drove north was in 1872, for a man named O. J. Baker. Everything went well until we got to Kansas. We stopped our herd 15 miles west of Ellsworth, near the Kansas Pacific Railroad. We wanted a day to rest and clean up. Next morning, about sunup, I heard a gunshot down by the creek and saw two Indians on mules riding away as fast as they could go. They had shot a white man with a gun and several arrows. He came dragging up to our camp with one arrow still sticking in him. One of the boys pulled it out and we carried him to a tent.

The trail drivers had many narrow escapes. They were exposed to hail and lightning storms, cyclones, and all kinds of weather. With the stampedes of cattle, there was always the danger of riding over ditches and bluffs in the night. Some of the boys never came back. They were buried along the trail, wrapped in their own bed blankets, with coyotes howling in the evening to keep them company.

———

WILLIS FRANKLIN CUDE was born on April 4, 1844. He served as a Texas Ranger and Confederate soldier during the Civil War. After the war he tried freighting, between Indianola and San Antonio, then turned to driving cattle. He married Mary Harrell in 1872 and they had 10 children. He died on Nov. 7, 1932, at the age of 88, and was buried in Pearsall Cemetery.

46

THE VIGILANCE COMMITTEE

R. H. Williams

ADVENTURER, SOLDIER, RANCHER

I was sitting on the gallery of our ranch house by the Medio Creek, 15 miles from San Antonio, when a two-horse ambulance with five men drove up. A man named John Atkins, whom I had met before, and two others got down, shook hands, and asked for drinks of whisky. As the other two remained in the ambulance, I saw there was something up. I asked Atkins what it was.

He said they had been on a rare hunt after a damned horse thief and had found him at Fort Clark, where he had enlisted for a year's service, putting his (Atkins') horse in as his mount. They recovered the horse, which was tied behind the ambulance, and were taking the thief to San Antonio.

But his manner as he said this aroused my suspicions. Besides, I knew him for what he was, a prominent member of the dreaded Vigilance Committee. I said, "I hope you are not going to hang the poor wretch before you get there." He laughed and said, "You've hit it, my boy, first shot. You get on your horse and come along to see the finish. You bet we won't take him much further now."

One of the two men in the ambulance left it and came to the house. The prisoner sat quietly on, apparently unconcerned. No suspicion of his impending fate seemed to have dawned on him. The human ghouls who had brought him 250 miles had played cards with him at each camp and were now going to murder him in cold blood.

It made my blood boil. Mr. John Atkins never guessed how near he was to getting a bullet through his heart. But if I could have killed all four of these bloodthirsty wretches and released their prisoner, I should have had to flee the country, or their fellow-murderers of the committee would surely have hanged me.

I mastered my wrath as best I could and used every argument that I could think of to induce Atkins to at least let his captive have his chance of a trial in town. In vain; neither argument or entreaty could move him. I had said as much as I dared, and more than was good for my own security. I could do no more.

Sick at heart, I walked over to the ambulance to speak to the poor young fellow. He was no more than 25, a well-dressed, good-looking fellow. He told me his name was Jack Young and said he was innocent of the charge, that he had bought the horse from a Mexican on the Medina, and was confident of being able to produce him at his trial. His trial, poor fellow! How little he knew. I couldn't tell him of the terrible fate awaiting him, and it was best not. It could only prolong his agony.

But I would try once more to sway his captors. I might have spared my breath. They were as hard as the nether millstone. The sun was setting and the murderers were anxious to start, that they might finish their evil deed before dark.

The victim asked for whisky, which I had forgotten to offer him, so I brought him a tumbler. He shook me by the hand, hoping to meet me again soon. I knew I would never see him alive again. They drove away, the prisoner in custody was cheery and unconcerned, his escort laughing and chatting with him, as if they were the best of friends. In less than half an hour the brutes would hang him.

I watched them, in the crimson glow of the setting sun, until they disappeared around a mott* and then turned back to the house. I slept badly and at daybreak was on my horse, following the trail of the ambulance. I was drawn by some irresistible attraction, feeling sure of what I would find, and yet hoping that perhaps the murderers might have relented.

I RODE FOR ABOUT three miles then saw what I had expected — Jack Young hanging from a China tree hard by the trail. I went on into San Antonio and reported to the city marshal what I had seen. The deed was recognized as the handiwork of the all-powerful Vigilance Committee and no one dared to interfere. Some men were sent out by the city authorities to cut down the victim and bury him where he died. And so an end, as far as the world's justice is concerned. I have seen others die by the same Lynch Law, but never so cold-blooded a deed as this one.

It was later in the summer of 1861 that I was a witness of another deed perpetrated by the Vigilance Committee. It almost surpasses, in cool villainy, any of its other doings.

I was in San Antonio staying with some friends. It was a lovely evening and many people were strolling about the Plaza. Under the shade of the trees that surrounded the Plaza were numbers of Mexicans seated at tables playing monte. A young Ranger from the camp, with perhaps too much aguardiente in him, began to jump over and upend the monte tables. Five or six of the city marshals ran up and after a big fight arrested him and carried him off to jail. A

---

* A mott meant a clump or grove of trees, usually by a river or creek.

simple drunken row, common enough in those days, but it was to have a tragic ending.

Next morning, about 10 o'clock, I walked over to the courthouse with my host, Mr. Sweets, the mayor of San Antonio. We were much surprised to see a large crowd in the Plaza fronting the court and jail.

I sat by Sweets' side while he performed his duties as magistrate and disposed of several trifling cases, amongst which was that of the drunken Ranger, who was charged with creating a disturbance. His case was dismissed with a caution, and the next case was called. But the young Ranger, though he had been acquitted, begged the mayor to keep him in custody. He gave no reason for the request. The mayor said he had no power to hold him and that he must go.

Then I remembered the crowd out front and stepped to the door to see what was going on. It had gathered thickly round the door, as though patiently waiting for something or somebody. At the back of the crowd I saw two well-known members of the Vigilance Committee.

I went back and told Sweets there was some mischief afoot. I don't know that he heard me for about then the Ranger was again asking, more earnestly than before, to be kept in custody. Sweets' answer was short. "Nonsense, my lad. You have been acquitted. I have no power to keep you." The Ranger didn't say another word. He shrugged his shoulders, turned on his heel, and marched out to his doom.

The moment he stepped outside, the human wolves, waiting for their prey, dragged him across the Plaza, put a rope around his neck, and strung him up to a tree in less time that it takes to relate. I saw it all, but was powerless to stop it. I rode off, fast as my horse would carry me, to the Ranger camp to tell the tale to the victim's comrades, in the hope they would muster to avenge their friend's murder. They ran to get their arms, but the general called out two regiments of infantry and marched them into town to keep order. Otherwise, I believe the villainous committee would have had to mourn the loss of some of its leading members that day. But the excitement died down and the committee's evil power remained unshaken.

The young Ranger's drunken escapade had nothing to do with his hanging. It only gave his enemies the opportunity of catching him away from his comrades at the Ranger camp. It seems that two years before, the Vigilance Committee had hanged a brother of his on some pretext or other. The young Ranger had openly threatened to shoot Asa Minshul and Solomon Chiswell, the Vigilance Committee leaders who had murdered his brother. These rascals therefore, to protect their own skins, had organized the hanging I had witnessed.

IT MADE ONE'S BLOOD boil to think that these cowardly villains could murder with impunity anyone they had a grudge against. They took no part in the war, and not a one of them fired a shot in defense of their country, but they stayed at home and ruled over those who did the fighting by their terrible secret power.

The leaders of this secret society were well-known, but the rank and file, who obeyed their behests without question, were difficult to identify. Some were known and shunned, as much as those outside the organization dared to. But the terrible part of the thing was that you never knew whether the man you met on business or pleasure might be a member and denounce you. It was a terrible state of society, truly. No private organization could hope to cope with it, and in those disturbed times public law and order were in abeyance. Asa Minshul,* a well-off storekeeper in San Antonio, was head of the Vigilance Committee. He was the man who pulled the strings. When I first met him, he was about 50, short, stout and florid. He

---

* The leader of the San Antonio Vigilance Committee during the Civil War was Asa Mitchell, a prominent merchant, rancher and preacher at San Antonio. Robert Williams changed the name to "Minshul."

looked like what he was, a prosperous merchant. Moreover, he was a shining light among the Wesleyans, in whose church he preached and prayed with much unction. His two daughters gave pleasant parties and I had been in his house, which was about the best in town.

When I discovered what terrible power the man wielded, and how necessary it was for my own good health to be friendly with him, I confess with some shame that I cultivated his acquaintance. I attended the Wesleyan church and listened to the old hypocrite's long-winded discourses. This was somewhat ignoble and not a thing to boast about. But there was always the rope the old fellow was said to carry in the tall white hat he invariably wore. One would do a good deal to keep it away from one's neck.

There was a story current in San Antonio that Asa Minshul was preaching one hot Sunday afternoon and as he vehemently denounced sinners, the perspiration trickled from his forehead and he reached down to retrieve a handkerchief from inside his hat on a chair beside him. But in seizing the handkerchief he also pulled out with it the end of a coil of rope.

R. H. (ROBERT HAMILTON) Williams, an English adventurer, emigrated to Kansas in 1852. He came to Texas in 1861 and, with two partners, bought a ranch on the Medio Creek near San Antonio. This ranch was sold and with the proceeds a larger ranch on the Frio was purchased. Williams joined the Confederate army and saw much service on the frontier and along the border. After the war ended, he joined a company of Texas Rangers and was promoted to captain. He returned to England in 1868 and, 40 years later, wrote an account of his adventures in Kansas and Texas, titled "With the Border Ruffians, or Memories of the Far West, 1852-1868." He died on Aug. 3, 1904, at age 73, and was buried in St. Margaret's Churchyard, Essex, England.

47

SIBLEY'S RETREAT

Theophilus Noel

INDIAN SCOUT, CONFEDERATE SOLDIER

There may have been an order issued by the general in command (Brig. Gen. Henry H. Sibley) for our retreat. One thing is sure, it was never read out on dress parade. After the battle of Valverde on Feb. 21, 1862, the army of invasion (Sibley's Brigade) marched north, leaving Col. Edward Canby in Fort Craig with some 4,000 federal troops in our rear, and between us and our supplies and our reserves.

We reached Albuquerque two days later. Since the war with Mexico, there had been stored there some six million dollars' worth of commissary, quartermaster, and medical supplies. The torch was applied to this immense storehouse of army provisions. Why it should have been done, I never knew. Nor did anyone else, unless it was because our men were getting drunk on the whisky and Sibley, our commander, had never been sober.

It was a furious fire, on the dark night of Feb. 26, fed by burning bacon, brandy and whisky, quartermaster supplies, with the bursting of bombs and the terrific explosion when the fire reached the powder magazine. That night, the condition of our 'red-eye'-loving Texans can better be imagined than described.

From Albuquerque we went to Santa Fe, where the same burning act was repeated. A mistake like that can have major repercussions. In less than five days, we would be suffering the agonies of starvation from our own acts of vandalism. There was no excuse for burning these supplies. It was the act of a maddened brain, a case of "whom the gods would destroy they first make mad."

We were told there was only a small federal force, one company of regulars, at Fort Union, 35 or 40 miles northeast of Santa Fe, at the head of Glorieta Canyon. I have often thanked my creator that I was not in good standing with Sibley, my commanding general, as a scout at this time. Therefore, none of the murders could be laid at my door, for what happened was no better than murder.

Eight hundred men were sent up Glorieta Canyon to attack Fort Union, where Col. John Slough and 6,000 northwest plainsmen (Pike's Peakers) were waiting at the mouth of a trap. The 380 men who had answered their last roll call — whose bodies and bones were left near the mouth of the canyon — were victims of Gen. John Barleycorn. Sibley (of Sibley's Tent fame) was an old army officer whose love for liquor exceeded that for home, country or God.

The retreat of the Army of New Mexico, or rather Sibley's Brigade, from Santa Fe to Socorro, was like that of the skedaddling of a crowd of urchins who had been caught in a melon patch. Col. Canby moved up from Fort Craig and set a torch to every burnable article that we had.

Sibley: "Our commanding general had never been sober"

Without guide or compass, track or trail, much less a road, we started up over that tall mountain westward. We made a detour of 200 miles over that desert, striking the Rio Grande again near old Fort Thorn, where we got the mail from loved ones in Texas and 60 pack mules loaded with dried buffalo meat, without which every one of the 1,400 men would have perished. The only thing I regretted about this was that the cause of all our misfortune was also kept from starving.

From old Fort Thorn to El Paso, a distance of 375 miles, we walked and staggered along, like the reeling, hungry, and thirsty wretches that we were. There was nobody to direct or command us. The Dog Canyon Apaches followed in our wake. They would scalp the poor unfortunate boys whose blistered feet and weakened frame made it impossible for them to march further. The memory of those days, as well as the next 800 miles' march, can never be effaced. No army or body of men on the American continent ever suffered as did the men of Sibley's Brigade on this retreat.

WE TOOK UP THE line of march from El Paso to San Antonio on April 26, 1862. The route was 740 miles over hot desert country. The men had thrown away their guns, though a few still carried six-shooters. There were six or eight horses and a wagon with four mules traveling with the first party of 600 men.

After a long and weary march of 100 miles, there was a well of fresh water waiting at Eagle Springs. The well, with circling steps around it, was 40 feet deep, fed by an artesian spring. We filled our water barrels and trudged on toward the next watering hole, Van Horn's Well, which was 22 miles away. The well at Van Horn's had been purposely fouled, filled with dirt and dead sheep. Who did it is one of the mysteries of the war. It was supposed that Indians instigated by Union scouts were to blame.

From here it was 38 miles to the next watering spot at Dead Man's Hole. We marched over a desert road, under a hot burning sun, with southwestern winds blowing over the parched plains with a heat that, once felt, can never be forgotten or adequately described. Twenty Apaches could have massacred the entire body. As I dictate this, the pictures before me portray the suffering, starving, perishing men, strung out for 20 miles along a desert road, crazed with their condition, reeling along like they were mad or drunk. The landscape itself had a tired and famished look.

The best walkers were the first to reach water. That was about midnight. They passed the words back to the next man and he to the next. By daylight, all were supposed to be present, though there was nothing like a roll call. As each individual quenched his thirst, he would like down on the road, the only place to lie, for both sides of the road were covered with cactus, sagebrush, and catclaw. The men lay on the road on their backs, the sun shining on their faces.

At three o'clock in the morning, myself and two others started out to pick our way to Wild Rose Pass to see what we might learn of the enemy's intentions. We saw smoke signals on Olympia Mountains, which were interpreted as, "Pursue the enemy no further." We were the three happiest mortals on earth. These were the last Indian signs I ever saw.

The brigade, what was left of it, was reformed. What became of Gen. Sibley I never knew, or much cared, though it was generally supposed that he crawled into a hole somewhere and pulled the jug and the hole in after him.

THEOPHILUS NOEL was born in 1840 at Berrien Springs, Mich. His father moved the family to Seguin in 1854. Theophilus left home at 14 to work cutting railroad ties and later worked as an Indian scout on the frontier. He enlisted as a scout in the 4th Texas Cavalry, which became part of Henry Sibley's brigade in the New Mexico campaign. After the battered brigade was reformed, Noel saw action in Louisiana and with Gen. Magruder at Galveston. He was later captured and paroled. Noel's "Old Sibley Brigade," published in 1865 and his autobiography, published in 1904, shed light on the disastrous Sibley campaign. Noel died at Berrien Springs, Mich., on April 10, 1918.

48

MATAGORDA COWBOY

Charles A. Siringo
COWBOY

In the fall of 1861 our teacher at the Dutch Settlement on Matagorda Island, Mr. Hale, broke up school and left for Yankeedom to join the bluecoats. Freed from academic custody, from that time on I had a regular picnic, doing nothing but studying mischief. Billy Williams was my particular chum and we were constantly together doing some kind of devilment.

The old women used to say we were the meanest little imps in the Settlement and that we would be hung before we reached 21. Our three favorite pastimes were riding the milk calves, coon hunting, and sailing play boats on the bay off the shoreline.

Shortly after school broke up, I wore my first pair of britches. Uncle Nick and Aunt Mary, mother's brother and sister-in-law who lived in Galveston, sent us a trunk full of clothes and among them was a pair of white canvas britches for me.

In 1862, a year after the war broke out, the Confederates rounded up all the cattle on the Peninsula of Matagorda and drove them to the mainland, where they were turned loose with many thousands of wild cattle already there.

Their idea was to keep the Yankees — whom they knew would hold the lower part of the Peninsula, they having the best gunboats — from getting fresh beef to eat.

There was only one cow left in the Dutch Settlement where we lived, and that was our old Brownie. Mother had pleaded with them to leave Brownie, for she knew we children would starve to death if we had to survive on cornmeal mush without milk.

WHEN THE WAR BROKE UP everybody was happy. We cheered for joy when Mr. Joe Yeamans brought the good news from town. With the war over, all the men and boys who were large enough went over to the mainland to gather up the Peninsula cattle. On their arrival they found it was a bigger job than they had figured on, for the cattle were scattered over two or three hundred miles of country and were as wild as deer.

My friend Billy and I thought it very hard that we could not go and be cowboys too. I was 10 then. But we had lots of fun by ourselves, for we had an old mule and two or three ponies to ride, so we practiced riding in anticipation of the near future, when we would be big enough to be real cowboys.

After having been gone to the mainland for three months, the Peninsula crowd came back, bringing with them several hundred head of cattle which they had gathered. Among them were about 20 head belonging to mother.

The crowd went right back after more. This stimulated Billy and I to become a crowd of cowboys all by ourselves. We put in most of our time lassoing and riding wild yearlings. We hardly stayed at home long enough to get our meals. Mother had to get her own wood in those days, for sister had gone to school in Galveston. Of course, I always had to come home at night, when mother would get satisfaction out of me with the black strap, for my waywardness and trifling habits.

In the spring of 1867, when I was 12, a cattleman named Faldien brought his family over to the Peninsula and rented part of our house to live in.

After getting his wife and babies settled in their new quarters, he started back home, in Matagorda, to make preparations for spring work. He had to rig up new outfits and so on. He persuaded mother to let me go with him and learn to run cattle. When she consented, I was the happiest boy in Dutch Settlement, for my lifelong wish was about to be gratified.

———

CHARLES A. SIRINGO was born on Matagorda Peninsula on Feb. 7, 1855, the son of an Italian father and Irish mother. Siringo went to work as a cowboy on coastal ranches at a young age. He worked for "Shanghai" Pierce and then became a trail driver in the 1870s. From there he worked on the LX Ranch in the Panhandle and during this period led a posse in pursuit of Billy the Kid and a herd of rustled cattle. In 1886 Siringo was hired by the Pinkerton Detective Agency and tracked down wanted men all over the West. He wrote several books based on his experiences, including "A Texas Cowboy," "Riata and Spurs," and "A Cowboy Detective." J. Frank Dobie wrote that, "No other cowboy ever talked about himself so much in print but no other cowboy had as much to talk about." Siringo died in Hollywood, Calif., on Oct. 18, 1928, and was buried in Inglewood Park Cemetery.

49

THE BATTLE OF
CORPUS CHRISTI

Francis Richard Lubbock

GOVERNOR, 1861-1863

At 9 a.m., Aug. 13, 1862, Captain Kittredge, commander of the federal fleet before Corpus Christi, approached the wharf in a launch under a flag of truce.

He stated that he had come, as ordered by the United States government, to examine the public buildings in the city. Every proposition to land, under whatever pretext, was peremptorily rejected. He then demanded that the women and children should be removed beyond the limits of the town within 24 hours, as he intended to land a force and execute his orders.

Forty-eight hours were finally allowed for the removal of families from town, which time was found amply sufficient for the purpose.

The ships Corypheus, Reindeer, Belle Italia and a steam gunboat from the enemy's fleet had taken positions on the previous day.

The Confederates had a battery near the water's edge that consisted of two guns (a 12- and an 18-pounder) which was supported by Capt. John Ireland's company and Maj. A. M. Hobby's battalion.

"At daylight on Aug. 16, wrote Maj. Hobby in his report, "we opened fire on the enemy. Six shots were fired on the federal fleet before they replied. The enemy shelled the battery and the town furiously, doing, however, but little damage. At nine o'clock, we drove him from his position. Beyond the reach of our guns, he repaired damages and mended sails rent by our shot. At three o'clock he returned and when within reach of our battery it opened fire, striking two of the ships, which compelled them to withdraw beyond the reach of our guns. They contented themselves with shelling the battery during the remainder of the day.

"Mr. William Mann, a volunteer commander of the battery, greatly distinguished himself by his skill and bravery.

"By guns of inferior caliber and a smaller force than their own, they were driven from their position. Five shots were seen to do execution. The enemy fired 296 times."

Only one Confederate, a private in Capt. Ireland's company, was wounded.

"On the morning of Aug. 18 (Monday), continued Maj. Hobby's report, "the enemy again opened on our battery, bringing his whole force to bear on it. Failing to silence our guns, a portion of his fleet withdrew and landed a 12-pounder rifled gun, supported by 30 or 40 well-armed men, who approached our battery by way of the beach, under the cover of a continuous fire from their gunboats.

"They attempted to enfilade our battery, their balls passing just above our entrenchments. I immediately ordered 25 men to charge the rifled gun, which they did in gallant style. After leaving the cover of our breastworks, they entered an open plain and rapidly neared the gun, whereupon the gunboats of the enemy opened a heavy fire upon them.

Thomas Noakes' painting of the battle of Corpus Christi

They were undaunted and pressed onward. When within range of small arms, I ordered them to fire, which they did, still advancing. The enemy in the meantime retreated double-quick, carrying with them their rifled gun. They left behind an ammunition box, hatchet, and rat-tail files (intended for use, I presume, to spike our guns), a hat and rifle cartridges scattered along the beach. We chased them to their gunboats, to which they retreated without delay.

"Whenever a ball from our battery would strike the boats of the enemy, our men would rise up and cheer, regardless of the fire to which were exposed. The enemy, taking position in front of the city, avenged themselves by shelling a few unoffending houses. A few shots from our guns drove them off, and on the following morning they stood away for Aransas Pass."

In September 1862, a second attempt was made to capture the place. Capt. Kittredge, commanding the United States fleet in Aransas Bay, visited Corpus Christi under a flag of truce and asked leave to take aboard the family of E. J. Davis. Maj. E. F. Gray, commandant of the port, referred the matter to Gen. Bee, and informed Kittredge

Texas' Gov. Francis Richard Lubbock

that an answer could not be expected under 10 days.

The federal commander then withdrew and proceeded with his ships down the coast towards the salt works on the Laguna del Madre. Capt. Ireland and Capt. Ware, with their respective companies, were dispatched in the same direction to watch the movements of the enemy. That night, Capt. Ireland prepared an ambush in a vacant house near the shore, off which the federal fleet had anchored.

Early the next morning, the federals shelled the houses and surrounding points for some time. Then, the ground being apparently unoccupied, Capt. Kittredge, accompanied by some of his sailors and marines, landed and approached the house. Our men being concealed, the adventurous officer fell into the trap set for him. Kittredge and his whole party were taken prisoner. As soon as the capture was discovered, the enemy gunboats opened a rapid fire of shell and grape on the command, which passed over our men and prisoners without damage to either.

Kittredge was immediately escorted by Maj. Hobby to headquarters at San Antonio, where he was paroled. The capture of this bold and energetic leader was especially gratifying to Gen. Bee, who described him as "an honorable enemy."

As to the citizens, Gen. Bee said, "Too much praise cannot be given to the patriotic citizens of Corpus Christi. They removed out into the woods with their families, out of fire, and in tents and under trees calmly awaited the result. They have suffered many inconveniences and privations, especially for the want of water, as the drought of this section has been unprecedented. Yet they have set a laudable example to their countrymen. It is worthy of remark that the citizens of surrounding counties, for a distance of 100 miles, attracted by the fire of cannon, repaired to the scene, with their rifles in hand, and tendered their services to the commanding officer. This demonstrates that when the emergency arises, their country can depend on them."

FRANCES RICHARD LUBBOCK was born in 1815 in Beaufort, S. C. After his father's death, when he was 14, he quit school and worked in a hardware store. He moved to Texas in 1836, opened a store in Houston and began ranching operations in the 1840s. Lubbock was elected clerk of the Harris County district court and served from 1841 to 1857. He won the governorship in 1861 by 124 votes. When his term of office ended, Lubbock was appointed lieutenant colonel and served as assistant adjutant general on the staff of Maj. Gen. John Magruder. The town of Lubbock was named for his brother, Thomas S. Lubbock. At the end of the war, Francis Richard Lubbock was imprisoned in Fort Delaware before being paroled. He died in Austin on June 22, 1905.

50

STRIFE AND STRUGGLE

Rosalie Hart Priour
TEACHER

It was in 1862 when my mother went to live on her ranch on the Aransas River. Some of my older children went with her but I kept the youngest with me in Corpus Christi. Federal ships sailed into the bay and threatened to shell the town. Women and children were told to evacuate. I had gone for a visit to my mother's ranch the week before. My husband sent all our Negroes to Britton Motts, eight miles southwest of town.

My husband described the evacuation. Every carriage, cart, and wagon in the town was pressed into service and even handcarts and wheelbarrows were used to carry furniture and household goods. In every direction, Mr. Priour said, you could see women and children loaded down with chickens, wash-pots, kettles and every imaginable article they could carry. One young lady carrying a wash-tub yelled back, "Mama! Don't forget the looking glass!"

Mr. Priour stayed at the Salt Lake where we had built a frame house. Here we had all our furniture and Mr. Priour would not leave the place. There was also a good crop of vegetables in the garden. He dug a cave where he put his money and valuables and there he went to sleep.

The Confederates placed their forces along the beach, determined to defend the place. The federals, with their gunboats and cannons and plenty of ammunition, could shell the town until the last house was destroyed.

While the federal ships were bombarding the town, I was at the ranch on the Aransas River. We went down to a hollow near the river where we could hear every shot fired. The river emptied into the bay and the sound followed the water. What surprised me was to feel the ground tremble, and this was 20 miles away.

Men brought news of the battle and told me that Mr. Priour was well. After a few days, I returned home.

IT WAS ALMOST IMPOSSIBLE to procure provisions. One time when I was sick Mr. Priour offered a dollar a pound for flour, not in Confederate money but in gold or silver, and could not get it at that price. Coffee was a dollar and 50 cents a pound; sugar was 50 cents a pound, not in paper, but gold or silver.

We had a severe drought to augment the misery of the war and nothing could be raised west of the San Antonio River.   We were forced to haul flour and corn from 300 miles away. If a man left home with a wagon and horses, he was in danger of losing them, for Confederate authorities would seize a team and wagon to carry cotton to Brownsville.

Under the circumstances, Mr. Priour thought it would be best to send the family to my mother's ranch.

I made an arrangement with the neighbors around the ranch to teach their children in return for provisions. I was

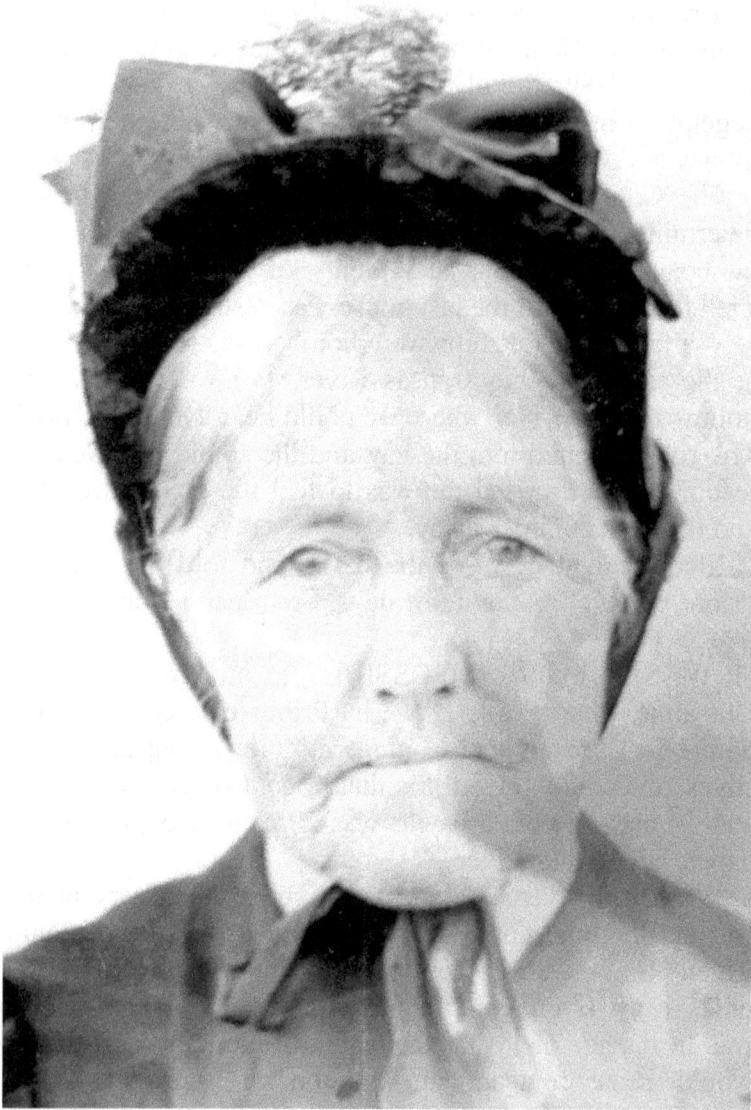

Rosalie Hart Priour, schoolteacher during the Civil War

able to keep my mother and children from suffering for
what was absolutely necessary. My mother was sick for

about six months; there was no disease, just a failing of strength.

During this time, I walked four miles to the schoolhouse, taught school all day, and in the evening came home and helped to do the housework. My nervous system became exhausted. I would arrive at the school so weak, and would tremble so much, I would have to sit and rest before ringing the school bell. I couldn't ride to school; our horses had been stolen.

When I could no longer walk so far and still teach, I took some bedclothes to the school and slept on the benches. I had the youngest of the children with me. We would go to the school every Monday morning and stay there until Friday afternoon.

The first two weeks that I was teaching school there was no corn or flour to be found within 20 miles. I got a few bushels of corn which had been badly eaten by weevils and smelled awful. But it was better than nothing. I sifted the best of the meal, ground it on a hand mill and made bread for mother and the children. I carried the hulls to the school to make bread for myself.

On Dec. 20, 1863 my mother breathed her last, as one going to sleep. We buried her under a large live oak tree, a place she had selected herself. There was no lumber to make a coffin; we tore off planks from the side of the house to use.

EVERYTHING ABOUT THE RANCH brought my loss to mind. I did not care for anything. I was in despair. We left everything as it was and returned to Corpus Christi.

There was only one ferry across the Nueces River, at San Patricio, so instead of a journey of 20 or 25 miles, we had to travel 70 or 80 miles, and on the worst kind of roads. The mud in some places reached the wagon hubs and we could only get a few feet at a time before we had to stop to let the horses rest.

It was cold and sleeting and I was afraid my children would be frozen before we reached home. We camped out two nights. We arrived at home two hours after sundown. It was as dark as it could be; we stopped at a neighbor's to borrow a lantern to find our way home. I was so weary that I longed to rest in my grave from all the strife and struggle of this troubled life.

I had been at home a few days when friends begged me to teach the boys and girls. They promised to furnish me with provisions. The federals (on Mustang Island) gave or sold provisions to families who belonged to their side. I began to teach in the house on Water Street in which my mother had formerly kept a store.

We moved our furniture down from our dwelling house at the Salt Lake, a mile from town. We intended to remain in town but were glad before long to return to the Salt Lake house. The town was sometimes occupied by one side and sometimes by the other.

I watched my children as close as possible but when I would think they were asleep they would slip out through the window and join the other boys. Confederate soldiers would see them in the day and appoint a place of rendezvous for that night.

When the town boys were assembled, the soldiers would go into someone's pen and get the best beef they could find, then the boys would surround it and drive it to the Salt Lake to be slaughtered. This was the only way the Confederates could get meat. The soldiers received half rations and even with the meat they killed they suffered from hunger.

My husband went to Austin for a load of flour and sugar but it took all he made to cover expenses. He ran into debt and I had to pay it with my school money.

James Hatch, my son-in-law, took pneumonia and was sick for three months. As soon as he was able to get up, he was compelled to go to Brownsville with a load of cotton for the government. While he was away, my daughter stayed with me. She was sick.

When my son-in-law came back from Brownsville, he had another load of cotton to take back, but he was so sick he couldn't go. We were without provisions and did not know what to do, so George Craven begged me to let my oldest son go in his place. I consented and went down to the commanding officers and asked for a pass.

The provost marshal was Mr. Charles Lovenskiold, one of our former teachers, and he knew Julian's age exactly. He said, "Julian will be 18 tomorrow." The date was Dec. 17, 1863. He spoke with someone and said he could not give a pass since Julian was old enough to go into the army. I told him that we were without food and had no means of getting any. His answer was: "If Julian tries to leave town, he'll be put in irons."

I told him Julian had neither horse nor saddle and he knew very well our horses had been taken. He said he would furnish us with provisions and find a horse and saddle for Julian. As a newly conscripted soldier, the first duty Julian had to perform was to guard the office. For this purpose they gave him a gun that couldn't be fired. He was told not to allow anyone to go into the office except the colonel. When one officer tried to get into the office, Julian stationed himself in the doorway and told him if he tried to enter, he would knock him down with the gun. They all thought this a good joke. After this, they put him to guarding prisoners with the same gun. Every chance he got, he worked at the wharf and brought me provisions from what he earned.

MR. PRIOUR had to go to Brownsville with cotton. He had four loads and he took Ambrose with him. The oxen in his team were wild and hard to handle. They ran away and he fell in such a way that two of his ribs were broken. A Negro driving one of the other teams picked him up and made him a bed in his wagon. Mr. Priour stayed in Brownsville and kept Ambrose, who was 11, with him. He planned to rent a place there and send for the family. Before he could find a suitable place he learned that the war was over.

The North sent two Negro regiments, commanded by white officers, to take possession of Corpus Christi. They were the most lawless set of people I have ever seen.

After our gardens at the Salt Lake had been raided over several nights, Mr. Priour went to town and informed the general of the way we were being annoyed by his troops. The general's name was Russell. He ordered the posting of guards to watch our gardens and this ended our troubles. It became a great source of pleasure for me as the captains, and their wives, came out every day.

The wives were two of the best ladies I have ever been acquainted with. They were well-educated and I could enjoy their conversation on every subject. They were from the North, but I loved them as I have loved few strangers.

The government ordered the soldiers to pack up and leave for some other place. Now came the pain of parting from Mrs. Steadman and her friend. To me, it was real grief. It was like parting with a part of my own family. I knew I would never have the happiness of seeing them again, that it was a final parting. Before leaving, they gave me two chickens and a white cat — and as long as they lived, they were among my greatest treasures.

———————

ROSALIE HART CAME to Texas from County Wexford, Ireland in 1832. They were members of the James Power colony. After her father died, her mother opened a store in Corpus Christi. Rosalie was sent to a convent school in Mobile, where she married Jean M. Priour. They returned to Corpus Christi to make their home. Rosalie Hart Priour died on Aug. 20, 1903. She left a large family. Her second son, John M. Priour, became well-known as a naturalist, featured in the book "A Man from Corpus Christi."

51

ELYSIUM

Arthur James Lyon Fremantle

COLDSTREAM GUARDS

April 19, 1863. For several days now, as we were traveling from Brownsville to San Antonio, I had heard of King's Ranch as some sort of Elysium, as it marks the termination of the hot sands and the commencement of comparative civilization.

We halted in front of the house. After cooking and eating, I walked up to the "ranch" which is a comfortable, well-furnished wooden building. Mr. and Mrs. Richard King had gone to Brownsville but we were received by Mrs. Hamilton Bee, wife of the Confederate general in Brownsville. She had heard I was on the road.

She is a nice little woman, a red-hot Southerner. She glories in the facts that she has no Northern relatives or friends and that she is a member of the Church of England.

Mr. King first came to Texas as a steamboat captain. Now he owns an immense tract of country with 16,000 head of cattle. However, his tract is situated in a wild and almost uninhabited region. King's Ranch is distant from Brownsville only 125 miles, but we have been six days in reaching it.

After drying our clothes after the rain of last night, we started again at 2:30 p.m. We entered a boundless and fertile prairie. As far as the eye could see, cattle were feeding. Bulls and cows, horses and mares, came to stare at us as we passed. They looked to be sleek and in good condition, yet they get nothing but what they can find on the prairie.

I saw a man on horseback kill a rabbit with his revolver. I also saw a scorpion for the first time. We halted at 5:30 p.m. We had to make our fire principally of cow dung. Wood is very scarce on the prairie.

April 20. I slept well last night. And that was in spite of the wolves which surrounded us, making a most dismal noise. We started at 5 a.m. and had to get through some dreadful mud. One of our teamsters, Mr. Sargent, was in an awful bad humor and using terrific language.

WE WERE MUCH DELAYED by this unfortunate rain. It converted a good road into a quagmire. We saw a rattlesnake crawling along this morning. I'm told that there are not nearly as many of them in this country as there used to be.

We halted at 9 a.m. and made a fire for cooking. Two Texas Rangers rode up while we were at breakfast. These Rangers all wear the most enormous spurs I ever saw.

We resumed our journey at 12:30. We reached a creek called Agua Dulce at 2 p.m. We got out before crossing to forage at some huts close by. We got two dozen eggs and some lard. We halted at 5 p.m. The heat from nine to two is pretty severe. But in this part of Texas there is generally a cool sea-breeze, which makes it bearable.

April 21: We started at 5 a.m. and reached a hamlet called Casa Blanca. We procured a goat, some Indian corn, and two chickens in this neighborhood. We had now left the flat country and entered an undulating, or rolling, prairie, full of live oaks of respectable size. We had also got out of the mud.

Our mule drivers, Mr. Sargent and Mr. Judge, got drunk again. But it had a most beneficial effect on our speed. We descended the hills at a terrific pace. As Mr. Sargent expressed it, we were going, "Like Hell beating tan bark."

We stopped at noon at a small creek. We made a pretty good afternoon's drive through a wood of post oaks. We saw another rattlesnake, which we tried to shoot.

We halted at Spring creek at 6:30 p.m. Water was rather brackish and there was no grass for the mules. We are now living luxuriously upon eggs and goat meat, and I think we made about 32 miles today.

April 22. We got underway at 5 a.m. The mules were looking rather poor for want of grass. We reached the Nueces River. The banks are very steep and bordered with a beautiful belt of live-oak trees. They were covered with vines of mustang grapes.

On the other side of the Nueces River is Oakville. It is a miserable settlement consisting of about 20 wooden huts. We bought some butter there. The women at Oakville were most anxious to buy snuff. It appears that the Texas females are in the habit of dipping snuff. This means putting it into their mouths instead of their noses. They rub it against their gums with a blunted stick.

* * *

APRIL 27. I LEFT SAN ANTONIO by stage for Alleyton at nine p.m. The stage was an old coach, into the interior of which nine persons were crammed on three transverse seats. In addition, there were several others on the roof.

I was placed on the center seat, which was extremely narrow and I had nothing but a strap to support my back. An enormous fat German sat facing me and a long-legged Confederate officer was in my rear. Our first team consisted of four mules; afterwards we got horses. My fellow travelers were military men or connected to the government. Only five out of nine chewed tobacco during the night, but they aimed at the windows with great accuracy and did not splash me.

April 28. We got a very fair breakfast at Seguin, which was beginning to be a well-to-do place when the war dried it up. It commenced to rain at Seguin, which made the road very woolly and annoyed the outsiders a good deal.

The country through which we had been traveling was a good deal cultivated. There were numerous farms and I saw cotton fields for the first time. After the rain stopped, we amused ourselves by taking shots with our revolvers at jackrabbits which came up to stare at the coach.

April 29. Exhausted as I was, I managed to sleep wonderfully well last night. We breakfasted at a place called Hallettsville and changed coaches. Here we took on four more Confederate soldiers as outsiders. We were now 18 in all. Nowhere but in this country would such a thing be permitted. The coach, owing to this great weight, swayed like a ship in a heavy sea.

WE PASSED THROUGH cotton fields and beautiful Indian corn, much of which had been damaged by hail. We crossed several rivers with steep banks and dined at a farmhouse. We crossed the Colorado and reached Alleyton, our destination, at 7 p.m. The distance from San Antonio to Alleyton is 140 miles; time, 46 hours.

May 2. I left by railroad for Galveston. In the cars I was introduced to Gen. Sam Houston, the founder of Texas Independence. Houston told me he was born in Virginia 70 years ago, that he was a United States senator at 30 and the governor of Tennessee at 36. He emigrated to Texas in 1832 and headed the revolt of Texas and defeated the Mexican army at San Jacinto. Though Houston is evidently a remarkable and clever man, he is extremely egotistical and vain. In appearance he is a tall handsome man, much given to chewing tobacco and blowing his nose with his fingers.

I was also introduced to another character, a man named Capt. Chubb who told me he was a Yankee by birth and served as coxswain to the United States ship Java in 1827.

He told me he was afterwards imprisoned at Boston on suspicion of being engaged in the slave trade, but he escaped. At the beginning of this war he was captured by the Yankees, when he was in command of the Confederate steamer Royal Yacht. He was taken to New York in chains, where he was condemned to be hung as a pirate, but he was eventually exchanged. I was afterwards told that the slave-trading escapade of which he was accused consisted in his having hired a colored crew at Boston and then coolly selling them as slaves when the ship arrived at Galveston.

ARTHUR JAMES LYON FREMANTLE of Her Majesty's Coldstream Guards made a tour of the Confederacy in 1863. He arrived at Brownsville, rode up the Cotton Road to San Antonio, and traveled across the South. At Gettysburg, he watched from the forks of a tree while Gen. Lee met with his generals to confer about the course of the battle. After Gettysburg, Fremantle sailed for England, convinced the South would win the war.

52

THE LOST BLANKET

John C. West
SOLDIER, LAWYER

When I left Waco in April 1863 to join Hood's Brigade in the army of Northern Virginia, I had with me a large shawl and a very large blanket. This blanket was made of pure wool, grown, spun and woven in McLennan County. It was the handiwork of Mrs. Powell, who lived near Bosqueville, north of Waco. It was striped after the fashion of Mexican blankets, which were quite common in Texas at that time. The colors were green, red and yellow, so intermixed and interwoven in stripes as to be quite unusual and noticeable.

My prudent wife took the precaution to write my name, company and regiment on a piece of white tape in indelible ink, and sew it securely in a corner of the blanket.

At Kingsville, South Carolina, this blanket and shawl were under the seat on which I sat, but when the train reached Columbia they were both gone. I have never seen the shawl since that day. I regarded them as lost to me and my heirs forever. I remained in Columbia a day or two and was supplied with a blanket and articles by my sweet mother-in-law, Mrs. Thee Stark.

I went to my company on the Rapidan, then to Culpepper, and through the Gettysburg campaign. Marched up and down the beautiful and picturesque defiles of the lovely Shenandoah Valley with its bright and shining waters until the mountain trails from Snigger Gap to Ashby Gap became familiar roads, and wading the river two or three times a day was a pastime, but in September 1863, four months after my blanket disappeared, we went with Gen. Longstreet to Chickamauga's bloody field and after gaining that Pyrrhic victory we moved to the foot of Lookout Mountain near Chattanooga and held a long line up and down Lookout Creek for two or three weeks in October.

WHILE IN CAMP HERE I learned that my old college friend, Gen. Martin W. Gary, was within a mile of our brigade. I got permission to visit him and found him at his headquarters on a gently sloping hillside.

There had been a very hard rain the night before and hundreds of blankets and other articles were spread and stretched out to dry. While we chatted, I viewed the interesting scene — one of the most unique and striking in army life. Some distance away I spied my Texas blanket and said to Gary, "Yonder is a blanket I lost in South Carolina several months ago."

Mart Gary was disposed to be profane and replied, "The hell you say." I called his attention to the blanket spread out in the sunlight on some bushes with its gaudy colors glistening in the sun. He said, "Well, let's go down there and see about it."

We went and I showed him the piece of tape in the corner with my name on it. By being wet the wool had shrunk and made a sort of roll on the edge of the blanket so that this mark could not be readily seen. Gary looked around and said in a loud tone, "Where is the man who claims this blanket?"

Someone answered, "He's out yonder at work on the redan.* " And Gary said, "Well, tell him here is a man from Texas who claims this blanket." We walked away to headquarters with the blanket and then some man said — just like a soldier will — in a distinct but somewhat suppressed tone, "Where is the man that stole the Texas man's blanket?"

Then someone else — just as a soldier will — in a little louder, more distinct tone, said, "Where is the man that stole the Texas man's blanket?"

And then two, three, 100, 500, took up the chorus, with higher inflection, until the woods resounded in every key with the cry, "Where is the man that stole the Texas man's blanket!" The echoes from the foot of Lookout Mountain answered back, "Blanket! ! !"

I had not seen Mart since my graduation in 1854. We talked of reminiscences of college days and of present hopes and fears for an hour or more and parted never to meet again.

I RETURNED TO MY CAMP and on the next day was visited by a Mr. Horton of Lancaster, South Carolina. I think he was a sergeant. He said, "I am the man who had the Texas man's blanket and I have come to tell you how I got it."

He was very pleasant in his manner and we talked for some time. The substance of his story was that his wife had received the blanket from a soldier in the Lancaster district. The soldier was sick and stayed a day or two at the house and gave her this blanket as he had more than he needed. (I

---

* Redan: fieldworks used to cover a camp or the front of a battlefield. Military Dictionary, H. L. Scott.

suppose he had the shawl also). Mr. Horton said his wife had sent him the blanket from home and he had it only a few days before I found it. We parted very pleasantly.

His statement seemed reasonable and I was satisfied he stated the real facts. This was about the 20th of October, and this wandering blanket served its purpose well during the severe winter campaign in East Tennessee, protecting me from many a wintry blast, warding off snow, sleet and rain.

I brought it back to Texas in May 1864 and kept it for many years. In 1868 1 took it on a hunt trip on Manos Creek, about 15 miles from Waco, and while we were absent from camp, the blanket disappeared, and I have never seen it since. Some months afterwards a citizen informed me that he was sure that Mr. — —, known as a shady character, carried the blanket with him to the Indian Territory.

———————

JOHN CAMDEN WEST JR. was born in Camden, South Carolina, on April 12, 1834, the son of John Camden and Nancy Clark (Eccles) West. He graduated from the University of South Carolina and moved to Texas in 1855 to join his brother, Charles S. West. He returned to South Carolina to marry Mary Eliza Stark of Columbia on April 14. They became the parents of three children. West read law in his brother's office and passed the Texas bar in 1858. He moved to Waco in 1859 and, in 1861, enlisted in the Confederate Army as a private in Company E, Fourth Regiment, Hood's Texas Brigade. He fought at Gettysburg, Chickamauga, and Knoxville before being honorably discharged in February 1864. After his discharge West returned to Waco and set up a law practice. He published his war letters and the diary he kept in a volume titled "A Texan in Search of a Fight." He died in Waco on July 12, 1927 and was buried in Oakwood Cemetery.

233

53

CAPTURE OF FORT SEMMES

Edwin B. Lufkin

PRIVATE, E COMPANY

Nov. 15, 1863, Point Isabel. We remained in bivouac, not far from the lighthouse, till about noon when the regiment embarked on the steamers "Matamoros" and "Planter," six companies on the former and four on the latter.

The "Matamoros," a stern-wheel steamer, was built at Pittsburgh for use on the Rio Grande and had been loaned to Gen. Banks by the Mexican general Cortina. The "Planter" was an Alabama River steamer which had been captured by the blockading fleet while trying to run across from Mobile to Cuba with a cargo of cotton.

The advance of the expedition consisted of the 13th and 15th Maine and two companies of the 20th Iowa commanded by Gen. T.E.G. Ransom. After the troops were embarked, the steamers went down to the bar, where they remained till nearly night then crossed. Most of the men on the "Matamoros" were transferred to the "McClellan" and then the "Matamoros" was taken in tow by the "Monongahela" (a gunboat) and the expedition started up along the coast.

About sunset on Nov. 16 we reached Corpus Christi Pass. It had been the intention of Gen. Banks for the "Matamoros" to cross the bar and land the troops on the inner side of Mustang Island, but the water on the bar was not deep enough so a difficult landing was made through the surf. The 13th took the lead. As soon as the landing was completed, which was considerably after dark, the troops started along the beach towards the northeast end of the island.

The marching was very tiresome on account of the men having had their feet and clothing wet while landing. But only short halts were made till four o'clock the next morning, when the men were allowed to rest till daylight. The distance marched during the night was about 18 miles.

As soon as it was light the march was continued, and after going about three miles, some of the enemy were discovered. The 13th was deployed as skirmishers and rapidly pressed back the enemy, who were much inferior in force. They fell back to the end of the island where they had a battery of three heavy cannon, built to command Aransas Pass. The Confederates called this post "Fort Semmes."

They saw it was useless to oppose such superior force and surrendered. One of them lost an arm but none of our men were injured. We captured nine officers, 89 men, three cannon, about 100 small arms, one schooner, 10 boats, 140 horses, and 125 head of cattle. The prisoners belonged to the 8th Texas Infantry and 3rd Texas State Militia.

––––––––––

EDWIN B. LUFKIN, born in Weld, Maine, in 1841, was a private in Company E of the 13th Maine. The regiment took part in the expedition commanded by Gen. Nathaniel Banks in late 1863 which resulted in the capture of Brownsville, Fort Semmes on Mustang Island, and Fort Esperanza on Matagorda Island. Lufkin died in 1903.

54

BURYING THE DEAD

A. J. H. Duganne

UNION COLONEL, WAR PRISONER

Sept. 10, 1863, Camp Groce. The bad news of the battle of Sabine Pass reached us on our return from the Masonic burial of Surgeon Cummings of the Massachusetts infantry. The ceremony was an impressive one and was fraternally participated in by Masons belonging to our Confederate guards.

Together, with white aprons and bearing willow wands, the men of North and South walked behind the bier. Together they surrounded the grave and listened to the beautiful ritual of burial. Together they cast the "ashes to ashes and dust to dust" and dropped sprigs of evergreen upon the dead. Together they uttered the solemn adjuration — "Amen! So mote it be!"

In this Masonic interchange, war and strife for a brief space were forgotten and charity was united in the hands and hearts of those who had been created one family by the

Camp Groce prison camp was near Hempstead

Sublime Architect of souls. The preliminaries of the funeral had been arranged at a meeting of free-masons, called by one of our guards who held high rank in the fraternity.

About the middle of September, we began to get acquainted with that peculiar visitor known as a "norther." A "norther" gives little warning of its coming. Noon may be fair and cloudless, with a promise of a balmy evening, when suddenly a low wind whistles across the prairie and swelling into strength and fury lashes the forests like a flail and sweeps with a roar toward the coast.

Sometimes the "norther" is dry and cold, freezing the marrow in one's bones, and sometimes charged with gusty rain that deluges the country, swelling the rivers and making the roads impassable.

Woe to a forlorn traveler who is overtaken by a frigid "norther" while crossing a wide prairie. Horsemen have been found in the saddle, chilled to death by this icy wind, and herds of beef cattle have perished in the arctic cold of a December "norther" in Texas.

The routine of camp life had been wearisome enough, but with the sick and dying constantly in our midst, a mental despondency began to prey upon many who were not physically ill.

Once a week, at least, we were called upon to follow the pine coffin of some poor captive. Our rough burial ground in the timber spread quickly with graves of federal prisoners, marked by wooden headboards on which Lt. Eddy painted the name and age of the departed.

Lt. Eddy was also an invalid and he had to prop himself up on a pillow in his bunk while he traced out the record of death in silver-white paint.

In the first week of October, Dr. Sherfy, our tireless surgeon, reported 120 prisoners on his sick list. The little mounds of prison-dead accumulated fast.

WE LOST ANOTHER of our officers, Lt. Ramsay, of the 175th New York Volunteers. He had been lingering long, with dysentery and pneumonia, and was wasted to a mere skeleton when he died.

Shortly after Ramsay's death, we lamented the sudden loss of Lt. Hayes, of the same regiment, a favorite with all of us. I had become personally attached to Lt. Hayes, attracted by his many amiable traits of character.

The low Texas forests were bending and sighing under the first blast of a "norther" as we walked, two by two, to bury the remains of our genial comrade. Two by two we followed the mule cart, which contained the coffin of rough yellow pine. The wagon wheels jerked heavily over stumps and uneven ground. The Negro driver sat at one end of the coffin. We walked behind the wagon and our ever-present guards, with loaded muskets, marched on either side.

Climbing to the grave that had been dug by the sailors of our company; standing at the edges on red clumps of earth; looking into the gaping hole as the coffin was lowered;

listening to the rattle of clods as they fell on pine boards; so proceeded the burial of our friend and comrade.

A brother officer read the burial service and we turned back into the face of winds that came howling over the prairie. How we prayed, in our hearts, for a "norther" that would sweep over this rebel country like a tornado.

AUGUSTINE JOSEPH HICKEY (A.J.H.) DUGANNE was born in Boston in 1823. He was a novelist and poet, served a term in the New York Legislature, and was one of the founders of the "Know Nothing" political movement in the 1850s. In 1862 he helped raise the 176th New York Volunteers and was commissioned its colonel. He was captured by Confederates in Louisiana in June 1863 and spent more than a year in Texas prison camps. He was paroled in July 1864 and mustered out for disability. After the war he was on the editorial staff of the New York Tribune. His wife, Priscilla Elkin Duganne, died on April 14, 1884 and he died six months later, on Oct. 20, 1884. He was buried in Cypress Hills National Cemetery, Brooklyn.

55

DINNER PARTY

Charles C. Nott

UNION COLONEL, PRISONER OF WAR

We were moved from Camp Groce, the Confederate prison encampment near Hempstead, to Camp Ford at Tyler. We arrived in time for Christmas 1863.

We found the prisoners at Camp Ford a poor and dispirited group of men. They possessed no supplies to sell and in manufactures they had not risen above carved pipes and chessmen. They lived on their rations and cooked them in the simplest manner. Half of them had no tables. Plates and spoons did treble duty, traveling from "shebang" to "shebang," as they called the hovels they built and occupied.

A few days passed in the work of improving our own "shebang." We were in the middle of the Christmas holidays. Thoughts of home pressed heavily on us and made the present seem darker than it really was. "Something must be done," said one man, "to raise these fellows up. They are completely down, and if we don't get them up, they will pull us down too."

"I never saw such fellows," said another. "They don't seem to have done anything to keep themselves alive but cook, and not much of that."

"And that's the remedy," said another. "Let's give a dinner party and astonish them."

"Well, why not? Didn't some of us celebrate the Fourth at Brashear? Didn't we have a Thanksgiving dinner at Camp Groce? Why can't we have a New Year's dinner here?"

On Dec. 30, Lt. Dane, of the signal corps, and myself went to the gate and asked the sergeant of the guard if we could see Col. Allen, the camp commandant, on private business.

The Confederate colonel, when we were taken in to see him, smiled pleasantly at our request and wrote us out a pass.

The lieutenant and I returned to our quarters and hung around our necks several canteens and three or four haversacks. We presented our pass to the sergeant at the gate and stepped out of Camp Ford on parole.

WE WALKED half a mile down the road and came to a big white house with slave cabins, a plantation. At the door we met a sour-faced man.

"Good day, sir. Have you any dried fruit to sell?"

"No."

"No apples?"

"No."

"Nor peaches?"

"No."

"Any eggs?"

"No."

"Nothing to sell for cash, at the highest prices?"

"No."

"Good day, sir."

A prisoners' log hut ("shebang") at Camp Ford at Tyler

It was two miles walking to the next house. A plain-looking woman invited us in. As ill-luck would have it, her two sons had been captured by Union forces. When they were ill, they were placed in different hospitals and someone with petty tyranny in his heart had refused to let one brother visit the other. The old lady said she would have forgiven anything but such gratuitous cruelty. Still, she gave us a pumpkin and allowed her servant to sell us some sweet potatoes from his private supply.

At the third house we had the same conversation we had at the first one. It began to rain and we debated about whether to turn back. We decided to go on.

Three miles more and we came to another house, owned by another old lady. She said she had nothing to sell, but her black overseer came in at that time and said that he had

243

some dried peaches for sale. We gave him $5 for a peck. We asked if he had any milk and he said no, but a thought struck him. He had some cider vinegar he made himself and reckoned it was worth $1 a quart. He filled our canteens with this precious liquid.

Retracing our steps, we noticed a small log-house where a woman was barbecuing beef under a little shed. We asked about making various purchases and a dozen eggs were produced and she sent her boys to catch a certain young fowl that could be sold.

Now we faced the task of walking six miles back in the rain. "This haul is a prize, Colonel," said the lieutenant. "The vinegar is a treasure, and the peaches are worth their weight in Confederate notes. How many should we ask to dine with us?"

"I think we can squeeze in six on a side and one at each end — 14 in all. But 10 eggs and one chicken won't make much of a dinner for 14 men."

WE TRUDGED ALONG in the mud on a rainy day, loaded with a bag of sweet potatoes, a big pumpkin, a couple of overstuffed baskets, and several haversacks and canteens. We were afraid that our appearance might produce a sensation in camp, but the rain and mud had driven all inside their hovels.

We walked rapidly past the closed doors of the "shebangs" till we reached our own. After a savage attack on cold beef and hot corn dodger, we hung our wet clothes before the fire and wrapped up in blankets. Before we fell asleep, someone came in and said it was freezing and the ground was white with snow.

The rest of the men in our mess, who had been abashed at our foraging, became interested and joined in the work by manufacturing a table and chopping an immense pile of wood for the evening.

"Happy New Year's" came bright and clear. The prisoners followed the old Dutch custom of wandering around and wishing each other happy returns.

At our "shebang" we had three fires in full blast — one in the fireplace, one in the stove, and one under an independent pot.

We placed the table directly in front of the fireplace and hung blankets from the roof to the floor to curtain-out the cold. We used our last three candles to light up the festive board.

When all was ready the door was opened and our guests marshalled in. They seemed fairly dazed with the splendors of the apartment. They sank into their seats and talked in subdued tones.

The first course consisted of soup and wheat bread. The soup plates were removed by one waiter while another placed the second course on the table. This was a composition of beef and sweet potatoes which a naval officer called "scouse."

At the other end of the table were turnips, boiled potatoes, squash, and cranberry sauce.

THE NEXT COURSE was a magnificent chicken pie, filling an immense pan and crowned with a brown crust. There were mince and pumpkin pies and the climax was a Lafayette cake, sometimes called "jelly-cake" and we closed with coffee (not parched corn, but real java).

That ended the great dinner.

The soup was made of boiled beef bones. The turnips and spareribs were a present from the Confederate Commissary. Dried peaches were used, with repeated experiments, to make cranberry sauce.

The mince-pies were made of peaches and minced meat. The pumpkin was cut into small pieces, stewed and seasoned with sassafras, prickly-ash, cloves and nutmeg to become pear preserves.

The cake was made, mostly, of cornmeal with a little flour and sugar. The cake was not a success. We might fool our guests with some of the dishes, but not on corn dodger. When they tasted dodger, they knew dodger.

Overall, the dinner was a grand success. Our guests retired from it wiser and better men. Manufactures sprang up and trade began. Some men made caps from rags and hats from straw. Others built a gymnasium, some started a garden, and a few musicians made banjos. One officer used a file, a screw, and a couple of old horseshoes to make a good turning lathe. We soon counted more than 40 items of camp manufacture that were made, chiefly, like our dinner, out of nothing.

CHARLES COOPER NOTT was born on Sept. 16, 1827. He graduated from Union College in 1848 and was admitted to the bar in New York in 1850. He was promoted to colonel of the 176th New York Volunteers and was captured by Confederate forces at Brashear, La. (now Morgan City) and held at Camp Groce, near Huntsville, then at Camp Ford, near Tyler. After the war, in 1867, he married Alice Effingham Hopkins and they had four children. He was appointed chief justice of the U. S. Court of Claims by President Grover Cleveland in 1897. He died on March 6, 1916 and was buried in Williams College Cemetery, Williamstown, Mass.

56

CHASING DESERTERS

Cliff Cates

LAWYER, HISTORIAN

A few days before Gen. Lee's surrender on April 9, 1865, the force in command of the post at Decatur, Texas, in Wise County, was thrown into a fever of excitement by the reception of orders to join in the pursuit of a fleeing band of 100 or more deserters from the Confederate ranks who were believed heading for New Mexico territory.

The order came from Gen. James Throckmorton, commander of the district, and accompanying the order was the information that a large band of soldiers had deserted the Confederate Army somewhere in East Texas and, with saddle horses and equipment, were trying to escape to regions beyond the jurisdiction of the Confederacy.

There were many such desertions with the end of the war in sight. There was a general despair in the Southern ranks and when an opportunity came, some took their chances and deserted. Many of these had been good loyal soldiers who had borne their part in the war. Another leading cause of the widespread desertions was a fear that cavalry forces would be dismounted and their horses taken from them. To prevent this, some deserted and left for regions beyond Confederate control.

Col. James Diamond and his forces from the Red River Station in Montague County were already in pursuit of the deserters when the order reached Col. G. B. Pickett, in command at the Decatur post, to join in. On Saturday, April 2, Pickett and a company of 100 men left, heading in a northwesterly direction. They were joined en route by another company from western Wise and Jack counties.

Late on Sunday afternoon, April 3, the command reached the Wichita in the Panhandle. They had followed the trail of the fleeing soldiers. The deserters were mounted on fine cavalry horses while their pursuers were mounted on inferior stock, even mules.

THIS WAS TEXAS STATE MILITIA in pursuit of a force of regular Confederate soldiers who had deserted. At the foot of a high ridge which separated them from the Wichita River, the command paused for the night. Supper was prepared and the horses staked out.

Next morning, a detail went out to bring in the horses. Presently, they heard the clear sounds of a bugle from the other side of the ridge, next to the river. The men after the horses hastily returned and reported the occurrence. "My God," said one, "I couldn't have felt any worse if I had heard Gabriel blow his horn."

The entire camp grew animated. The fact of them being in the immediate vicinity of the deserters was not in doubt. The two forces had slept through the night on either side of the ridge without the knowledge of the other's presence.

Three scouts were sent to the top of the ridge and could look down on a large camp, pitched in true military style, in a draw near the river. Their horses were grazing near the camp and they were busy preparing their breakfast.

Col. Diamond was hesitant to make an attack. Col. Pickett suggested making a raid on the camp to steal their horses. Diamond agreed. Twenty-four volunteers were sent, riding hell-for-leather and yelling like banshees, down the ridge and into the deserters' camp.

There was a great commotion among the deserters, who grabbed their rifles and began firing. But the charging men were able to capture all the horses and drive them back over the ridge.

With their horses gone, the deserters raised a white flag. Col. Diamond went to parley. The deserters threatened to kill him if the horses were not returned. The white flag had been a ruse.

Col. Pickett then went down and met with similar threats. A long discussion followed and finally the deserters were convinced that their position was useless. They surrendered and threw their weapons in the river. They were mounted and escorted back to the settlements. Some of them were taken to the post at Red River Station and some went to the post at Buffalo Springs. They were not held in captivity long. They were all freed with Lee's surrender.

———————

CLIFF (DONOHO) CATES was born on Oct. 19, 1876, the son of Charles D. and Rowena Cates. Cliff Cates was a lawyer and secretary of the Decatur Chamber of Commerce. He never married. He wrote the 1907 edition of "Pioneer History of Wise County: from Red Men to Railroads—Twenty Years of Intrepid History." He died at the age of 73 on Aug. 10, 1950.

57

GOING HOME

Joseph P. Blessington
CONFEDERATE SOLDIER

On the morning of May 1, 1865, a federal officer named Col. Sprague arrived at the mouth of the Red River with dispatches for Gen. Kirby Smith. The troops heard that Gen. Smith was about to surrender. They gathered in groups everywhere to discuss the matter.

Angry and bitter curses fell from the lips of those not accustomed to using such language. Some of the officers and men swore never to surrender. It was such a scene as one seldom cares to witness. The depth of feeling — shown by tight lips, pale faces and hard eyes — told a fearful story. The humiliation was unbearable.

For nearly four years Walker's Texas Division battled for the South. For nearly four years of horrors, suffering, toil, and bloodshed, the soldiers of the division had trod the soil of Arkansas and Louisiana, and left their dead on the hills and plains of those states. Now, back in their own native Texas, they were to witness the final overthrow of the Confederate government and must turn over their arms.

On the morning of May 19, most of the troops were preparing to leave. They were allowed to take one wagon for each company. On the evening of May 20, the balance of the troops that remained were discharged from the Confederate army. The parting among the troops was most affecting. Many put their arms around each other's necks and wept like children. Others gave a strong grasp of the hand and silently went away, their hearts too full for utterance. And still others would mutter a husky "goodbye" or some deep oath. Such were the farewell scenes.

THESE MEN IN TORN GRAY uniforms had been together in battle, in camp, in sunshine and in storm, in suffering and in pleasure, in sorrow and joy, on the weary and toilsome march — no wonder that their hearts were linked by ties that are unspeakable, inexpressible. No wonder that the parting — perhaps for years, perhaps forever — wrung their souls with such agony.

I hope our worthy foes will do us the justice to acknowledge that the private soldiers of the Southern army — like the soldiers of Walker's Texas Division — were never defeated, never whipped, just overpowered.

JOSEPH PARMER BLESSINGTON was born in Ireland on April 21, 1841. He arrived in New York in 1857, at age 16, and moved to Texas. In the Civil War, he enlisted in the 16th Texas Infantry, which served in Walker's Texas Division in campaigns in Texas, Louisiana and Arkansas. His book on the campaigns was described by one Texas scholar as "one of the best war histories written, as to Texas troops." Blessington died on Dec. 19, 1898, at age 57, and was buried in Holy Cross Cemetery, Waco.

58

VISITING THE DEAF

Elizabeth Bacon

MRS. GEORGE ARMSTRONG CUSTER

Before we reached Austin, several citizens sent invitations for us to come to their houses. I knew that Gen. Custer would not accept and, cold as the nights were, I felt unwilling to lose a day of camp life.

We pitched our tents on rolling ground in the vicinity of Austin, where we overlooked a pretty town of stucco-ed houses that appeared summery in the midst of the live-oak's perennial green.

The state house, land office, and governor's mansion looked regal to us, after so long bivouacking in the forest and on uncultivated prairies.

The governor offered for our headquarters the Blind Asylum, which had been closed during the war. This building possessed one advantage in that there was room enough for all the staff.

Gen. George Armstrong Custer

It was a great relief to find a southern state that was not devastated by the war. The homes destroyed in Virginia could not fail to move a woman's heart, as it was women and
children who suffered from such destruction. In Texas nothing seemed to have been altered. The roads were smooth and the surface rolling.

There was one high hill, called Mount Bonnell, where we had picnics and enjoyed the fine view. We would take along one of the bands of the regular regiments. Mount Bonnell was so steep we had to dismount and climb part of the distance.

As the band played the "Anvil Chorus" the sound descended down through the valley. The Colorado River below was filled with sandbars and ugly on close examination, but from Mount Bonnell it looked like a silver ribbon.

We even went once to the State Insane Asylum, taking the band. The attendant asked if dancing music might be played, and we watched with wonder the quadrille of an insane eight.

THE FAVORITE RIDE for my husband was across the Colorado to the Deaf and Dumb Asylum. There seemed to be a fascination for him of the children, who were equally charmed with the young soldier that silently watched their pretty exhibitions of intelligent speech by gesture.

My husband riveted his gaze on their speaking eyes, and as their instructor spelled out the passions of love, hatred, remorse, and reverence on his fingers, one little girl represented them by singularly graceful gestures, charming him, and filling his eyes with tears, which he did not try to hide.

The pupils were from 10 to 16 years of age. Their supple wrists were a delight to us. The general held a small child of the matron's who, with its tiny hands, talked in a cunning way to its playmates who, it knew, could not comprehend its speech.

It was well that the professor of the asylum was hospitality itself and did not mind a cavalcade dashing up the road to his facility. My husband, when he did not openly suggest going, would use some subterfuge as trivial as going for watercress, which grew in a pond near the asylum.

The children knew him and welcomed him with lustrous, eloquent eyes, and went untiringly through their little exhibitions, learning to bring to him their compositions and maps for his commendation.

How little we thought then that the lessons Gen. Custer was taking, in order to talk with the children, would come into good use while sitting round a campfire and making himself understood by Indians. Of course, the Indians' sign language is wholly their own, but it is the same method of using the simplest signs to express thought that the general was learning on his many visits to the Deaf and Dumb Asylum at Austin.

ELIZABETH (LIBBIE) BACON, born on April 8, 1842, married George Armstrong Custer in 1864. At the end of the war, she joined her husband who was assigned to occupation duty in Hempstead and Austin, Texas. In February 1866 he was transferred to Fort Riley, Kansas. After Gen. Custer's death in 1876 at the Battle of Little Big Horn, she became a lecturer and author. One of her books was "Tenting on the Plains: Or, General Custer in Kansas and Texas." She died April 4, 1933, at the age of 90, and was buried alongside her husband at West Point.

59

OUT OF SORTS

H. H. McConnell
SERGEANT, SIXTH CAVALRY

On Monday, Jan. 14, 1867, at about three in the afternoon, we came in sight of Jacksboro, and as sorry and forlorn a place as it was, it loomed up as an oasis does to the traveler in the desert. For there, the white tents clustered on the public square, was our regiment at last, or at least the battalion of it to which we were assigned. Our recruit days were over.

We marched on to the parade ground just as the bugles were sounding retreat, were informally inspected by the officers who were present, had supper, and were handed over to the first sergeants for assignment to quarters.

The troops were quartered in "A" tents, some of them pitched on the square. The stables stood on the south side of the square. The commanding officer, Major (and Brevet Colonel) S. H. Starr, had his headquarters in a tent at the southwest corner of the square, surrounded by a picket stockade.

Colonel Starr, known as Old Paddy, had been represented to us as a real terror. And a terror he was, to evil-doers, but a braver, more just, or more honorable officer never wore the uniform. His peculiar disposition was such that, like the Irishman, it might be said of him, "He was never at peace only when he was at war."

Colonel Starr was indeed an odd character, who seemed always to be out of sorts. He had lost one arm during the late war, had met during his long years of service many setbacks in rank (the result of his temper), together with his having seen scores of younger men promoted over his head, and all these things had soured his disposition and made him irascible, unreasonable, cranky and crabby.

OFFICERS WHO CAME INTO frequent contact with Old Paddy soon had their edges rounded off. But as he was stricter with the officers than the enlisted men, he stood in high esteem with the latter.

Owing to the anticipated incursions of hostile Indians, a line of guards had been posted around the camp. Old Paddy issued orders that no one could "pass or repass" without permission. I had a permanent pass, because of my various duties. One pleasant Sunday afternoon I took a seine, went down to the river, and in a short time had a nice lot of fish. I selected a fine fat one and sent it to the colonel. I went to my quarters with the thought that I had done a good thing for myself.

A day or two afterwards, Old Stoop, the colonel's orderly, appeared and said the colonel wanted to see me right away. At his tent, I found him in a rage. "Who gave you permission to go fishing last Sunday?" he shouted.

"No one, sir. I have a pass, and go and come at all times."

"Very true, sir, but your pass does not apply to going fishing. Don't let it happen again!"

257

I returned to my quarters, a sadder and wiser man.

Later, having occasion to report to him, I found him in another rage. He was trying in vain to patch and mend a damaged map of Texas that had been ripped during a storm. Having but one arm, he succeeded badly in getting it to lie smooth and at each motion of the flatiron he tore it worse. I offered to take it to my office and repair it, which I did. I returned it to him nicely mended; he was much pleased and thanked me. Then he followed me to the door and shouted, as I departed, "Sergeant, please observe, sir, that were it not for the loss of my infernal arm, I could have done this as well as you, sir!"

A newly installed sutler (post trader) thought to put himself in solid with Old Paddy. He sent over a nice lot of sundries — cigars, beer, choice can goods — to the colonel, with his compliments. When the colonel returned and found all these delicacies on his table, he ordered Old Stoop to get the sutler to report.

"Take these things away, sir!" he ordered the sutler. "You cannot afford to make presents to the officers unless you are robbing the men, and if I hear any more of this, I will drum you and your shop out of camp, sir!"

ONE DAY I WENT to Old Paddy's quarters to submit a paper on a man of my company about to be sent to the Ship Island military prison. Looking it over, the colonel pushed it toward me, saying, "Take it away, sir! It is not properly made out!"

Knowing that it was perfectly correct, I replied, "In what particular, sir, is it incorrect?"

He shouted, "Go and inform yourself, sir!"

Returning to my room, I found the paper was all straight and correct in every way, all the t's crossed and all the i's dotted. I marched back with it, completely unchanged, and gave it to the colonel again. He scrutinized it minutely, could find no apparent fault and motioned me to leave. No sooner was I outside than he called me back, pointed at random to a certain place on the document with his finger, and said, "Put a comma there, sir! Now go!"

Such was the old fellow, captious, querulous, and cranky. Notwithstanding all of which, he possessed a lot of traits that endeared him to the men, for they knew he was every inch a soldier and a just and honorable man. As distance and years have passed, I cannot say that, "With all his faults I learned to love him." Yet I surely learned to respect his integrity and his honor in even the most trifling matters. When he went on the retired list, and was succeeded by another officer of the regiment, every man felt the loss of Old Paddy.

I doubt not that traditions of the old fellow linger yet around the campfires of the Sixth Cavalry, handed down from one soldier to another.

H. H. (HARRY HALL) McCONNELL was born in 1837 in Pennsylvania. In 1866, after the Civil War, he enlisted in the regular army at Carlisle, Pa. and was assigned to duty with a battalion of the Sixth U.S. Cavalry, then stationed at a camp at Jacksboro, Texas, before the new post of Fort Richardson was built. McConnell kept a diary of his time on the Texas frontier and wrote about his experiences in "Five Years A Cavalryman" published in Jacksboro in 1889. After he left the army, McConnell returned to Jacksboro and for a time was the editor of Frontier Echo. He married Jeannette Desire Conner and they had two sons. He died July 31, 1895 and was buried in Oakwood Cemetery, Jacksboro.

60

NAMES OF THE DEAD

Joseph Almond

CARPENTER, SHEEP RANCHER

July 24, 1867. Mr. Williams told me this morning that Andrew Fisher was very sick. There are a number of others who have lately taken sick. On the third of this month, a Mr. Snyder died at Ziegler's Hotel of yellow fever. He came here from Indianola where yellow fever has been so bad and I am of the opinion that was the cause of the sickness here, which has spread on all sides, though there have been no other deaths besides Snyder's.

Last night I called to see Andrew Fisher. I stayed all night with him. About 10 p.m. I was told that Mr. Drinkard died. He has long been sick of dyspepsia but the cause of his death was the bursting of a blood vessel.

July 27: Rev. McPhail died yesterday. He was a Methodist minister who came here a month or six weeks ago. This was the first death by yellow fever in which the infection was caught here. Mr. J. N. Morgan died today.

July 28: Mr. Perry, Mr. Sterne and a Pole, name unknown, died today.

An Englishman from Manchester and partner in a dry goods store here, named H. H. Eastman, died on July 30 and Rev. William Mitchell, a Presbyterian minister, died on Aug. 1.

Mr. Palmer, a carpenter and native of Canada, died on Aug. 4. Next day, Samuel Clymer, also a carpenter who worked with Palmer, died. Mr. Clayton died; he was a business partner of Mr. Perry, who died a week ago. The child of Mr. Larken died.

Aug. 6: Marcella Swift, Mrs. McClanahan, and Pat Dunn died today. Three weeks later:

I WAS TAKEN sick on Aug. 7, after sitting up all night with James and Ben Gibbs. I learn that on that day, these died: Mr. G. W. Smith, Daniel Cahill, a Pole, name unknown; Jane Marsh, and Mrs. Dunn. The next day, Aug. 8, the list of the deceased included John Scott, Mrs. Clark, Christopher Dunn, husband of Mrs. Dunn and brother of Pat Dunn, who died on the 6th and 7th); James Rankin, F. J. Cromer, Frank Stillman, H. Fisher, Rebecca Hughes, a child, and Mr. Lawrence the painter.

Aug. 9: James and Ben Gibbs both died, along with Mrs. Hughes, sister of the Gibbs' brothers and mother of the child who died the day before.

The list of deaths for Aug. 10 include F. Ritter, Owen Clymer, brother of Sam Clymer, who died four days before; Gregory Headen, McFarlane, Mrs. A. Dunn. On Aug. 10: Henry Sinclair, Carrie Sims, two Poles, Mrs. Kelly, John Kelly, a child, Charles Fields, Dr. G. F. Johnston, Mary Grace Maltby, sister of Marcella Swift, who died three days before; George Meuly, Mrs. Weidenmueller, John Pollan Jr., Mr. George Robertson, druggist; Agnes Rankin, daughter of James Rankin, who died on Aug. 8, and my own boy, Jo Almond, who was seven years old.

Aug. 11: Mr. Stone, Lizzie Riggs, Louisa Dryer, Mrs. Vetters, a Mexican, and Mrs. Ludewig.

Aug. 12: Dr. E. T. Merriman, the last of our doctors; A. DeRyee, the last of our druggists; Mrs. Schultz, J. M. Sims, father of Carrie Sims, who died two days before.

Aug. 13: Mrs. Matthew Headen, Mrs. Gibbs, wife of Ben Gibbs, who died on Aug. 9; Mrs. John Dunn, mother of Pat and Christopher Dunn, who died on Aug. 6 and Aug. 8; Mrs. Ridder, wife of F. Ridder who died on Aug. 9; J. M. Myers, G. A. Ludewig, husband of Mrs. Ludewig, who died on Aug. 11; the infant of Dr. G. F. Johnston, Michael Whelan, Mrs. J. Whelan.

Aug. 14: John Callahan, Renaldo Allen, children of William Ashton, John Whelan, brother and husband of the two Whelans who died the day before.

Aug. 15: Mr. Vetters, son of Mrs. Vetters who died on Aug. 11; Mrs. Doorly, William Norris, August Holthaus, Nascerio Morales, Dora Cody, and Jo Egan.

Aug. 16: Mrs. Garner, Matthew Lewis, Sarah Lewis, mother, son, and daughter; F. Attion, John Henry Moore, who died of cancer; John Kelly, husband of Mrs. Kelly who died a week before.

Aug. 17: Joseph Hagan, Mrs. Howard, Mrs. Helen Evans, Mr. Toomey, Henry Armstrong, Beatris Chaleron, John Ludewig, father of G. A. Ludewig who died, along with his wife, one week before.

Aug. 19: Mrs. Smith, Augustus Moore, druggist who came in from the country to DeRyee's store.

Aug. 20: Son of Mrs. Meuly, brother of George Meuly, who died on Aug. 10; Bridget Fernisa, a child of Mr. Beasley, A. Weir, and Rev. J. P. Perham, whose death is a severe loss to the community. Rev. Perham was president of the Howard Association* and made himself useful in visiting the sick and burying the dead. He belonged to the Methodist Church and was one of the very best preachers I have ever heard anywhere.

Aug. 21: Antonio Salazar, a German, name unknown; Ralph Gregory, Fenega Chabeai.

Aug. 23: Frank Clark, son of Mrs. Clark, who died two weeks ago.

Aug. 25: Susan Headen, Christiana Perham, W W. Worrell. About three or four weeks before his death, his two brothers were murdered at John Dix's ranch on Ramirena Creek, 50 miles from Corpus Chrsti; they were murdered by their own shepherds.

AUG. 26: ANOTHER CHILD OF Mr. Beasley, James Wallace, Mrs. Matthew Dunn, Mr. Stone, the son of Mr. Stone who died two weeks before.

Aug. 27, Peter Parker, infant of J. B. Mitchell.

Aug. 28: Child of Mat Dunn.

Aug. 29: Child of the late James Ranahan; a Catholic priest staying with Father Gonnard.

Aug. 30: A Frenchman, name unknown. There were no other deaths today.

Sept. 1: There was one death, Ysidro Casas.

Sept. 3: Jesus Gonzales.

Sept. 5: Rev. J. Gonnard, a Catholic priest, who was a native of France and about 40 years old. He was very much devoted to the cause of religion and education. He has gone to his grave deeply lamented.

Sept. 6: Ruperta Garza.

Sept. 7 and 8: No deaths.

Sept. 9: Perry Doddridge's son, four years old.

---

* The international Howard Association of volunteers was named for British philanthropist John Howard. The Corpus Christi chapter of "Howards" maintained a pest house where some yellow fever victims were taken.

Sept. 10: Samuel McComb.

Sept. 14: Since Aug. 10, there have been two Poles and a Mexican who died; I do not know their names. Number of deaths to date, 144.

Sept. 17: Edwin McLaughlin died today.

Sept. 21: There have been no more deaths since that on Sept. 17 of Edwin McLaughlin. We had an increase in family this morning. About six my wife Lizzie gave birth to a girl (Josephine). Both Lizzie and Josephine are doing well.

———————

JOSEPH ALMOND, from Newcastle-on-Tyne, came to Corpus Christi in 1852 with his wife, Elizabeth (Lizzie) Wade and her family. Almond, a carpenter, built some of the early homes in Corpus Christi. In February 1867, he moved the family from Nuecestown to Corpus Christi, where he had several carpentry jobs. That summer, with an outbreak of yellow fever, he visited the sick and recorded in his diary the names of those who died. His own seven-year-old son, Joseph (Joey), was among the victims. Before it was over, he listed 135 who died of the fever. Almond later established a ranch at Palo Hueco Creek. His wife Lizzie died in 1876 and he died at midnight on Christmas Day 1887 at the St. James Hotel.

61

IN SHALLOW GRAVES

Anna Moore Schwien

TEACHER, LAUNDRESS

Many lives were lost in the yellow fever epidemic of 1867 and Corpus Christi would have been swept as clean as a pin if it hadn't been for E. J. Davis bringing Dr. Kearney here from Havana at his own expense after the three doctors — Dr. Merriman, Dr. Robertson and Dr. Johnston — all died of the fever.

Many mean things have been said about Mr. Davis, but he certainly deserves credit for what he did for Corpus Christi at that time.

Dr. Kearney, a celebrated physician, had his hands full looking after the sick. His treatment consisted of having the patient put his feet into a mustard bath up to the knees then go to bed. The patient was given warm teas of any kind. For nourishment he was given clabber or whey from boiled buttermilk. Dr. Kearney didn't use as much whisky in treating yellow fever as the other doctors did.

Anna Moore Schwien recalled yellow fever outbreak in 1867

So many people died that the lumber that was stacked on the bluff to build the Presbyterian Church had to be used to make coffins. The bodies of the dead were hauled to the cemetery in drays. There wasn't time to dig the customary six-feet-deep graves, so they were buried in shallow graves, only about three to four feet deep.

I REMEMBER the death of Dr. Johnston's baby, which was only eight months old. One day I took the baby's clothes to Mrs. Johnston (my mother was a laundress) and the baby was sick with the fever. Mrs. Johnston put it in my arms and it died while I held it. She took it from me and laid it on the bed. But I didn't take the fever. Mrs. Johnston also escaped.

Dr. Robertson had a drug store in Corpus Christi. He lived at the corner of Chaparral and Schatzel streets. He was the father of Mrs. Jessie Clark and Mrs. Eli Merriman. He lived at the corner of Chaparral and Schatzel streets.

Dr. Kearney lived on Chaparral Street in the 600 block in a little cottage that the DeRyees owned later. After the yellow fever epidemic, he sent to Havana and got four rose bushes that he planted in his front yard, two on each side. They were so sweet you could smell their fragrance when you reached that street. The plants were so vigorous and hardy that even the coldest weather didn't kill them. The Kearney roses were cabbage roses, very large, and were much in demand by the young men of the town, who wanted them to take to their sweethearts.

It was a number of years before we had another yellow fever scare; that was in 1873. Many years later, in 1897, there was another scare and many people left, going in different directions. Saltillo was an especially popular place to go and a number of families, including the Weils, went there. But the scare passed over very soon.

———————

ANNA MOORE SCHWIEN's mother, Malvina, was a slave owned by Forbes Britton, a wealthy merchant and rancher who was later state senator. Anna was born on May 15, 1856. She named her father as Sam, a slave owned by John M. Moore, who took the name of Sam Moore. After the Civil War, Anna Moore attended a Freedman's Bureau school and became a teacher and later a laundress. She married a German named Schwien who fled town after he was threatened for marrying a black woman. Anna kept his name and never remarried. Anna Moore Schwien died at age 89 on April 19, 1946 and was buried in Old Bayview Cemetery.

62

DIARY OF A TRAIL DRIVE

Jonathan Hamilton Baker
CATTLEMAN

Thursday, Sept. 2, 1869. The herd of about 1,250 head (480 mine) left the Slaughter Ranch for Kansas, starting in the direction of Flat Top Mountain. J. R. Powell, P. E. Slaughter and myself took the tally, came to Jacksboro and had it recorded. We then went out west of town a few miles and camped.

Friday, Sept. 3. We started as soon as it was light enough to see how to ride. After riding some 10 miles we ate breakfast. We then rode on to Flat Top Mountain where we were to meet the herd. Failing to find it, we rode entirely around the mountain until we struck the trail. We found the herd five miles west of Flat Top. Parson Slaughter, who has made this trip before, is trail boss.

Saturday, Sept. 4. Last night was my first turn at guarding the herd. I stood guard from midnight to daylight. Here Dick Jowell and some of the boys turned back. We are now in the vicinity of West Fork, moving in the direction of Buffalo Springs. We picked up a stray mare today. Traveled about 10 miles.

Sunday, Sept. 5. Picked up two more stray horses today. Drove 10 miles toward Buffalo Station on the divide between West Fork and Little Wichita. Good grass, no cattle lost.

Monday, Sept. 6. Rain began at daybreak and continued until 10 a.m. We drove to Buffalo Station. Damp and cold all day. Our cattle stampeded during the afternoon and it was several hours before we stopped them. Do not think we lost any.

Tuesday, Sept. 7. It is clear this morning. Cattle were restless during the night. Kept all hands busy. It was cold. We came to a stream where they got water, in the vicinity of Victoria Peak.

Wednesday, Sept. 8. A cool night, cattle quiet. Drove eight miles to Victoria Peak. Camped 10 miles from Red River.

Thursday, Sept. 9. Drove to within two miles of Red River Station and struck camp. I have a sore eye.

Friday, Sept. 10. We reached the river about 10 a.m. and swam our herd across.

IN CROSSING, one of our hands, William Cowden, came very near drowning. It was with difficulty that he was rescued. We camped about three miles from the river.

Saturday, Sept. 11. Started before breakfast and made fine progress. Made 10 miles.

Sunday, Sept. 12. Looks like rain. My eye is better. Broke camp and made three miles which brought us to Muddy Creek. It took the rest of the day to cross the cattle.

Monday, Sept. 13. A tremendous rain last night. It was so dark we could not see the cattle. We were compelled to turn them loose. Set out early to gather them and spent the whole day at the job.

Tuesday, Sept. 14. Started early and traveled eight miles and camped on the prairie.

Wednesday, Sept. 15. Started early and soon struck timber. Have been in the timber all day. Crossed several boggy creeks.

Thursday, Sept. 16. Started early and drove through the bottoms of Caddo Creek. After these muddy creeks we crossed several clear ones with gravel bottoms. We camped not too far from Fort Arbuckle.

Friday, Sept. 17. Foggy and misty rain this morning. About eight miles brought us to a small post on the Washita River garrisoned by two companies of U.S. troops. Made camp about three miles east of Fort Arbuckle.

Saturday, Sept. 18. Crossed the Washita without difficulty. Traveled up the river in the direction of Cherokee town.

Sunday, Sept. 19. A good rain in the night. Came by Cherokee town today. We learned that three other herds are behind us, of about 900 head each.

Monday, Sept. 20. We traveled in the Seminole Nation today. Crossed the South Canadian and made camp at an old church.

Tuesday, Sept. 21. Misty rain last night and cloudy today. We herded most of the day and made camp near some Seminole settlements.

Wednesday, Sept. 22. Started early and traveled in timber all day. Passed several Indian settlements. Considerable dissatisfaction among the hands because of the ill temper of the trail boss.

Thursday, Sept. 23. Now in the Shawnee Nation. Crossed the north fork of the Canadian and made camp.

Friday, Sept. 24. Traveled over prairie today and into Osage country.

Saturday, Sept. 25. A norther blew up this morning. It is cold. The cattle are inclined to run.

Sunday, Sept. 26. Clear and cool this morning. Two miles travel brought us to the deep fork of the Canadian, a pretty stream with a rock bottom. After crossing we had dinner and put a new tongue on one of the wagons.

Monday, Sept. 27. Heavy dew this morning. We turned the cattle off the road to get water and night overtook us before we could find the road again. We camped on a high hill without our wagons and without supper.

Tuesday, Sept. 28. When daylight came we found we were near our wagons. We drove our herd down the hill and ate breakfast. We called the hill where we spent the night Mount Rough-It.

Wednesday, Sept. 29. Cool this morning. Traveled most of the day on high prairies. Fairly good sedge grass. Timber very scarce.

Thursday, Sept. 30. Cloudy and cool, south wind blowing. The cattle are grazing on good mesquite grass.

We made camp on a hill one mile from where we crossed Grapevine Creek.

Friday, Oct. 1. A heavy rain last night. The cattle are grazing while breakfast is being prepared. In the afternoon we came to the Arkansas. We drove the herd across without swimming. It is a clear stream about 600 yards wide.

Saturday, Oct. 2. Frost this morning. Started at 8 a.m. and drove till nearly sundown. Poor land, with occasional patches of mesquite grass. Myself and horses are much fatigued.

Sunday, Oct. 3. Clear and tolerably warm. Traveled over high rolling prairies and camped on the north side of Clear Creek. It is said to be Osage land. We have seen none of them yet and have had no beef demanded of us.

Monday, Oct. 4. Started early and crossed several muddy tributaries. William Cowden is chilling.

Tuesday, Oct. 5. Morning clear and cool. About 12 miles brought us to the top of the divide. An extensive view presents itself. On every side, far as the eye can see, extends the prairie. Camped and had dinner near the forks of a creek.

Wednesday, Oct. 6. Morning is fine. We crossed a creek and are traveling northwesterly, over a high rocky prairie. No settlements of any kind.

Thursday, Oct. 7. A brisk wind from the south today. Crossed Prairie Creek late in the afternoon. Camped on a high prairie. Good mesquite grass.

Friday, Oct. 8. A cold norther with rain blew up just before day. The norther blew all day. Made camp near the Kansas line. We find that 20,000 head of cattle are being grazed in the vicinity, waiting for buyers.

* * *

SATURDAY, OCT. 23. THERE IS a tremendous frost this morning. Very cold. The sun is beginning to melt the snow and we hope for better weather. We find many herds here waiting for buyers. Traveled 15 miles and arrived at Smoky River, about sunset, two miles or so from Abilene.

Sunday, Oct. 24. A tremendous frost this morning and very cold. We did not move camp today. A buyer came to look at the cattle but made no decision.

Monday, Oct. 25. A heavy frost. All hands have gone to town except Hunt and myself.

Tuesday, Oct. 26. Frost again this morning. I went to town and ordered a pair of boots to be made. I also looked at some wagons, harness, and ready-made clothing with a view to making purchases to take home for speculation.

Wednesday, Oct. 27. Two of us held the herd last night and I am holding it today. The prairie is on fire and burning all around. Considerable damage is being done.

Thursday, Oct. 28. Lost 28 head of cattle last night on account of the prairie fire. Some of the hands are hunting them while the rest drive the remainder of the herd to town to ship, as they have been sold. Only three head of the lost cattle were found.

I HAVE LOST 25 head here, besides several on the way. My sales amount to $4,664. That leaves me, after paying my hands and other expenses, $4,068.

Friday, Oct. 29. Came to town and spent the entire day getting our affairs in order. Drove about five miles from Abilene, to Turkey Creek, and made camp.

Saturday, Oct. 30. Went to town, had some horses shod, and dined at the Cottage Hotel. Bill 75 cents.

Sunday, Oct. 31. John Slaughter, John McKinney, and I started at nine a.m. to look for lost cattle. We did not find them. We did find a Dutchman housed in a hole dug out of the ground.

Monday, Nov. 1. Started early and found seven head of cattle in McCoy's herd; cut them out and drove them to Abilene and then returned to camp.

Tuesday, Nov. 2. Went to town and bought a bill of goods from a Dutchman, $320.17. I swapped horses and paid $40 to boot. Bought a wagon and harness for $153 and came back to camp.

Wednesday, Nov. 3. Went back to town, bought some more goods and had the sheet (covering) put on my wagon and went back to camp.

Thursday, Nov. 4. Hunted horses until noon and spent the balance of the day preparing to go home. I think all are ready to start in the morning.

Friday, Nov. 5. About nine a.m. the train consisting of 12 wagons and 19 loose horses with two hands to drive them started from the old camp on Turkey Creek to our home in Texas . . . After an uneventful trip, reached home at Palo Pinto on Saturday, Dec. 11, 1869.

JONATHAN HAMILTON (HAM) BAKER, born July 13, 1832, came to Texas from Virginia in 1858 with his brother, G.W. Baker. Baker first taught school in Fort Worth, where he was stricken with malaria, then moved to Palo Pinto County. He opened a school there and kept a detailed diary. His journal covers the day he left Virginia and continues to 1918. Baker led a company of local men to defend the area against Indian attacks and was with Sul Ross in the recapture of Cynthia Ann Parker. Baker was also an open-range cattleman and, in 1869, began driving his herds to the Kansas market. Baker served in various elective offices in Palo Pinto County, from tax assessor to district clerk. He married Nancy Ann Doyle Arnett. The couple moved to Granbury in 1890. He died Oct. 18, 1918 and was buried in the Granbury Cemetery.

63

UP THE CHISHOLM TRAIL

John Taylor Allen
COWBOY

Ever since I learned to ride a horse I was trained to work with herds and care for horses and cattle on my father's homestead near Honey Grove in Fannin County. Even before I could ride, I herded a large flock of sheep. In those days, wolves were so bad it required the utmost vigilance to keep the sheep from being killed and eaten. Sheep were necessary to us then, and profitable. From their wool we carded, spun and wove our clothing and we depended on mutton for our meat. Many a woman made a suit of clothes for her husband and sons from the wool of their own sheep.

As I grew older, I had to herd cattle and horses. On the prairie the luxuriant grasses grew in such abundance that it was profitable to raise cattle. There were no railroads then and to market our stock we would drive them to Kansas.

For several months we would not be under a roof. We slept out in the open, exposed to the weather, through storms and rains, thunder and lightning, and often had to deal with stampeding cattle.

The first trip up the trail I took I shall never forget. I was used to the comforts of home, with plenty of good milk, butter and eggs, chicken, fruits and vegetables, and at night I had a nice soft feather bed to sleep on. But, oh, my! What a change when I started up the Chisholm Trail to Kansas. How I longed for my comfortable home.

It required all my courage and determination to keep me on the way. The brackish water, the coarse cornbread, the fried fatback, the badly made coffee, were no substitutes for the food at home. For the first few days of the drive I almost starved. The cowboys and the cook called me the parson.

They would taunt me because I would not eat their crude food. "Parson," they said, "you will come to your appetite in time." And I did. Often after a long hard day, I would arrive in camp, exhausted after chasing cattle in a stampede, with lightning and thunder and rain or sleet beating in my face, and sit down to a meal of corn-pone and fatback, washing it down with bad coffee.

How it lingers in the memory. I would come in tired and ready to eat only to find that other cowboys came in before me and left nothing. The cook would say, "Wait, Parson, and I'll start a fire and soon have some bread and coffee."

Another scene comes to mind in vivid detail. The night was so dark and the storm so menacing that we could not see beyond the length of our arms, except in the brief flashes of lightning. We were feeling our way along, not knowing what we might run into. The frightened cattle were rushing ahead of us, invisible except when lightning pierced the darkness. We had to press on, for fear the cattle would be lost. For three days and nights we had been in the saddle nearly all the time. How we longed for a good sound sleep.

During this stampede my brother's horse stepped into a deep hole and its feet stuck, throwing the horse and my brother Loss somersaulted over the horse's head. The horse turned over on my brother as he fell, seriously hurting him.

The horse stepped in a hole and fell on brother Loss

I stopped to help him but he said, "No, go catch my horse." After falling, the horse got up and ran after the stampeding cattle.

With the steady use of the quirt and spurs I succeeded in reaching the herd and finally found the horse and brought him back to my brother, who was badly crippled by the fall. With some difficulty I got him into the saddle and back to camp, where our wagon and mess tent were. For several days he had to ride in the wagon before he was able to mount his horse again. This accident, I believe, shortened his life, for he never fully recovered from the injury he sustained.

It was hard sometimes to get the herd across a stream, but after we would get one started it would usually result in the rest following without trouble. It was on one of these occasions when I almost lost my life.

We had to swim the rivers on horseback and we usually constructed a raft on which to float across our wagon. The

Big Walnut Creek, in the Osage Nation near the Kansas line, was rapidly flowing. We were anxious to cross before night. On the opposite bank was a log raft tied to a tree. I told my brother Loss that I was going to swim across for that raft so we could ford our wagon and grub across.

I TOOK HOLD of the rope with my teeth, after tying two 30-foot lariats together, and started to swim across. I got along first-rate until I reached the middle of the stream. The weight of the rope in the water began to tire me and I was pulled under. I was not frightened and kept my presence of mind. My brother yelled for me to let go of the rope, but I was determined to carry out my plan. I would hold my breath when I went under so I would not strangle.

I only had a short distance to go when my strength gave out. I made one strong effort and was just about ready to give in when I found my feet could just touch bottom. I made one more effort and after two or three strokes I got hold of the limb of a bush hanging on the edge of the bank. It saved me from going under.

I was so worn out that I just lay there, half-drowned, holding on to the branch until I gathered enough strength to crawl up on shore. I did not take long to get the raft over and ferry our traps and grub across, but it sure seemed an age when I was swimming across that dangerous stream. I have often thought that if that river had been a yard wider, I would have reached that other shore, that undiscovered country from which no traveler ever returns.

———————

JOHN TAYLOR ALLEN was born on Oct. 29, 1848 in a log cabin on his father's homestead six miles northwest of Honey Grove in Fannin County. He married Mary Emma "Mollie" Finch in 1878 and they had seven children. John Taylor Allen died in 1927, at the age of 79, and was buried in the Allens Chapel Cemetery. His wife "Mollie" died two years later.

64

LAND WAS DIRT CHEAP

W. G. Sutherland
TEACHER, HISTORIAN

When I first came to this country in 1870, southwest Texas was a vast expanse of open prairie, a rolling sea of green grass. There was no timber except along the creeks and the river bottoms. In a few places there were clumps of trees that were called motts. Land was valued at from ten to 15 cents an acre. In many instances, a Spanish league (4,428 acres) sold for $500.

Long before my time, many early settlers pre-empted 160 acres near a watering place. Although many of these early settlers were the owners of thousands of head of cattle and horses, only a few were shrewd enough to buy land.

This may seem strange to the present generation, when they consider that a large farm could have been bought for less than the price of a pair of shoes. But men of that older time had good reasons for not buying land. The range was free. There was no benefit to be derived from buying land and paying taxes on it when the whole country was open to public use.

Few people were able to look ahead and see the future. Most of them thought the boundless West would never be fenced, that the open range would last forever.

Fifty years ago, when I was a new emigrant, northwest Texas was about as well-known as Central Africa. The country south of the Nueces was designated as "the range of Comanches, wild cattle, and mustangs." The northwest was known as "the great American desert," the "Staked Plains," or the "Jornado de Muerte," the journey of death.

Indian or bandit raids occurred frequently. Nearly every month, about the time of the full moon, vast herds of cattle and horses were stolen from South Texas ranches and driven across the Rio Grande into Mexico. From 1874 to 1878, at least 40 stores were robbed and more than 100 people murdered between the Nueces and the Rio Grande.

THERE WERE NO railroads, telegraphs, telephones and no fences or farms. Such things as electric lights, automobiles and flying machines were never dreamed of. Merchandise was hauled from Indianola to San Antonio in wagons or ox-carts, and from Corpus Christi to Laredo, Monterrey, Saltillo and Monclova by the same primitive manner.

There was hardly any limit to the width of roads and at certain seasons the depth was uncertain. When creeks flooded, travelers unyoked their teams and camped by the side of the stream until the flood abated, sometimes for weeks. Schools and churches were few and widely scattered. In 1874, I think there were only seven public schools in the territory that now includes Nueces, Kleberg, Willacy, Jim Wells, Duval, Brooks, and Jim Hogg counties. Catholic priests and a few Methodist ministers traveled hundreds of miles to visit isolated settlements.

Men who would ride 20 miles to a post office to get their mail once a week considered themselves fortunate. If a rash man hinted at the possibility of making a living by farming, he was looked upon as having a weak spot in the head. In general, a few patches of corn, beans, watermelons and pumpkins were planted for home use, not to market.

Uriah Lott began the construction of a railway known as the Tex-Mex in March 1875. Trains were soon running from Corpus Christi to Banquete and by 1879 the rails reached San Diego. Shortly after this the railroad was sold to a syndicate that completed the line to Laredo.

In 1886 the building of the San Antonio & Aransas Pass Railroad (SAAP) was begun. In 1888, the branch of this railroad from Skidmore to Alice was completed. In May of that year, the first house was erected in the county seat of Jim Wells. In 1904, the St. Louis & Brownsville Railroad was built and Kingsville founded.

From 1860 until 1890, the raising of cattle, sheep and horses was the most important industry south of the Nueces. Beeves were worth $8 to $10 and tens of thousands were killed for their hides and tallow. In Nueces County, packing houses were located at Corpus Christi, Nuecestown, Tule Lake, El Oso, and Santa Gertrudis. In 1875, some 250,000 cattle from this region were sent up the trail to Kansas. Capt. King of Santa Gertrudis sent up 60,000 head himself.

In 1879, there were more than a million sheep in Nueces County. Corpus Christi was one of the top wool markets in the world, exporting annually from 10 to 11 million pounds of wool. Sheep were divided int*o flocks, each containing from 100 up to 1,200 head under the care of a pastor or shepherd, usually a Mexican-American who was paid $10 a month with rations of one bushel of corn, three pounds of coffee, three pounds of sugar, and all the cabrito he could eat. He would sleep in a jacal, a small shelter. Few sheepmen would hire a shepherd unless he had to advance him from $60 to $200 to pay his debts. The amount of his indebtedness was the criterion by which his character and ability were judged. A man without debt was not trusted.

Sheep were sheared twice a year. Companies of shearers, each under the control of a jefe came up from Mexico in April and remained for about two months. They would come again in August and stay until the end of September. Nearly all of these companies had contracts which bound them to work for only one or two ranchers. Shearers were given board and paid from two to three cents for each sheep shorn. The average amount earned was about $2 a day.

From 1872 until 1884, Corpus Christi was one of the busiest towns in the country. Several merchants were rated as millionaires. A steamship made weekly trips from Corpus Christi to and from Morgan City (called Brashear then). Col. Norwick Gussett, a Corpus Christi wool merchant, had three schooners that made monthly voyages to New York City. Hundreds of ox-carts and great Chihuahua wagons drawn by up to 30 mules brought wool, hair and hides from northern Mexico and carried back cargoes of flour, sugar, coffee, dry goods and lumber.

Beginning about 1876, vast tracts of land were fenced. A fleet of schooners brought pine lumber from Florida every week. Nearly all the pastures were originally fenced with lumber at a cost of $600 per mile. With valuable fencing, the grass was not burned each spring, as it had been in the past, and the brush grew up and spread. Then the sheep-raising ceased to be a profitable industry in Nueces County.

W. G, SUTHERLAND was born in Elgin, Scotland in 1852. He came to South Texas in 1870 when he was 18. He taught school for 21 years, mostly around the Bluntzer community in Nueces County. He was known as an authority on the history of the region and called "the Sage of Bluntzer." His wife Sara died in 1930 and he died Oct. 26, 1931. Both were buried in Tom Mathis Cemetery.

65

OUTLAWS AND GUNFIGHTERS

Carroll C. Holloway
AUTHOR

Lawlessness after the Civil War was widespread. Poverty and despair, carpetbag rule and the natural psychological state of the beaten war veteran were not conducive to a reduction in crime. Law enforcement in Texas was generally lax during reconstruction and crime gained such a foothold it required 20 years or more to stamp out gun rule.

Nearly all cowboys had some of the skills of a gunfighter. Most, fortunately, did not have the required disposition that involved indifference to loss of life, the ability to think clearly in moments of great excitement, the art of coolly squeezing off a shot when utmost haste was a matter of life and death and, above all, the temperament to remain constantly prepared and alert.

There was a class of gunfighters who were bandits, trigger men, robbers, murderers, rustlers, horse thieves and cut-throats. They really can't be classified. A cross section of the criminal element of 1870 would probably reveal the same strata of motives and mental processes shown by the criminal element of today.

There would be one exception. The courage that existed in the old-style outlaw cannot be questioned. When he entered a town to rob a bank, he knew there would be stiff opposition. Most citizens carried guns and could use them. Modern bandits need not fear the unarmed public.

A member of the Dalton gang, riding out of Longview, Texas, after robbing a bank and engaging in a full-scale battle with the citizenry, was shot in the face with a light load of birdshot. Whirling quickly to fire at his assailant, the bandit saw that it was a young boy. The lad, mouth agape, was partly hidden by the huge front gate post before his home. Smoke curled from the barrel of his father's shotgun.

The Dalton bandit wiped the blood from the side of his face, dismounted to recover his big black Stetson, and grinning at the frightened boy, said, "Look out there, bub, you're liable to hurt somebody with that gun." Men were dead back there on the streets of Longview and he was not yet out of town, but he was calm and good-humored, even after being shot in the face.

Texas had long been a refuge for wanted men. During reconstruction, many Johnny Rebs throughout the South ran afoul of the law and left for Texas, though Texas outlaws needed no reinforcements. The State Treasury in Austin was robbed in 1865 by local talent. With the out-of-state help, the robbers' roosts filled and became a major problem. Many of the gangs operated out of Indian Territory (Oklahoma) or New Mexico, both more sparsely settled than Texas.

Billy the Kid's gang moved back and forth across the western border of Texas. Horses stolen in New Mexico were sold in Texas. Cattle rustled in Texas were sold in

Belle Starr and her friend "Blue Duck"

New Mexico. Billy's business was so prolific the ranchers put gunmen on his trail, including men such as James H. East, Lon Chambers, Leigh Hall, Cal Polk, Bob Robinson, Tom Emory, George Williams, and Charles Siringo. The Kid's gang consisted of Tom Pickett, Charley Bowdre, Tom O'Folliard, Bill Wilson and Dave Rudabaugh.

The pressure led to Billy's death at the hands of Sheriff Pat Garrett. Garrett, with the influence of the pleased Texas ranchers, obtained a captain's commission in the Texas Rangers.

Myra Maybelle Shirley, called Belle, was born on a farm near Carthage, Mo. After her family moved to Texas, she married Jim Reed, a member of the Jesse James gang. After Jim was killed in a Texas gunfight, Belle married Sam Starr and they made their home in Younger's Bend in Indian Territory. Sam was an outlaw also, which did not displease Belle who, by her forceful personality, shrewdness and unscrupulous character, became the leader of the gang and a thorn in the side of north Texans.

Belle Starr was killed by Edgar Watson, another outlaw, who used a sawed-off shotgun loaded with "blue whistlers." She was 43. Her gang suffered a somewhat similar fate. Sam Starr, Dan Evans and Felix Griffin were killed in gun battles. Jim French was killed resisting arrest. Jack Spaniard and Blue Duck, both half-breed lovers of Belle, were slated to hang. However, Blue Duck escaped the noose in favor of the cell by the narrowest of margins.

The Cook-Skeeter gang, the Dalton gang, the Younger boys, Jesse James' gang, the Doolin gang and the Hole-in-the-Wall gang dipped in and out of Texas in a flurry of violence. The Rangers broke up Bill Cook's gang of bank and train robbers which ranged in the Panhandle.

Bob Dalton was the leader of the Dalton gang. He and his brother, Grattan, after a career of crime, were killed during a bank robbery at Coffeyville, Kansas. Emmett Dalton went to the penitentiary. Bill, a brother too young for the gang, grew up and joined the Doolin gang, but soon died with his boots on. Frank Dalton stayed on the side of the law and became a deputy U. S. Marshal. But he, too, died in a gunfight.

The Younger and James gangs used Texas as a place of refuge, refraining from robberies within the state. In financial embarrassment, the James gang finally robbed a Texas stagecoach, which applied the heat to them all.

The Youngers were headed by Thomas Coleman Younger, known as Cole. His brothers were James, Robert, John and Bruce. Other members of the gang were Clem Miller, J. F. Edmundson, Bill Chiles, Bud and Tomlinson McDaniels. Most of them died of gunshot wounds, or in prison. The James gang was headed by Jesse and Frank. Other members were Jim Reed, the first husband of Belle

NOTICE!

$5,000 REWARD

will be paid for the capture of

COLE YOUNGER

MEMBER OF THE NOTORIOUS JAMES BAND!
: WANTED FOR TRAIN ROBBERY :

The St. Louis Midland Railroad offered $5,000 for the capture of Cole Younger, the equivalent of $116,000 today

Starr, Charles and Robert Ford, Charley Pitts, Bill Chadwell, Hobbs Kerry, Clell Miller, Arthur McCoy and Bill Greenwood. Their fate was similar to the Youngers except more of them were shot down, and fewer went to prison.

The Hole-in-the-Wall gang, one of the most famous in the west, ranged over Montana, Wyoming, Nevada, Utah,

Idaho, Colorado, Oklahoma, New Mexico and Texas. Members of the gang were frequent visitors to Fannie Porter's whorehouse in San Antonio. The leaders of the gang, George Parker, known as Butch Cassidy, and Harvey Logan, called Kid Curry, along with Harry Longabaugh, the Sundance Kid, all committed suicide at various times to avoid arrest.

George "Flat Nose" Curry, Will Carver, O. C. Hanks, Lonny Logan, a brother of Harvey, all were killed resisting arrest. John Logan, another brother, was killed in a gunfight. Ben Kilpatrick, "the handsome Texan," was killed during a train robbery. Robert Lee, the only member who did not die by the gun, served a long prison sentence for train robbery.

Bill Doolin led a gang closely allied to the Daltons. Doolin was killed by Marshal Hack Thomas. When Doolin drew his revolver, the Marshal hit him with 21 buckshot. Charles Pierce, Charles Bryant and George Newcomb, members of the gang, were also killed resisting arrest. Bill Powers and Dick Broadwell, other members of the gang, were killed in the same bank raid. Retribution was pretty certain.

Why did they turn to outlawry? Some were naturals; some started small but once outside the law they robbed to live; some began their decline with whiskey. With Joel Collins it was gambling. Joel led a group of trail drivers from Texas to Kansas where he sold a herd. The herd had not been his, the money from the sale had to be returned to Texas. Joel lost this money at poker and dared not return without it. He decided to rob a train to recoup his loss. His fellow cowboys agreed to help him. Their haul was rich enough to spoil them, $60,000 in gold coin.

Instead of going home and paying off the debt, these young men decided on a career of crime. But Joel Collins, Jim Berry and Bill Heffridge were killed resisting arrest. Jack Davis disappeared in New Orleans and may have gotten away.

Sam Bass and John Underwood, "Old Dad," returned safely to Texas. Bass proceeded to organize a band of Texas train robbers. Arkansas Johnson was Bass's lieutenant. James Murphy, Frank Jackson, Bill Collins, a cousin of Joel's, Henry Underwood, brother of "Old Dad," Sam Pipes, Albert Herndon, Jack Davis, Tom Spotswood, Billy Scott, and Seaborn "Sebe" Barnes were members who spread terror among Texas railroads. The hauls were small so the robberies had to be frequent. Probably Sam was too fun-loving to be leader of such a desperate enterprise.

AS THE GANG STRUCK furiously, and train after train was robbed, large rewards soon were offered, and intensive manhunts kept the boys on the jump. The Texas Rangers killed Arkansas Johnson at Salt Creek. James Murphy betrayed the gang for personal immunity, and then regretting the scorn of fellow Texans, killed himself.

A bank was to be robbed in Round Rock, the old stage station near Austin. The Rangers were tipped off by Murphy, who managed to avoid the company of his three companions while in that town. These three men, the residue of the gang, were Sam Bass, Sebe Barnes and Blocky Jackson.

A local officer tried to beat the Rangers to the quarry, and touched off the battle prematurely. This officer tried to disarm Bass and company and was instantly killed. The outlaws took to their horses, the bank forgotten. The Rangers, who were scattered around town, went into action. Ranger Dick Ware shot Sebe Barnes to death, Ranger George Harrell shot Bass from his saddle.

Then Jackson did a heroic thing. He was in the lead and had almost ridden from range of the guns into safety. He turned back, saw that Barnes was dead and that Bass was wounded. He dismounted, and as the rifles and six-guns pumped at him, he lifted Bass on a horse, remounted and led Bass's horse out of town on a run, while some of the best shots in Texas were firing at him, undoubtedly doing their best to miss such a courageous man.

Frank Jackson was never seen again. Sam Bass was found not far away, dying. Bass has captured the imagination of Texas and remains its favorite outlaw. Bass loved his joke and was quite humorous. He was not a killer by instinct. He was brave even in death, that is, "he died nice." Texans admire all these traits. But Sam Bass had to go.

Frank Stevenson's gang, the Sand Creek gang, the Daniel and Robert Campbell gang, the Joe Beckham gang, the Sid Woodring, the Bill Brookens, the Kimble County gangs all made their splash, created excitement, shed their blood and died. Burt Alvord, the Baker gang, the Marlow brothers, Ham White, Joe Horner, Jim Moon were six other desperate gangs of outlaws. The McCampbell gang, the John Kinney gang add to the list. Each of those names is a story in outlaw history.

ONE NAME STANDS OUT, that of King Fisher. In 1876, he was a young man of gaudy dress and few scruples. He affected the silver-studded clothes of the Spanish Dons. The excessive cost of his clothes, horses, hacienda and ranch in Dimmit County did not concern him greatly.

He had parlayed personality, gun skill, diplomacy and aggressiveness into a southwest Texas empire. Both the criminals and the courts in half a dozen counties in this section paid him homage and followed his orders. Never less than 50, often over 100 gunmen, rode at his command from Castroville near San Antonio to Eagle Pass on the Rio Grande. But King Fisher did not hide behind his wall of gunmen. He led them. They respected him as a leader and as a dangerous man, for he boasted 26 notches on his own guns.

The Texas Rangers were assigned the task of reducing Fisher's organization. The Rangers, unaware of Fisher's control of various courts, undertook to capture him after obtaining enough evidence for conviction. This feudal lord was bearded in his den. Ranger Leander McNelly captured him after a dangerous campaign. But seemingly Fisher was immune from justice. He was freed by the court, recaptured and again freed by a different court. At last the Rangers managed to jail him in San Antonio, where he had less influence. He was confined there only eight or nine months before his influence or money had him back in the saddle with his guns tied down.

At last a woman accomplished what the Rangers had not. His love for a good woman and her proper guidance reformed King. Willingly, he destroyed his empire of crime and violence and became an officer of the law in Uvalde, under a court he no longer controlled.

A night away from home, a short fling with former friends, and he was killed. On March 11, 1884, with his friend Ben Thompson, Texas' most famous gunman, King attended a show at the Vaudeville Variety Theater in San Antonio. His companion for the evening was ill-chosen, for Thompson had been marked for death at his next appearance there. When the gun slugs cut down Thompson, the domesticated King Fisher was also slain.

THE DEATH TOLL OF individual gunfighters of Texas, and all the West, was exaggerated. If a man possessed the qualities of a gunfighter, he was known to be dangerous. Such a man need not have a record of past performance, among those who knew him. He could perform and this was recognized. To exaggerate is a human trait. Reports circulated orally are apt to be distorted.

The fame of the gunmen outgrew accuracy. Ben Thompson was as dangerous a man as ever lived. He was an ex-convict, gambler, Confederate soldier (during the war he killed three Confederates and no Yankees), railroad guard and peace officer. Reputedly dozens of men were killed by him. Actually, he is known to have killed six men, none of them his equal in handling a gun.

If, however, the occasion had offered, he doubtless would have done everything, and more, that legend attributes to him. He shot up Leadville, Colorado, when that rough camp was at its toughest. He stood off Ellsworth, Kansas, and all its fighting men. He was feared in Abilene, the town dominated by Wild Bill Hickok. No, Ben Thompson had no private cemetery, but it was the other fellow's caution and not Ben's reticence which was responsible.

Bill Longley probably killed 18 men, though he is credited with 26. He is called "Father of the Quick Draw," though only two men died at his hands in quick-drawing contests.

John Wesley Hardin is credited with 40 notches. Of Hardin's victims, at least a dozen were murders, pure and simple. His quick-draw killings are more numerous than any other Texan's — seven. Both Hardin and Longley rate with Thompson as conscienceless killers. Billy the Kid killed a lot of men; nearly all of them were murders rather than combats. He has been called "a sure-thing killer."

We are not depreciating Ben Thompson, *et al*, as gunfighters. We are merely depreciating their supposed accomplishments, those deeds of fantasy rather than fact. Their bravery cannot be doubted. But their fame is based as much on oral embellishment as on real accomplishments. It is easy to say that Wild Bill Hickok killed a hundred men. But who were they? Where were their homes? Where are they buried, and who are their relatives? In answering these questions, the number of notches in each case necessarily must be scaled downward.

———

CARROLL CAIN HOLLOWAY was born on Dec. 15, 1904. His wife, Mary Elizabeth, was born in 1911. Holloway's "Texas Gun Lore" included this chapter on gangs and gunfighters, which was published by the Naylor Company in 1951. Holloway died on March 11, 2000 and was buried in Hallsville Cemetery.

66

MY LAST STAMPEDE

James T. Johnson
COWBOY, TRAIL-DRIVER

I was six months old, in October 1852, when my parents left Jackson County, Miss., and landed at Corpus Christi. My father was county clerk there for one term. My mother took sick on the ship coming to Texas and lived only six weeks after reaching Corpus Christi. My grandfather, who came to Texas with the Irish colony, served in the Confederate Army, was wounded and came home on a short furlough. He died soon afterwards of blood poisoning.

At the tender age of nine, I was left an orphan. I was sent to live with the Bookman family, where I was treated as one of their own children.

For two years I enjoyed myself in the homes of these good people, but an uncle in Falls County sent for me to come and live with him. I was abused so much there that I went to live with another uncle, who was just as bad, so I drifted out into the wide world on my own at the age of 13.

I worked for Cade Lewis, in the town of Bremond, hauling water and freighting to the town of Kosse. I stayed two years in this job, earning $400 in wages due. When I went to collect, I had to be satisfied by exchanging my saddle, worth $9, for his, which was not worth more than $15.

I began to work for the widow Thomas, gathering and herding range horses, where I learned my first work on a ranch. I then hired to Wash Grey to bring a herd of cattle to Goliad County, delivering them to his brother, Bob Grey. I remained in Goliad and worked as a freighter again, hauling supplies from Indianola to Goliad and Sutherland Springs.

THE OX TEAMS we had to drive were too slow for a boy my age and I longed to get back on a ranch chasing down mavericks. For the next four years I worked for H. A. Lane, 12 miles west of Goliad, and received $20 a month for breaking broncs and gathering and branding cattle.

When I was 22, I left Goliad with a herd of mixed cattle for H. A. Lane and J. Gus Patton, and drove these cattle over the Chisholm Trail to Dodge City. We only had two stampedes on the entire trip.

One year later I again went up the trail with a herd of mixed cattle of over 3,000 head for Patton. On this trip we had Patton for boss, with Sidney Chivers, Uncle Billie Menefee and Will Peck as cowboys.

When I returned I gathered wild horses in Goliad, Victoria, Refugio, Bee, Live Oak and Karnes counties. I gathered several thousand head for various ranches.

In the winter of 1871 and 1872, I helped skin dead cattle on the prairies in Goliad, Victoria and Refugio counties, as the cattle were starving to death by the thousands and very few grown cattle lived through that terrible winter.

I have seen as many as a thousand head of dead cattle in one day's ride on the prairie near Lamar. Horses, cattle, deer and sheep suffered awfully during these times.

In 1876 I again went up the trail with 4,500 head of aged steers for Dillard Fant, with Charlie Boyce as herd boss. On this trip we had the worst weather I ever experienced, losing cattle in blizzards, with the most vivid electrical displays you

can imagine. We had seven stampedes on the way. This was my last trip up the trail to Kansas, and my last stampede.

I returned to Limestone County, near Pottersville, where I married Martha Thomas in 1876. We settled near the Manahuilla Creek six miles north of Goliad.

I experienced quite a lot of difficulty trying to stay neutral in the Taylor-Sutton feud, as my sole desire was to work for wages and not get mixed up with either side.

All the schooling I ever got was about two weeks a year for three years. I did not have a chance to attend school, as other boys did, but I realize what I missed out on and it has been one of my greatest desires to make sure that all my children get a good education. My farm near Charco was on land I once roamed over as a cowboy.

JAMES THOMAS JOHNSON, born in Jackson County, Miss., arrived in Texas with his parents 1852 and became an orphan at nine. He worked as a freighter and ranch hand before trailing cattle to Kansas. He married Martha Ann Thomas in 1876 and the couple had 10 children. He died on Jan. 8, 1928 and was buried in Stockton Cemetery; she died in 1941 and was buried in Glendale Cemetery, both in Goliad County.

67

THE ART OF DAVE GAMBEL

Ruth Dodson

WRITER, HISTORIAN

I do not know whether Dave Gambel was tall or short or light or dark. I do know he was Irish and a unique personality. I have known something of Dave Gambel from my earliest years, and I have added a little to that knowledge as time has passed.

The house in which I was born and reared was painted by Dave Gambel. That was in 1872. The painting was pronounced a good job by my parents. After many years the walls were still rather white and the ceilings a decided blue. The house would have been designated as a red house with white gallery posts, 13 of them in all. "Such a good painter!" my parents would lament, such a pity that wood alcohol that he drank as an experiment when he was out of anything else to drink should have put an end to his talent.

Dave Gambel was not only a house painter. He also painted portraits. Two of these were in our home for many years, each one a yard square. There being no artist's canvas available, heavy unbleached domestic was used instead. This domestic not being so durable accounts for the fact that not one of the many portraits that Dave Gambel painted is in existence today. It seems that when he painted a house, he would also paint portraits if the customer so desired.

In my mother's bedroom hung a portrait of one of her brothers, with his little son standing at his side. I do not know how well-pleased she was with the portrait of Uncle Martin Culver, but we children did not fully appreciate the gifts of the artist and saw room for criticism. The red apple, about the color of the outside of the house, that the little son was holding in his left hand could not possibly have been peeled with the dull-looking table knife he held in his right hand. We wondered why he didn't borrow his father's pocketknife, as any of us would have done.

The other portrait hung in the living room over the fireplace. This one included a startled-looking young man wearing a neat string tie of a pale blue color. By raising the eyes one could compare the blue of the tie with the blue of the ceiling. The ceiling was just a shade lighter, which a little white paint could have brought about. The young man with the blue tie was another uncle, and a young lady of fully 20 years that was sitting at his side was, my mother explained, a little niece who was actually six years old.

The best endorsement that I have had of the portrait-painting of Dave Gambel was when an old lady told me that he had painted a portrait of her grandfather and it looked "sorter like him." One time I went with my mother to visit an old friend whom she had not seen in years. We went into the living room of the friend and my mother exclaimed, "Maggie, I see you still have the picture of your father and mother. How well it has lasted." I knew that the picture of the old Irishman holding a Bible on his knee, with the title "Holy Bible" turned so that the observer would have no doubt as to the nature of the book, and the

Ruth Dodson on Dave Gambel*'s masterpieces*

little old lady with the cap on her head and holding a rosary in her hands, were none other than my Grandpa and Grandma Pugh.

I also knew, from listening to my mother's reminiscences, that Grandma Pugh was in character with a rosary but I was not so sure about Grandpa Pugh. I had heard my father reminiscence about him, but it had nothing to do with his reading the Bible.

I had forgotten Dave Gambel's masterpiece until a few years ago. J. Frank Dobie, the author, called on my brother and me. My brother told us the story of it: Henderson Williams, who had a ranch on the Lagarto Creek in Live Oak County, had Dave Gambel paint his house. By way of making something extra of the job, it was completed by his painting a camp scene above the fireplace. The main figure of the scene, my brother said, was that of a young cowboy, supposed to be the likeness of the son of the owner of the ranch, who had roped a calf and was dragging it up to be butchered.

This ranch became the property of Frank Shaeffer and he moved the Williams' house to his ranch and added it to his house there. The room with the Dave Gambel mural became the dining room. As long as Mr. Shaeffer lived, those who ate there could enjoy the scene of Hedge Williams with the roped calf. But after the death of Mr. Shaeffer, his widow had the dining room painted and the mural was covered with fresh paint.

Frank Dobie remarked, "The fools!"

I thought that Dobie should have seen the mural before deciding that it should have been preserved for posterity.

In our home the family Bible rested on a center table in the living room. In this Bible were kept such funeral notices as the family had collected through the years. Once in a while, when I was growing up, I was given permission to look at these. One that attracted my attention was that of Dave Gambel. I don't recall the entire announcement, but I do recall that the burial was in Oakville, and that the time was in the early 1870s. But no mention was made of the cause of death, the wood alcohol.

RUTH DODSON was born on Sept. 3, 1876 on Rancho Perdido on Penitas Creek, in today's Live Oak County. Her father was Milton Milam Dodson and her mother Mary Susan Burris. Miss Dodson wrote articles for Southwestern Review, Frontier Times and other publications. Her book on Don Pedrito Jaramilla, "The Healer of Los Olmos," was published in 1934. She died July 19, 1963 and was buried in Tom Mathis Cemetery in Mathis.

68

SHOOTING A DOG

E. H. Caldwell
HARDWARE MERCHANT

I found myself in Corpus Christi wishing for some ice during the long hot summer. The principals at the Doddridge Bank, where I worked, and several other merchants, decided to buy a cargo of ice and have it brought in by schooner from the North Atlantic coast. A company was incorporated to do this and I took a share for $100. This was in 1873.

The cargo was purchased and an insulated warehouse was constructed to receive it. There some loss from melting during the voyage down and the poor insulation of the storage facility resulted in more loss. Given the high local demand, despite the high price of five to 15 cents per pound, we soon realized the shipment would not last the entire summer.

To buy another cargo, the ice company tried to assess each stockholder a 45-percent contribution, based on his original subscription.

E. H. Caldwell was fined $50 for shooting a dog

I paid up but the other stockholders refused to put any more of their money into ice. No other shipment was contracted. I asked for my payment to be refunded, but the company was broke and had no cash.

I was told that I could have the value of $45 in the ice that was left, at 15 cents a pound. Our family could not possibly use that amount of ice before it all melted. I decided to give an ice-cream supper for the ladies of the Temperance Society. I would furnish the ice and they would furnish everything else. I lost the value of my stock, true, but that supply of ice made me quite a reputation for a time.

Not long after the ice episode, I decided to leave my job with the Doddridge Bank and go into sheep-raising. Seeing the cash deposits made by sheep men opened my eyes to the profit potential of this business.

On my last day of work at the bank, I put my pistol in my hip pocket to carry home. The bank was always at risk of being robbed, so I kept a loaded pistol right under the receiving and paying window.

I was riding home by horseback when a big yellow dog, owned by one of our neighbors, ran out barking and snapping at my horse's hooves. I resented this indignity and, foolishly, I took out my pistol and shot the dog dead.

Within half an hour, the neighbor filed a complaint in district court against me for carrying a concealed weapon. The sheriff came to our house and asked me to accompany him to court which, as it happened, was already in session. I followed him through town on my horse.

The judge read the complaint and asked if I were guilty. I had to respond that I was. He gave me a fine of $50, assessed by the jury. This was the minimum under the law. I thanked the jury and added the observation that I had no doubt that more than half of them were at that very moment carrying concealed weapons. This was almost certainly the case. In those times, nearly everyone carried weapons, concealed or openly. I had to pay just the same, and even got my name in the newspaper. Half a century later, that same article was re-published in the section called "Men and Events of Fifty Years Ago." I paid twice for my crime.

————

EDWARD HARVEY CALDWELL was born on Aug. 13, 1851 in Cleveland, Tenn. He moved to Corpus Christi in March 1872 when his father became minister of the First Presbyterian Church. E. H. Caldwell worked for the Doddridge Bank until he established a sheep ranch in Duval County. After his marriage to Ada Lasater in 1880, he returned to Corpus Christi and opened a hardware store. He died on March 14, 1940 and was buried in Rose Hill Cemetery.

69

SHOOT THE SCOUNDREL

John Wesley Hardin
COWBOY, GUNFIGHTER

On April 9, 1873, I started to Cuero on business connected with shipping cattle. As I was about to start, John Gay told me they were opening a new road from Cuero to San Antonio and the road went by Manning Clements' place. Gay told me if I would follow this furrow across the prairie I would save time and get to Cuero without any trouble.

I got about 18 miles from home, opposite the Mustang Mott, when I saw a man riding a gray horse 200 yards away. As I got closer, I could see he was carrying a Winchester and two six-shooters on the horn of his saddle. He turned in his saddle, as if looking for cattle, I suppose to put me off my guard, but it made me more alert. I checked up and he got down from his horse. I got down also, apparently to fix my saddle, but really to give him no advantage over me.

His weapons and appearance gave me the impression he was on the dodge or an officer of the law. He then mounted his horse and I did likewise. We were face to face. He said, "Do you live around here?" I told him I was on my way to Cuero and was following the furrow. I asked him how far it was and he said seven miles.

Then he said he had just been over to Jim Cox's to serve some papers on him. "I'm sheriff of this county," he said.

I had thought that Dick Hudson was the acting sheriff of DeWitt County and said, "I suppose your name is Dick Hudson?" No, he said, Dick Hudson was his deputy and that his name was Jack Helm. I told him my name and he said, "Are you Wesley?" At the same time he offered me his hand, which I declined to take. I told him he now had his chance to take me to Austin.

"You have said I was a murderer and a coward, and have had your deputies after me. Now arrest me if you can."

"Oh, Wesley, I am your friend. My deputies are hunting you on their own account, not mine."

I drew my pistol. He begged me not to kill him. I told him, "You have been going around killing men long enough. I know you belong to a legalized band of murdering cowards and have hung and murdered better men than yourself."

"Wesley, I won't fight you. And I know you won't shoot me down. I have the governor's proclamation offering $500 for your arrest in my pocket. But I will never try to execute that warrant if you spare my life. I will be your friend."

I told him his deputies were putting themselves to a lot of trouble about me and that I would hold him responsible. Well, I let him alone and we rode on toward Cuero. We separated about two miles from town and agreed to meet the next day and come to an understanding.

We did meet and he asked me to join his vigilante company, of which he was the captain. I declined. The people with whom he was at war were my friends. I told him all I wanted was for him to let my friends and I stay neutral. This was understood and we parted. We agreed to meet again in a week, on April 16. He would bring one of his men and I would bring Manning Clements and George Tennille.

I stayed in town and went to the bar room on the corner of the square. I took a drink with some friends and went to a back room where a poker game was going and joined the play. It was a freeze-out for $5 and I won the pot.

We went to the bar and a man named J. B. Morgan rushed up and wanted me to treat him to a bottle of champagne. I declined. He got furious and wanted to fight, starting to draw a pistol on me. Some of my friends held him and I walked out, saying that I wished no row. I walked outside and was talking to a friend. I had forgotten Morgan when he came up again and told me that I had insulted him and had to fight. He asked if I was armed and I said that I was. He pulled his pistol halfway out and said, "Well, it is time you were defending yourself."

I PULLED MY PISTOL and shot him above the left eye. He fell dead. I got my horse and left town. The coroner, I heard, held an inquest but what the result was I never learned.

In the year 1873, there existed in Gonzales and DeWitt counties a vigilante committee that made life, liberty and property uncertain. This vigilante band was headed by Jack Helm, the sheriff of DeWitt. His most able lieutenants were his deputies, Jim Cox, Joe Tumlinson, and Bill Sutton. Some of the best men in the country had been murdered by this mob. Pipkin Taylor was lured from his house one night and shot by Helm's men because he did not condone the killing of his own sons-in-law, Henry and Will Kelly.

Anyone who did not support their foul deeds incurred their hatred and it meant death at their hands. They were about 200 strong and were waging war against the Taylors and all their friends.

John Wesley Hardin: "Many of the best citizens of Gonzales and DeWitt patted me on the back"

One night, about the first of April, Jim Taylor shot Bill Sutton in a billiard hall in Cuero. Such was the state of affairs when Manning Clements, George Tennille and I went to Jim   Cox's house to meet Helm, leader of the vigilante gang.   When we got there, they took me off to one side and said they would get me out of all the trouble I was in if I would join them. They said there were two sides, either for them or against them.

I talked as if I would join them and they told me of a dozen or more of my friends whom they wished to kill. These were some of the best men in the community and their only sin was the fact that they did not support the vigilante committee's murdering. Helm's men told me they would have to do a lot of work to get me clear, so I would have to do a lot for them in return. They went so far as to say that if George Tennille and Manning Clements refused to join them, they, too, would have to be killed.

I told them that neither George or Manning or myself would join them, that we wanted peace. I told them that I would not swap sides and work for them, but that they and their mob would have to leave us alone. They agreed to this and said they would let me know if any danger threatened me. At the same time, they swore eternal vengeance on the Taylors and all their friends.

When they were gone, I told Manning and George what had passed between us. George remarked that it would not be a week before the murdering cowards made a raid on us.

About the third of April 1873, Jack Helm and 50 men came into our neighborhood. They inquired for Manning, George and me. They insulted the women and Jack Helm was particularly insulting to my wife because she refused to tell him the whereabouts of the Taylor party.

We were away hunting cattle at the time. When we came back and found out what had happened, we determined to stop that kind of activity. We sent word to the Taylors to meet us at Mustang Mott and concoct a plan of campaign.

There I met Jim, John and Scrap Taylor, while Manning, George and I represented our side of the house. It was agreed to fight mob law to the bitter end. Our lives and families were in danger. A fight came off near Tumlinson Creek and Jim Cox and Jake Christman, of the vigilante gang, were killed.

It was reported that I led the fight, but as I have never pleaded in that case, I will say no more, except that Cox and Christman were killed by the Taylor faction about May 15, 1873. Two days later, I was to meet Jack Helm at a little town called Albukirk in Wilson County. I went there, according to agreement, with Jim Taylor, a trusted friend, accompanying me. Helm and I talked some and failed to agree. He threatened Jim Taylor's life.

Later, I told Jim to look out, that Helm would shoot him because he had shot Bill Sutton. Jim asked me to introduce him to Helm or point him out. I declined to do this, but I referred him to someone who would.

I went to a blacksmith shop to have my horse shod. I paid for the shoeing and was about to leave when I heard Helm say, "Hands up, you damned son of a bitch." I looked around and saw Helm, with a large knife in his hand, advancing on Jim Taylor. Someone hollered, "Shoot the damned scoundrel!"

IT APPEARED TO ME that Helm was the damned scoundrel. I grabbed my shotgun and fired at Helm as he was closing with Jim Taylor. I then threw my gun on Helm's crowd and told them not to draw a gun and made one man put away his pistol. In the meantime, Jim Taylor shot Helm repeatedly in the head, and so died the leader of the vigilante committee, the sheriff of DeWitt, the terror of the country, whose name was a horror to law-abiding citizens.

Jack Helm fell with twelve-gauge buckshot in his breast and several six-shooter slugs in his head. All of this happened in the midst of his own friends and supporters, who stood by utterly amazed. The news spread that I had killed Jack Helm. I received many letters of thanks from widows of the men he had cruelly put to death. Many of the best citizens of Gonzales and DeWitt patted me on the back and told me it was the best act of my life.

JOHN WESLEY HARDIN was born in Bonham, May 26, 1853, the son of a Methodist preacher and his wife. John Wesley's criminal record began in 1867 when he stabbed a youth and, at age 15, killed a black man who insulted him. He went up the trail to Kansas as a cowhand, married Jane Bowen, and got entangled in the Sutton-Taylor feud. He was sentenced to 25 years in prison in 1877 and pardoned in 1894. He was shot to death by old John Selman in the Acme Saloon in El Paso on Aug. 19, 1895. He asserted throughout his life that he never killed anyone who didn't need killing.

70

TURKEY ROOST COUNTRY

Billy Dixon

BUFFALO HUNTER, ARMY SCOUT

Hugging the south side of the Canadian, we followed an old trail up to White Deer Creek, a beautiful clear-running stream. Opposite the mouth of this stream were the old ruins of the original Adobe Walls.

Crossing to the north side of the Canadian, we reached Moore's Creek, then went north until we struck the Palo Duro. Here we found quite a number of buffalo hunters camped for the winter. Our object in making this trip was to find a good buffalo range for the following summer. After lying around camp with the boys on the Palo Duro for several days, we headed for the Cimarron and then on to Dodge City.

In making a big circle — to Buffalo Springs, Red River, the ruins of Adobe Walls, and back to Dodge City — we saw very few buffalo, but there were abundant signs showing where thousands had been herding together, and we felt certain that they would come back to their old range in the spring.

We got back to Dodge in February 1874. We had seen enough to satisfy us that the thing to do would be to get down on the Canadian soon as the weather settled. The hunters at Dodge were convinced there would never again be a big run of buffalo that far north because of the enormous slaughter on that part of the range in 1872 and 1873.

The plan was that every hunter who wanted to pull down into good buffalo country, somewhere on the Canadian, should load his wagons with supplies. The organizers of this expedition caused much enthusiasm among the hunters at Dodge and many wanted to go along. Soon every man was engaged in gathering his equipment for the long trip to the new country.

Three or four days before we were ready to leave there came from the East a man named Fairchild. Naturally he was a neophyte, a tenderfoot. When he heard of our expedition, he shouted for joy and made arrangements to go along.

THIS FAIRCHILD WAS, by every indication, well-supplied with money. He was from Illinois and had been admitted to the bar, but yearned for western adventure.

When we moved out of Dodge, there were about 50 men and 30 wagons. There was never a happier lot of men in the world. We were all in rugged good health and ate like wolves. Spring was on the way, the air was light and buoyant, making the days and nights a delight.

The youngest of our party was "Bat" Masterson, who was to win a reputation not only as a member of this expedition, but in many other places in later years. It seems remarkable that finally Masterson should wander as far east as New York City and become a newspaper writer. He was a chunk of steel, and anything that struck him in those days always drew fire. In age, I was perhaps next to Masterson, being in my 24th year.

Best of all was when we camped at night. There would be singing, dancing, music and storytelling. After we had eaten, and the campfire was aglow, some fellow would stretch out and peg down a dry buffalo hide on which the men would dance, turn-about or in couples. The hide gave a much better footing for dancing than one might suppose.

After crossing the Cimarron we held a conference on the Indian problem and it was agreed that if we should encounter Indians and find them manifesting friendship, we would do likewise. This was their country and if they would leave us alone, we would be willing to leave them alone.

Since we left Dodge, Fairchild had hoped to get into an Indian fight and bragged about what he would do when the time came. We began to fear that he might fire on a peaceable Indian and get us all massacred.

We struck the Palo Duro at its mouth, where there was plenty of water. Here we camped and then moved into the Panhandle of Texas. We went south from the Palo Duro and struck Moore's Creek then followed this steam to the South Canadian River. We made camp about two miles from the later town of Plemons.

While camped on the South Canadian, we felt that something would have to be done about Fairchild who was so bent on killing an Indian, something to teach him a lesson and take the edge off him.

There was a large grove of cottonwoods above our camp where hundreds upon hundreds of wild turkeys roosted every night. When a turkey hunt was proposed, to take place at night, Fairchild was so eager to go and giddy with excitement that he could scarcely control himself. Three men slipped quietly out of camp and picked a place in the timber to have a fire burning. One of them returned to serve as a guide. Ostensibly, he was to lead the hunters to the best and biggest turkey roost, but actually he was to pilot them to the vicinity of the campfire.

Fairchild was impatient to start. It was difficult to persuade him to wait until darkness had fallen and the turkeys had settled down to roost.

I do not believe it would have been possible to find a man who loved practical jokes more than Bat Masterson. He was one of the three who slipped out to build the fire and he came back to camp, ready to pilot the hunters to a spot where they would find "a million turkeys."

Masterson started out with Fairchild close at his heels and A. C. Myers bringing up the rear. Masterson cautioned them to keep their eyes open and move softly and not frighten the turkeys.

Rounding a bend of the creek, the hunters found themselves slap-bang against a campfire in full blaze. Masterson waved them back into the timber.

THE THREE MEN held a consultation. Masterson was sure it was an Indian camp. Myers argued that he was wrong, but even if it was an Indian camp, he was willing to bet that Fairchild could whip all the Indians in the Panhandle, given a fair show.

Bang! Bang Bang! Bullets ripped through the branches above the hunters' heads. Myers took the lead, starting back to camp, yelling bloody murder at every step. Masterson came last, firing his six-shooter and yelling, "Run! Fairchild, run!"

At a bound Fairchild passed Myers and tore into camp like a tornado. He was half a mile head of Masterson and Myers.

Fairchild, gasping for breath, fell exhausted onto a pile of bedding. We crowded around, asking a thousand questions. Finally, Fairchild managed to squawk, in a hoarse whisper, "Injuns!"

"Oh, man, he must be shot," said one man. Another seized a butcher knife and ripped Fairchild's shirt down the back, looking for bullet wounds. Another, frantically yelling for water and finding none, emptied a pot of coffee on Fairchild's back, which alarmed him with the fear that he really had been wounded.

Masterson and Myers ran in, panting for breath, and upbraided Fairchild for abandoning them to the mercy of the Indians. We had asked Fairchild, when he first arrived, what had become of Masterson and Myers and he feebly replied, "Killed, I guess."

"How many Indians were there?" he was asked. "Did you see them?"

He said the timber was full of them.

Masterson stepped forward and, in great fright, said the whole turkey roost country was alive with Indians. Instantly, there was rushing around making preparations for defense.   All kinds of suggestions were offered as to what was best to do. Some were in favor of starting at once for Dodge City. Fairchild was firmly committed to the Dodge City plan. But those more resolute were in favor of fighting it out, even if every man should be killed and scalped. And they said the men should take turns standing guard until morning.

This plan was adopted. Fairchild was placed on guard nearest the river and warned to maintain a close and vigilant lookout, as the Indians might swim up the river and plug him when he wasn't looking. The guards were all stationed and, shortly afterwards, one by one, they drifted back to camp, all save Fairchild, who stood sentinel at his river post.

In camp, there was much noisy laughter over the trick we had played. When Fairchild failed to be relieved by the next guard, he became suspicious and drew near the camp. Then he heard the laughter and what we were saying. He came in with blood in his eyes. I have often thought that he was the angriest man I ever saw. We were too many for him, or else he would surely have crippled somebody over our innocent little deception.

Fairchild refused to eat breakfast and sulked, keeping his own company, for several days before he got over his wounded feelings. Ever afterwards, though, he was a good hunter and a good fellow. The last time I saw him he had his sleeves rolled up and was skinning a buffalo. He bore little resemblance to that tenderfoot I had first seen in Dodge City. And as for his great boastful ambition to kill Indians, we heard of it no more.

WILLIAM (BILLY) DIXON was born in Ohio County, West Virginia, on Sept. 25, 1850. He was orphaned at age 12 and lived with an uncle in Missouri until he left for Kansas, where he worked as a bullwhacker and muleskinner. He worked as a buffalo hunter and moved into the Texas Panhandle in 1874. Dixon was one of the participants in the second battle of Adobe Walls in 1874. After the battle, he became a scout for the U.S. Army. Dixon returned to civilian life in 1883 and built a home near the site of the original Adobe Walls. He married Olive King on Oct. 18, 1894 and they eventually had six children. He dictated his story to his wife who wrote the book, "The Life of Billy Dixon" published in Dallas in 1927. Dixon died on March 9, 1913 and was buried at the Adobe Walls Battlefield Site.

71

OUTRAGE IN REFUGIO

William L. Rea

JUDGE

(On June 8, 1874, sheep rancher Thad Swift and his wife were murdered at their ranch house on Saus Creek in Refugio County. Their bodies were hacked to pieces and left for their three small children to discover. The brutality and graphic accounts of the crimes enflamed the entire countryside.)

I was too young to join a posse, several of which were formed in Refugio, but I saw them leave and saw Edward Fennessey's contingent return with the body of Dan Holland.

Capt. Henry Scott, who was a neighbor of the Swifts, got his Minute Men together and scoured the country. Edward Fennessey was made captain of another contingent and took his men to the Moya Ranch on Mah-Arroyo Creek in

Goliad County. They went to apprehend one of the Moya boys, suspected of being complicit in killing the Swifts.

The Moya ranch house was constructed of palings filled in and daubed with moss and mud. Chink holes had been left in several places which could be used as loopholes for firing through. When the posse got there, one of the men, Dan Holland, went into the yard. The Moyas had seen the posse coming and were barricaded inside.

Holland called out and one of the Moyas shouted back, "What do you want?" Holland carelessly stooped down and yelled into one of the chink holes, "We want you."

A MOYA INSIDE fired into the hole and the bullet struck Holland under the left eye, killing him instantly. The posse laid siege to the house and fired into the chink-holes. While matters were in this condition, Phil Fulcord, sheriff of Goliad County, arrived and took charge.

Fulcord went to within hailing distance of the house and told the Moyas who he was and guaranteed them full protection of the law if they would give themselves up.

The Moyas came out. They were arrested by the sheriff, who took them and headed for Goliad. The Refugio posse, outraged over the slaying of Dan Holland, rode after the sheriff's party and caught up with it. They took the prisoners from Fulcord and in the melee that followed Marcello Moya and his father were shot to death.

The sheriff persuaded the Refugians to allow him to take the remaining prisoners to Goliad. Fennessey and his men returned to Refugio, carrying the body of Dan Holland.

Holland was a well-liked young man. He had lived with and worked for Jesse Williams on the Beeville road. He had no kin that we ever heard of, but he had the largest funeral I have ever seen in Refugio County.

Within in a week of the Swift murders, there were but few Mexican families to be found in Refugio County. The citizens were outraged over the murders of the Swifts and

Holland and every Hispanic suspected of complicity was arrested and brought to Refugio.

I remember that three men were brought in and chained up in the old wooden courthouse. One night a mob took the three men and hung them on Saus Creek. I had seen them in jail that very morning.

Most of the remaining Hispanics began an exodus toward Mexico and the roads were lined with ox-carts and wagons headed west. What struck the posse-men as being peculiar was that all the vehicles were driven by women. Not a man could be seen. When the carts were searched, the men were found hiding beneath bedding and household furnishings. Some of them were pulled out and taken to Refugio but in most cases the carts were allowed to proceed to the Nueces.

Capt. Henry Scott and his Minute Men tracked the main suspect, Juan Flores, who had worked for Thad Swift, to the Rio Grande. They found that he had already crossed the river into Mexico. Scott made a deal with Mexican authorities for the possession of the fugitive and brought him back to Refugio. He was indicted, tried and convicted.

Juan Flores was hanged on the outskirts of town, where the Fox gin was built later. It was the first legal hanging to take place in the county and a large crowd turned out. I was present with the rest. Flores approached his fate bravely and made a speech from the scaffold. He admitted his guilt and admonished the spectators not to act as he did, so they would not come to the same end.

WILLIAM LEWIS REA was born on May 31, 1862, in Louisiana. His family moved to Texas soon afterwards. Rea married Nancy Ellen Kelley and was later elected judge. He died on Aug. 6, 1940 and was buried in Mount Calvary Cemetery in Refugio.

72

THE LYNCHING OF MOSS TOP

John B. Dunn

TEXAS RANGER, VIGILANTE

One day in 1874, three or four of us Rangers left our camp to go to town, that is, the village of Concepcion* in Duval County. Our camp was two miles from the village.

On the way we met two of our boys riding back to camp. One of them was riding a racehorse that belonged to Lt. Ferguson. The rider was Mark Judd and he was full of booze. He began wallowing around on his horse and talking very loud. His actions excited the horse and as the other horses began to move he thought a race was coming off and wheeled and ran in the opposite direction, fast as he could go.

We knew it would only make matters worse if we tried to catch him. This would only make Judd ride faster and he

---

* Concepcion is 14 miles southeast of Benavides and 28 miles southwest of San Diego. Handbook of Texas.

John. B. Dunn, a Texas Ranger during violent times

was on the fastest horse in the company. In a few moments both he and the horse disappeared into the chaparral and we rode on in the direction of Concepcion. Later, when we came in sight of the captain's quarters, we saw the horse going there in a dead run. Mark Judd was hanging over on the horse's shoulder. He and the horse were covered with blood.

When the horse halted at the door of the captain's quarters, we eased Judd down and saw he had been shot in the eye with a small caliber pistol. One side of his face was laid open with a machete. He was unconscious and could say nothing.

We followed the trail of the blood to a Mexican jacal where even the door was splattered with blood. We found no men within but only women and children who denied any knowledge of the affair.

We put guards around this jacal and several others nearby until we could search the premises thoroughly. Dave Odem, Billie McKintosh, myself and one other man guarded the first jacal to which we had trailed the blood.

We were on a path overgrown with tall weeds when I heard a noise behind me. I turned and there was a man lying on his stomach with a machete in his hand. Ten feet away was another man grasping a club of mesquite wood. We captured and disarmed them and found they had crawled about 30 yards toward us before we spotted them.

The one who had the machete had a mop of frizzy hair that looked like a buffalo's mop. One of the boys, Chubby Cody, called him Moss Top. His body was covered with awful sores from which the stench was terrible.

WE LOST NO TIME in taking Moss Top to camp. When we arrived there, a scout under Steve Burleson came in and asked who we had. We told him the circumstances and he threw a noose around Moss Top's neck and began throwing the other end of the rope over a tree. Our captain, Warren W. Wallace, and some of the boys came running up.

Capt. Wallace tried to bluff the boys out of hanging the prisoner. When this didn't work, he gave his word of honor that if we would desist he would keep the prisoner under guard until the grand jury was in session and would turn him over to the law.

A few days later we learned that Moss Top had been freed. The boys put spies on his track and found that at a certain time every evening he took a rope and machete and went down to the creek to get firewood.

Next day, two of the boys hid in a gully that ran into the creek and caught him easily. They made him mount behind one of them and tied his legs under the horse's belly so that if he happened to fall or jump, he could not escape.

They struck a run for a small lake which was surrounded by mesquite timber. They could not find a tree large enough or high enough to swing him clear of the ground. After losing considerable time trying to find one, they saw a tree with two limbs that forked high enough from the ground.

They jammed Moss Top's head into the fork of the tree, took the end of the rope and put it around his neck and tied the other end around the horn of the saddle and made the horse pull until the man's neck was broken.

He was not found for several days and it was August. The body was soon swollen beyond recognition and emitting a terrible odor. The villagers were afraid to take him down and the Rangers refused to do so. Finally, a detail was summoned to come and bury him. Mark Judd recovered, but he was blind in one eye and carried a scar from his hair down the side of his neck.

JOHN B. DUNN was known as "Red John" to distinguish him from his cousin, also named John Dunn. He was born in Corpus Christi on Jan. 18, 1851. Dunn rode as a Ranger and vigilante during the violent years of Reconstruction. In later years he settled down to a quiet life as a dairyman, married Lelia Nias, and kept a private museum at his home on Shell (UpRiver) Road in Corpus Christi. His wife died on Nov. 12, 1920 and he died on Nov. 3, 1940. Both were buried in Rose Hill Cemetery.

73

BOOTS AND SADDLES

Dr. Robert T. Hill

GEOLOGIST

Many a frontier army post gained fame on account of some single experience or incident, but old Fort Griffin, on the banks of the Brazos River in the northeast of Shackelford County, achieved its reputation from three major events. Before the Civil War it was made an outpost near one of the several reservations which had been given to and taken away from the Comanche Indians. The post incorporated in its bosom as scouts the Tonkawas, another Indian tribe of Caddoan stock, members of which dared not get out of the protection of the soldiers' guns for fear that their hereditary enemies, the Comanches, would get them.

Fort Griffin was at various times the seat of famous army explorations. It was the sentry house which stood guard against the Western Plains Indians at the northwest door of Texas (1868-1874). It was the focal point of the wild slaughter of the great Southern herd of the American bison

(1874-1877), one of the most tragic events in North American history. It was the rendezvous and supply point for Col. Ranald S. Mackenzie's expeditions for finally ridding Texas of the Comanche and Kiowa Indians (1872-1874). Then it was, for a short period (1875-1880), a way station on the Western or Dodge City cattle trail.

I must confess my inability as a boy to distinguish one Indian tribe from another. And the Griffin Tonkawas gave me great annoyance. As with most Texans at that time, all Indians looked alike to me. Some have said the Tonkawas were cannibals. This may have been true but if so, it was a form quite different from what most people might suppose. The eating of small bites of human flesh was not for food, but was a religious ceremonial. They believed, I am told, that by tasting the flesh of a brave enemy one acquired his bravery and courage in battle.

Between 1872 and 1875, Fort Griffin was solely an army post. The place at that time presented no attractions for civilians. The post was not over a six-company command and consisted of a few stone houses on the highest level of the prairie. The "town" was below on the flat by the Clear Fork of the Brazos River. A dirt road led from the military camp above the town down to the river. Water was hauled up to the post in tank wagons by army teams of splendid mules.

The town was a nondescript affair. There were two or three stone buildings and many mud-roofed one-story houses built of vertical posts stood up in trenches in the ground. The space between the posts was chinked up with mud. There was one large stone mercantile house (Conrad & Rath's) with lodging rooms above.

The store carried everything a frontier man's heart could desire — guns, pistols, knives, blankets, frying pans, pots, kettles, hats, chaps, spurs, harness, saddles, and so on. Provisions of every kind were sold: rice, hominy, coffee, sugar, beans, dried apples and dried peaches (all in bulk), and flour by the sack. There were also Indian goods — the blue issue cloth, porcupine quills for breast adornment, beads, and the big black hats prized by some Indians.

The soldier days of 1872 to 1875 were busy ones. Forts Clark, McKavett, Concho and Griffin constituted a network a short distance from the eastern side of the Staked Plains. From these forts, troops in 1874 closed in upon the Comanches and Kiowas who had, almost from time immemorial, maintained permanent abodes in the secreted canyons which indented the eastern edge of the plains. These were west of the bitter gypsum waters.

This campaign in 1874 was not a tin-pan rattling affair, as some of the old frontiersmen delighted in calling the army's pursuit of Indians. It was a deliberately planned operation which absolutely ended the previously unbroken reign of the most warlike Indians in West Texas, against whom our frontiersmen had so long and so impotently battled.

IT WAS AN AUTUMN DAY in 1874 when a procession marched into Fort Griffin from the direction of the setting sun. Led by, surrounded by, and followed by campaign-worn troops of the Fourth Cavalry, it was the strangest and most motley herd of people Texas had ever seen.

The cavalrymen themselves did not look as if they had ever faced a military inspection. Their coats, capes, and hats were torn and dirty. The uniforms could be detected as such only by the occasional remnant of the yellow stripes that once decorated the blue trousers. The sun, wind and harsh climate during a four-month campaign left the white troopers hardly distinguishable from the black.

In the midst of this squadron of soldiers were the last of the hitherto unconquerable bands of Kiowas and Comanches. These were people who had hardly allowed a white man into their Staked Plains since Coronado passed through 400 years before. But at last they were captured, and completely broken, and were being taken from their canyon homes to live upon the reservation at Fort Sill.

324

Here, the handsome Sioux-like Kiowa braves rode beside their less-handsome Comanche allies. The latter, it was said, were the best horsemen and bowmen the West had ever known. Here, too, afoot or riding the tepee poles of the travois, were the Kiowa and Comanche women and their children.

It was a strange sight. It was the sight of a unique peoples and their ancient customs perishing before one's eyes. Arts, language, songs, myths, symbology inherited from the sun-god ages, priesthood, all the unique ethnologic traits that thousands of years had created, were coming to an end. They would all be gone in ten years.

Hardly had the dispossessed Indians moved out of Fort Griffin and on to Fort Sill, hardly had the soldiers time to riot away the back pay they had accumulated over four months in the saloons of "The Flat," before Fort Griffin received a new impetus to reach its zenith of debauchery.

With the Indians gone, there was nothing to prevent those slaughterers of the Plains, from Kansas and Nebraska, from getting at the long-coveted Southern herd of buffalo. From the earliest time, this great herd had lived in the vast country between the mountains of Oklahoma and the Rio Grande.

The slaughterers did not hesitate either — great burly ruffians that they were, with their huge globe-sighted buffalo guns of large caliber, and their wagon loads of camp followers to skin the butchered animals. They came in the hundreds. It had taken thousands of years to stock our American veldts with buffalo. It took the buffalo hunters three years to wipe them out, to leave those beautiful plains completely devastated.

Dead and dying animals, their skinless carcasses or white-boned skeletons, marked the prairie everywhere. In the only two towns in the whole buffalo country — Fort Griffin and Camp Supply — huge stacks of brown hides, as big as ordinary two-story buildings, rose towards the sky.

Fort Griffin on Government Hill looked down on "The Flat" and town below

The streets and saloons by day and night roared with the ribald oaths and curses of the hunters, skinners, and bull-team drivers. They were all of a caste so low down they were pariah to all but their own kind.

No description could do justice to their goings-on. In thick clouds of tobacco smoke and kerosene smoke the buffalo gang mingled with the soldiers, pimps, gamblers and danced the drunken hours away with the lowest of low women.

From Fort Griffin heading toward Kansas ran the vast caravans of hide-laden bull trains. There were 10 wagons to a caravan and 10 pair of oxen to a wagon. Bull teamsters with huge cracking whips walked beside each wagon. A train master on horseback bossed it all. Ox-team driving was the lowest caste on the frontier, universally looked down upon. When a man played out and proved himself a failure at soldiering, buffalo-hunting or skinning, the last place on the whisky trail was this profession.

HOW CHEAP LIFE WAS on the Southern Plains. One great river of blood flowed for three years and an orgy of brutal animal murder went on at our back door. The beautiful natural West was blighted as if it had been swept by a plague. And for what? The profits of this game went mostly to the saloons and pimps and underworld.

The last of the buffalo were expiring when the vanguard of another horde of animals was seen coming up from the south. It looked like a huge serpent two miles long as it moved north. Outriders rode up and down its sides, and as it passes it seems to be headed by a single leader, a monarch of the chaparral, a big Texas steer whose horns become him like an emperor's crown. The great Texas cattle trail moved westward from Fort Worth to just past Fort Griffin.

The bright lights of Fort Griffin's saloons which had burned for the buffalo killers glitter again for the Texas cowboy. Once more the fiddles whine, the ivory ball spins around the roulette wheel, the skilled monte dealer palms his "copas" and "espadas." Fort Griffin is mad wild again.

There is something about these Texas cowboys the Griffin underworld does not like. They were too fond of arguing with a trigger. They did not take kindly to certain epithets which were friendly words of badinage for saloon denizens and buffalo people. And the cowboys resented being cheated and insisted that games be on the square.

One day four of the trail-hands went into town and only two came back. But for their two that were lost, they left four dead, including Shackelford County's deputy sheriff, three others, besides a badly wounded district attorney. But the cowboy trade was good while it lasted.

Something else happened to Fort Griffin. John W. Gates brought barbed-wire fencing to Texas, which destroyed the free range and changed the whole complexion of life for the cowman. In addition to fencing, people commenced invading the West in wagons and settling in towns and on farms. They even started a new town as a rival to Fort Griffin, called Albany. These developments killed Fort Griffin. It was never born to be a farm town. It would have been something like a sacrilege to have made it so.

Sometime in the early 1880s the last reveille and the last "Boots and Saddles" were sounded at the old fort on the hill. The flag was raised, saluted, and lowered for the last time. The soldiers folded their tents and silently stole away. With the fort's closing, the parasites of the flat went too. I do not know what became of Scarface Fanny and Long Nose Kate, but I do know that Fort Griffin turned up its toes and died.

———————

DR. ROBERT THOMAS HILL was born in 1858 in Nashville, Tenn. He was orphaned in 1863 and raised in the home of his grandmother. Hill dropped out of school in the sixth grade. He left home at the age of 16 to work as a printer's devil for the Comanche Chief, *a newspaper owned by his brother in Comanche, Texas. From 1882 through 1885 he worked his way through Cornell University, where he received a B.S. degree in geology. In 1885 he began his career with the United States Geological Survey and became a pioneer Texas geologist. His "Physical Geography of the Texas Region" (1900) was the first systematized geography of Texas. In 1931 he became a feature writer for the Dallas Morning News. Hill died on July 28, 1941, in Dallas. He was survived by two daughters, one by his first marriage in 1887 to Jennie Justina Robinson, and one by his second marriage in 1913 to Margaret McDermott.*

74

DISASTER IN INDIANOLA

V. L. Manci

PASTOR, EDUCATOR

Sept. 15, 1875 was truly a dismal and terrible day for Indianola. It began with one of the largest funerals ever seen in the town, foreshadowing the catastrophe to follow. On seeing the great crowd of people at the funeral of Martin Mahon, whom we were mourning, I felt moved to say a word or two on the certainty of death's uncertain hour.

After the funeral, the sky darkened, and I was on the point of staying in Indianola but I had promised to go to Cuero where I had some children to baptize, some confessions to hear, and where I generally go at least once a month. As I stepped into the railway car, it began to rain and to blow as if to usher in the hurricane, of which we all had a presentiment.

I reached Cuero at half-past five in the evening, baptized some children, heard several confessions and, next morning, in a pouring rain, started on the return trip to Indianola.

We got to within 10 or 15 miles of Indianola, at about 10 a.m., when the train began to reduce speed. The track was covered with water and we proceeded slowly, for we ran the risk of running into the current beneath us.

At 11 a.m. we were half a mile from the station when a man came running up to us, telling us to stop because the tracks had been washed away. We came to a standstill.

You can't imagine how painful it was to hear the conductor say that the train could not go on and that it was impossible to reach the town, either by foot, horseback or by swimming. It fairly knocked the breath out of me. Was I to be cut off from my flock in this awful extremity? In my distress, I tried the church's exorcism on the tempest but the storm raged on with increasing fury.

The water kept rising, two or three feet every hour, and the violence of the wind was terrible. When I put my head out of the door, my spectacles were whipped off and blown away as if they were no more substantial than a straw.

WE SAW A FAMILY making signs for help. Some of us ran to their rescue and succeeded in saving two little boys with their father, mother and grandmother. In the meantime, we could not reverse course because the storm had destroyed the tracks behind us.

Here we were, in the midst of a surging sea, exposed to an unceasing blast. None but an eyewitness could have any adequate idea of the violence of this hurricane. People may imagine that it was somewhat like an inundation, but the inundation was nothing to the way in which it was produced and the wind which hurled the waves about.

The storm, with the power of the wind and the waves, wrenched up whole houses, whirled away roofs, and flung down persons trying in vain to keep their feet.

I tried to go out on the platform but I had to draw back immediately. The wind sucked my breath away and I was running the risk of being blown away like a leaf. The sensation was as if a powerful machine had thrown a bucket of water into my face.

We had to remain spectators of the storm till seven in the evening. Then we began to feel its effects ourselves. There were 18 of us in the passenger car and it was no longer safe. The rails began to slide from beneath the wheels and soon the car itself was overturned, hurried away by the waves, and broken into several pieces.

Before this occurred, we had taken refuge in the baggage car next to us. When we saw what the storm had done to the passenger car, which was much heavier than the baggage car, we knew we were in imminent danger.

The men on the train, except for the father of the two little boys that we rescued that morning, huddled together on the locomotive. I stayed in the baggage car with five children, their mothers and the grandmother of the two boys we rescued. I hoped to be able to baptize the children and go to heaven in their company. Never did death seem so near. Its approach could be seen on the faces of my adult companions, while the five little boys, lying on cushions, had fallen asleep, which, to all appearances, would likely end in the next world.

For about six hours we were in agony, helpless in the fury of the wind and waves. Our car would be lifted high, and almost overturned, but still it withstood the rushing flood. An invisible hand was holding it up. I believe it was the hand of St. Joseph, to whom I had made a special vow.

It was now midnight. Before, the storm and flood had been constantly on the increase. Now the wind veered and the water began to subside. It fell seven feet in five hours. With the veering of the wind, our immediate danger ceased, as the car was placed directly north and south. Not so for Indianola.

The northeast wind in its mad bout of 24 hours, together with the surging water, had laid bare the foundations of the buildings. The north wind did the rest. It toppled more than

250 houses, tilted almost all the rest, and tumbled about in the chopping waves 250 to 300 victims, about one-sixth of the population of Indianola. Of these 300 victims, some 230 were recovered. Many bodies were disfigured and bruised beyond recognition.

Daylight revealed the ruins of Indianola. I attempted to wade to the ruins of the town but could not do so until half-past one in the afternoon. What a sad sight. A few hours before it was a charming seaport, known for its health-restoring breeze, and now it was a heap of ruins, giving off an indescribable stench, owing to the dead bodies and carcasses of animals to be encountered at every step of the way. I reached the town, drenched from head to foot.

THE FIRST VICTIM I buried was a little girl, Blanche Madden, who was found drowned, her tiny arms gripping the neck of a cow. A mother, wishing to cross over in a boat with her children to another part of town, had to leave one of them behind until she could return. She came back just in time to see the child swept away in the rising waters.

One horse was the salvation of four people: two got on his back while the other two clung to his tail and they reached a house on higher ground 200 yards away.

One family escaped on their roof, which floated away undamaged; the house beneath it was completely demolished. A man, seeing his wife and children in danger, made them climb up to the roof. But the building was giving way. The wife and children were drowned; only he survived. There were many such tragic incidents and stories.

Some who had been mourned for dead turned up after three or four days, having been carried by the storm 10 miles or more from town. I saw the meeting of a sister with a brother whom she never expected to see again. They fell to hugging each other and crying in the middle of the street.

After the disaster, all the people of Indianola were brothers and sisters. They shared the little that remained.

One kitchen served two or three houses, one house sufficed for several families, one room for many persons. For a month, there were two or three sleeping in the same room as myself.

Some people were beside themselves with grief and distress. Quite a number of them could hardly recover their composure of mind. An extraordinary panic seized hold of many and in two or three days no less than 200 left the town, some on foot or in carts, others by steamboat for Galveston, Corpus Christi or New Orleans.

I cannot fathom how a hurricane could, in a few hours, wreak such awful destruction.

In several places of the town, it cut channels from seven to 10 feet deep and 200 feet or more wide. It swept substantial brick houses and huge masses of iron for a distance of seven or eight miles.

Had I remained at Indianola, instead of going to Cuero that day, I should doubtless have perished in the storm. My bedroom was destroyed, the roof of the house was torn away by the wind and the church, where I should certainly have rushed to, fell into ruins. Nor could I have been of use to anyone. The driving wind and water made it impossible to see a house 20 yards away. Those who could help each other had to be standing in the same spot. Otherwise, each person had to look out for himself.

REV. V. L. MANCI, Society of Jesus, was assigned to the Indianola parish in the absence of Rev. Joseph Ferro, who was in France at the time of the storm. Rev. Manci returned to Cuero where a small frame church was built and he became the first resident pastor of St. Michael's. He later moved to Seguin to become the president of St. Joseph's Academy. The date of his death and place of burial are not known.

75

COOLEY'S REVENGE

James B. Gillett

RANGER, LAWMAN, RANCHER

Mason and the adjoining county of Gillespie were settled by Germans in the early history of the state. These settlers were quiet, peaceful and made excellent citizens when left undisturbed. Most of the Germans engaged in stock-raising and were sorely troubled by rustlers and Indians, who committed many depredations on their cattle.

In late September 1875, Tim Williamson, a prominent cattleman in Mason County, was arrested on a charge of cattle theft by John Worley, a deputy sheriff. There had been complaints about the loss of cattle.

The Germans charged that many of their cattle had been stolen and the brands burned off. Much indignation had been aroused among the stockmen of Mason County and threats of violence against the thieves were common. The news of Williamson's arrest spread and a mob (or posse) formed and set out in pursuit of the deputy sheriff and his prisoner. On the way to Mason, Worley was overtaken by the posse.

Williamson, when he saw the pursuing men, begged the deputy to let him run to save his life. Worley refused. He drew his pistol and shot Williamson's horse, causing it to fall.

Williamson, unarmed and unmounted, was killed without a chance to protect himself and without any pretense of a trial. After the murder, Worley and the mob disappeared.

Whether or not Williamson was guilty of stealing cattle, he had friends who bitterly resented the deputy's refusal to give the cattleman a chance to save his life. His death caused a great deal of excitement in the county.

Scott Cooley, an ex-ranger of Captain Perry's D company, was a close friend of Williamson and his family. Cooley was no longer in the ranger service; he was farming near Menardville. He had worked for the dead man and had made two trips up the trail to Kansas with him. While working for the Williamson, Cooley contracted typhoid fever and was nursed back to health by Mrs. Williamson.

WHEN THE NEWS of Tim Williamson's murder reached Scott Cooley, he vowed to get even with the murderers of his friend. He saddled his horse and rode into the town of Mason heavily armed. He had devised a plan of his own and set out to put it into execution.

Cooley stabled his horse in a livery barn and registered at the hotel. He was unknown in Mason and remained there for several days without arousing suspicion. He proved to be a good detective and discovered that the sheriff and his deputy were the leaders of the mob that killed his friend. He also learned the names of the men in the posse that murdered Williamson.

Cooley rode out to the home of John Worley, where he found him cleaning out a well. He asked for a drink of water and, as Worley was drawing up the bucket, asked if his name was John Worley. When the deputy said it was, Cooley shot him to death, then stooped down and cut off Worley's scalp and rode away.

Cooley made a quick ride across Mason County to the western edge of Llano County, where he waylaid and killed Pete Border, the second man on his list of mob members.

These two murders struck terror into the hearts of nearly every citizen of Mason County. No one could tell who would be next. The people of the whole county rose in arms to protect themselves.

The sheriff, terrified lest he become Cooley's next victim, departed Mason and never returned. Tim Williamson had other friends eager to avenge him and the killing of Pete Border was their rallying signal. John and Mose Beard, George Gladden, and John Ringgold joined Cooley in his work of vengeance. The gang rode into the town of Mason and in a fight with a posse of citizens killed another man.

The governor of Texas, fearing an outbreak of a deadly feud in Mason County, ordered Major John B. Jones to rush to the relief of the frightened citizens. Major Jones rode to Mason with Texas Ranger Company A, commanded by Captain Ira Long, and 10 men from Company D. In all, Major Jones had 40 men to restore law and order in Mason County.

Before the rangers could reach Mason, the sheriff's party had a fight with Cooley's gang down on the Llano River and killed Mose Beard. On his arrival in Mason, Major Jones sent out scouts in every direction to hunt Cooley. He kept this up for two weeks, without any positive result.

Major Jones finally learned that nearly the whole of his command, especially the Company D boys who had ranged

Major John B. Jones reminded his force of rangers of the oath they had taken

with Cooley, was in sympathy with him. The rangers were making no serious effort to find him. It was even charged that some of the Company D boys met Cooley at night on the outskirts of Mason and told him they didn't care if he killed every damned Dutchman in Mason County who formed the mob that had murdered Williamson.

Major Jones drew up his whole force of 40 men and reminded the rangers of the oath they had taken to protect the state against all enemies. He told them that while Williamson had met a horrible death at the hands of a mob, that did not justify Cooley in conducting a private war of vengeance.

The major then asked for any ranger in sympathy with Scott Cooley and his gang to step out of the ranks and be discharged. Fifteen men stepped to the front. For all the others, Major Jones said he expected them "to use all diligence and strength in helping me to break up or capture these violators of the law."

After the discharge of the 15 Cooley sympathizers, the rangers went to work with a new vigor. They captured George Gladden and John Ringgold. Gladden was sent to the pen for 25 years and Ringgold got a life sentence. John Beard, it was reported, left Texas for Arizona. Scott Cooley was probably informed of Major Jones' appeal to the rangers for he became less active around Mason.

ONE DAY Ranger Norman Rodgers got permission from Captain Roberts to ride over to Joe Franks' cow outfit to swap his horse for a better one. When Rodgers rode into the cowboy camp, he noticed a man resting under a tree near the fire. The stranger called one of the cowboys over and asked him who Norman was. When Rodgers left the camp, the man followed him and asked if he was one of Roberts' rangers and then asked if he knew Reynolds. (Reynolds was known as "Mage" or "Major," a nickname he acquired in the Civil War.)

Rodgers replied that he did know "Mage" Reynolds very well. The man then declared that he was Scott Cooley and, reaching into his pocket, pulled out John Worley's scalp and said, "Take this to Major Reynolds with my compliments, but don't tell anybody you saw me."

Rodgers delivered the scalp and Reynolds cautioned him to say nothing about it. Forty years afterwards, at a reunion of old settlers in Sweetwater, Norman Rodgers mentioned the incident in a speech. He had kept his promise to Cooley and "Mage" Reynolds for all those intervening years.

Cooley went to Blanco County, where he was stricken with brain fever. He was nursed and shielded by his friends. He died without ever being brought to trial for his killings. That ended the Mason County War, but before the feud died some 10 or 12 men were killed and a race war was only narrowly averted.

———

JAMES BUCHANAN GILLETT was born in Austin on Nov. 4, 1856. The family later moved to Lampasas and Gillett started working at area ranches. In 1875, he joined the Texas Rangers, first serving with Captain D. W. Roberts Company D. In addition to fights with the Kiowa, Comanche and Apache Indians, Gillett as a ranger dealt with cattle thieves and outlaws. Gillett resigned from the Rangers In 1881 and was appointed assistant city marshal of El Paso. Six months later he became the Marshall of El Paso. In April 1885 he became the manager of the Estado Land and Cattle Company before establishing his own ranch in the Marfa area. Gillett married Mary Lou Chastain and they had six children. Gillett died on June 11, 1937 and was buried in the Marfa Cemetery.

76

THE RELUCTANT BULLS

Mrs. O. B. Boyd

SOLDIER'S WIFE

The quaint old town of Piedras Negras lay directly across the Rio Grande from our post of Fort Duncan. We were able to enjoy everything Piedras Negras afforded in the way of sightseeing, having arrived just before the big celebration of the year, the annual fiesta.

Piedras Negras, like all the towns that I saw in Mexico, was built around central squares called plazas. These were occupied during the fiesta with booths for the sale of curiosities and also for gambling. Any game could be indulged in, from roulette to three-card monte. Visitors could also partake of Mexican viands served by bashful senoritas in pretty Spanish costumes.

The climax of festivities were the bullfights, when the large amphitheater would be crowded with an excited audience. Having heard so much of these affairs, we were eager to see one. Our curiosity was soon satisfied, for a more tame encounter I never beheld.

The poor bull was unenthusiastic about risking his life. He refused to fight. After having been goaded and prodded with sharp-pointed spears, he kept wistfully turning toward the door by which he had entered, as if looking for a way out. Every now and then he would rush toward this exit only to be met with more spear-pricks which, though causing his blood to flow, only served to further intimidate the poor animal.

Amid the shouts of the people, the reluctant bull was finally dispatched and replaced by another, equally timid bull, that showed the same want of fighting spirit. It seemed a cruel sport, unworthy of its historic greatness.

The only delightful features connected with the so-called pastime were the performances of the Mexican band and the drilling of Mexican soldiers, who marched and counter-marched for at least an hour without a single order being given. They responded merely to a tap of the drum as each new movement was initiated. The band was superb. The music was sweet and so thrilling that we could have listened for hours without weariness.

FRANCES ANNE (FANNIE) MULLEN was in New York in 1848. She married Lt. O. B. (Orsemus Bronson) Boyd in 1867. She was stationed with her husband at forts in California, Nevada, Arizona, New Mexico and Texas, during which she had three children. Her husband died in 1885, when he was 41, and was buried in San Antonio National Cemetery. Her book, "Cavalry Life in Tent and Field" portrays the life of an Army family at Forts Clark and Duncan in Texas. She died in New York in 1926.

77

DOCTOR TURNS COWBOY

Henry F. Hoyt
FRONTIER PHYSICIAN

John Chisum told me the Panhandle was full of people, which was wrong. The smallpox epidemic soon faded away and there was little doctoring for me to do around Tascosa. There were all kinds of hunting, plenty of adventure and excitement, so I was enjoying life, but my income was diminished.

It was not long until a debonair young medico, the first to practice medicine in the Texas Panhandle, was flat broke. I was too proud to send home for funds, which would not have been an easy matter anyway. The nearest post office was Dodge City, Kansas, and the only communication with it was an occasional bull train or with Old Dad Barnes. He was an old-time cowboy who, every two or three months, would pick up letters for Dodge City at 50 cents a letter and retrieve answers at the same price.

Well, since I couldn't make a living at my own calling, I applied to Bill Moore, the superintendent of the LX Ranch, for a job. Moore was short-handed and took me on. He had a staff of about 50 men, a good part of whom were refugees, many under an alias and a few with rewards for their apprehension hanging over them. This even included Moore himself, though we didn't know that at the time.

Moore was a Californian raised on a cattle ranch. He was one of the best vaqueros I ever saw. During roundups Moore would watch some wild steer baffle every cowboy who tried to rope him and after all had failed, Moore would put spurs to his mount and dash in with his 60-foot riata. I never saw him miss.

We later learned that Moore had killed some member of his family and fled to Wyoming where he became the manager of a large ranch owned by the Swan Cattle Company. After a time he was angered by a Negro employee on the ranch and killed him. He then escaped to the Panhandle where W. H. Bates and David T. Beals had recently established the vast LX Ranch. They made him the ranch superintendent.

MY FIRST DUTY AS a cowboy was with a bunch of hands assigned to construct a large corral. We cut down cedar trees in the brakes and hauled the posts to a deep ditch we had dug around the outer edge of the corral. I was raised on a farm and had done my bit in digging and chopping, but my hands were now soft and this job produced a big crop of blisters.

Instead of putting me through the usual initiation accorded to a tenderfoot, such as hiding burrs under my saddle, I was treated rather royally, doubtless because I had doctored some of the boys during the smallpox outbreak and did not kill them.

The senior foreman on the ranch was Charles A. Siringo. He was one of the most expert cowboy riders, ropers and gunmen in the Panhandle and he taught me how to throw the riata and other tricks of the trade. We formed a strong friendship that continued until the day of his death in 1928.

After the corral was completed, I became a range rider, paired with Latigo Jim (if he had another name, I never knew it). We were located in a small log cabin on Bonita Creek, south of the Canadian, about the middle of the south edge of the LX Ranch, which had an area of 40 square miles. Our beat consisted of 20 miles, 10 miles east and 10 miles west. We patrolled the boundaries daily looking for any trails leading from the ranch and when we found such trails we followed the tracks and brought back the strays.

Our chuck was bacon, sourdough bread, black coffee with sugar, potatoes, jerked or fresh beef, alternated with wild game at our pleasure. We were both good camp cooks so we fared rather sumptuously. From the home ranch was issued green coffee beans, which we roasted in a skillet and ground at the bottom of a tin can with the end of a hammer handle. When this was brought to boil in a tin pot, we had coffee as fine as I have ever tasted.

Twice during my tour of range riding we were hit with a severe norther, each one starting just after dark. In a short time, cattle all along the line were drifting south with the storm. Each cowboy on the ranch went to the south boundary, doing his utmost to stem the tide and bring back the stragglers. But still a good many got away and kept on going.

When the grass sprouted in the spring of 1878, Bill Moore sent a party of eight men south across the Staked Plains to gather strays that had drifted south with the storms. The outfit included Latigo Jim and myself, a cook and chuckwagon, all under the supervision of Jack Ryan. He was the junior foreman on the ranch, a first-class cowboy, genial, cheerful, just the man for the place.

Going south as far as the headwaters of the Brazos and Concho Rivers, we picked up quite a herd and began to work out way homeward. Some of our supplies were getting low so Jack Ryan sent me ahead to the Charles

Dr. Henry F. Hoyt in 1876

Goodnight Ranch in the Palo Duro Canyon for the needed articles and told me to meet him at the head of the canyon as he came up with the herd.

I was told to ride straight north and that the Goodnight place was one day's ride away. I started out right after breakfast, without carrying any provisions as I expected to be at Goodnight's by supper time.

But someone blundered. It took me three days to reach the ranch. I didn't mind it the first day. That night I picketed my horse and with a blanket and saddle for a bed slept out under the stars. But by noon of the second day my appetite began sending signals of distress.

There were buffalo and antelope, but my horse was not fast enough for me to kill one with a Colt .45, which was the only weapon I had.

As I passed a big mesquite, I heard a whiz-z-z and my horse jumped sideways. I caught sight of an enormous rattlesnake and quickly shot its head off. I sat on my horse looking at that snake for some time. I had been told it was good meat. And I was surely hungry.

I picketed my horse and started a fire with buffalo chips. After skinning and cutting up the snake, I roasted a portion on the end of a split mesquite branch. I was agreeably surprised. The meat tasted like chicken or rabbit and was very palatable. I satisfied my hunger and had enough left for a couple of meals the next day.

Near sundown on the third day I sighted the walls of the Palo Duro Canyon and before dark I was made comfortable by Col. Charles Goodnight and his good wife. I was treated to one of the most enjoyable meals that I can remember.

When I rejoined our outfit I got a cordial reception. Jack Ryan had discovered his mistake in directing me and to make amends he cut my night watch from then on.

We reached the head of the brakes leading to the Canadian River, where we found an ideal spot for a camp. There was a fine spring at the bottom of a steep bank, from the crest of which spread out before us a magnificent panorama of the entire surrounding country.

The stream flowing from the spring supplied abundant water for our horses and cattle.

Ryan decided to leave the herd here while he reported to headquarters. He left Latigo Jim and I to see after the cattle. We had 15 horses, a chuckwagon, and were instructed to hold the cattle there until relieved from the home ranch.

Jim and I pitched our camp on the ridge above the spring. We had been in this spot a week when a horseman rode in from the east. He was a Ranger and told us the Comanches were off the reservation and that he had been sent up the valley to spread the alarm.

We found a shovel in the wagon and dug a trench and filled a bunch of gunny sacks with the dirt and placed them around the edge of our fort. We dug a tunnel through which we could crawl in or out and covered the fort with a tarpaulin. Ryan had left us with two Sharp's carbines and plenty of ammunition, along with our revolvers. We were snug and comfortable in our fortification and ready for any hostile outfit that might show up.

We waited for two weeks. No word came from the home ranch so we decided to make a move. We drew lots to see who would ride to headquarters and Jim won. He promised that someone would be back in three or four days.

I HAD A BIG BUNCH of cattle and 14 horses to look after, but the grazing was fine and they made little trouble. I kept one horse picketed at camp, saddled and ready to ride. The others were hobbled and never strayed very far, except once.

I crawled out of the fort one morning to find not a hobbled horse in sight. I had heard nothing in the night. The cattle were all right and I could discover no reason for the absence of the horses. Putting some dried corn and jerked meat in a saddlebag, I soon found the trail, which led south.

The horses kept well together and seemed to be traveling rapidly. The trail finally led to the bed of a dried-up lake and there the mystery was solved. In the soft muddy ground the tracks of wolves were plain to see.

I hurried along and about two hours before sundown I saw a strange sight. My horses were lined up in a formation almost as precise as that of a cavalry squad. They were fighting off with their hobbled forefeet two large gray wolves, which were snapping and snarling and doing their best to get a big meal after their long chase. The wolves were so intent on their prey that I was able to ride within 50 yards without being noticed.

I took my time and brought down one of the wolves with a shot through his spine. I hit the second wolf but did not bring him down. He was running away and turning and biting and snapping at himself near the hip.

The horses were in a sad plight where the hobbles had worn through the flesh. After removing the hobbles, I started back to the camp and, strange to say, the horses followed me like a pack of hounds. They did not have to be driven.

After being alone for 30 days, I was relieved by Bill Moore himself. He gave a number of reasons for the delay, but I was so pleased to see people again I paid little attention to them.

I then took part in the big roundup in which most of the ranchers in that section of the Panhandle participated. The work was hard and exciting.

I soon had recouped my funds sufficiently to return to civilization. I quit the cowboy life and went back to Tascosa, with plans to move on to New Mexico.

DURING MY COWBOY SOJOURN of about a year, Bill Moore, the ranch superintendent, was probably the most popular and highly esteemed cowman in the Panhandle.

A few years later he moved to New Mexico, west of the Rio Grande, and started his own ranch. Two brothers owned land adjoining his. This land had a fine spring of water that Moore coveted, but the brothers refused to sell. After sending them word that he was coming after them, Moore rode up to their home and shot both of them, with fatal accuracy.

He again made his escape and was not heard of again in that country. Many years afterward, one of the top foremen of the LX Ranch, Charlie Siringo, had become a Pinkerton detective and while chasing a wanted man in Alaska he met and recognized Bill Moore* although he denied his identity. But Moore had a peculiar cast in his left eye which could not be disguised. Siringo, who knew him well, said, "If a person ever saw him once he would know him again anywhere." Siringo was certain that he was the same man from the old LX days in the Texas Panhandle.

HENRY FRANKLIN HOYT was born on Jan. 30, 1854 in St. Paul, Minn. He began medical training with his uncle, John Henry Murphy, a doctor in St. Paul. In 1877, after prospecting around Deadwood, South Dakota, he made his way to the Pecos River Valley in New Mexico. Near Roswell, he stayed at the ranch of John Chisum, who told him that Tascosa in the Texas Panhandle needed a doctor. He arrived at Tascosa in the middle of a smallpox outbreak. Afterwards, he worked as a cowboy for the LX Ranch, along with Charles Siringo. He became friends with Billy the Kid. Hoyt returned to St. Paul where he became a surgeon and married Ella Owens Gray. At the outbreak of the Spanish-American War in 1898, Hoyt enlisted in the medical department as chief surgeon and served under Gen. Arthur MacArthur (father of Douglas MacArthur) in the Philippines, where he was wounded in action. Afterwards he practiced medicine in El Paso then moved to Long Beach, Calif., where he wrote his autobiography, "A Frontier Doctor," published in 1929. He died on Jan. 21, 1930 in Yokohama, Japan during a trip to the Pacific.

---

* Siringo also relates the Bill Moore incident in Alaska in "Lone Star Cowboy."

78

THE KICKAPOO RAID

Jean Stuart

MRS. WILLIAM H. STEELE

(It was called the Kickapoo Raid but the culprits were a mixed band of Mexican outlaws and hostile Indians, mostly Kickapoo, who left a bloody trail of murder and mayhem across South Texas. At William Steele's sheep ranch east of Fort Ewell, Jean Steele's two young sons were killed and scalped. During the attack, she hid with her small children in tall grass by the Nueces River. At least 18 people were killed and many more wounded in the Kickapoo Raid of 1878.)

I was living on the Palo Alto Ranch on the Nueces River, about 15 miles below Fort Ewell. On April 17, 1878, for some reason which I can't explain, I felt very much depressed and troubled in my mind. My husband, Mr.

Steele, had gone to Dogtown* and there was no one left on the ranch but his brother, John Steele, and myself and my children.

About 9 o'clock I went up on top of the house and I saw two men on horseback, about two miles away, in the open country. They seemed to be chasing something like a man on foot.

A few minutes later two other horsemen appeared, heading toward the house, but then stopped about half a mile away. John Steele had left the house a little before I went up on the roof. At this moment, he came into sight, out of the brush, and I saw three more men ride up and they got between John and the house.

I SAW ONE MAN fire a shot and John fell from his horse. Two of the men rode off in the direction of my two boys, one aged eight and the other 12, who were herding sheep. One of the men fired a shot before they disappeared out of sight.

I came down from the roof and took my three remaining children (the youngest was nine months old) and went down to the river. I put them on the loose branch of a tree and by wading and pushing the branch ahead of me crossed the river. We hid in the tall grass for about three hours.

I returned to the house after I heard the voice of a vaquero, who worked on a neighbor's ranch, calling for Mr. Steele. I found one of our Mexican shepherds, Venturo Rodriquez, lying on the ground, wounded in eight different places. All the wounds were made by arrows except for one gunshot. Another shepherd was lying in the house; he had been run by the Indians for a great distance and was exhausted.

---

* Tilden was once called Dogtown. One theory for the name holds that a cowboy riding through was set upon by yapping dogs barking at his heels. It was called Rio Frio, Colfax, then changed to Tilden in 1877 after presidential candidate Samuel Tilden.

Mr. Steele returned about 2 p.m. with a Mr. Hart, and they began to search for John Steele. They found his body half a mile from the house. He had been shot twice. He had a strong conviction against carrying weapons of any kind, and had none on him when he was killed.

The bodies of my two sons were not found until late in the afternoon of the next day.

JEAN STUART TAYLOR STEELE was born Jan. 23, 1846 in Aberdeenshire, Scotland. Her first husband, Alexander Taylor, died in 1877 and she married William Hutton Steele, a sheep rancher in La Salle County. Her two sons killed in the Kickapoo Raid were George Taylor, 12, and Richard Taylor, 8. born in 1870. She had four more children. She died Nov. 14, 1931 and was buried in Cotulla.

79

HANGING DAY

William John L. Sullivan
TEXAS RANGER

On Oct. 11, 1878 I witnessed the hanging of Bill Longley, who was executed at Giddings before a crowd of thousands for the murder of Wilson Anderson. The sheriff of Lee County, Jim Brown, who had charge of the execution, was the noted horse-racer who was afterwards killed in Chicago by a policeman.

A little before the execution, the sheriff read the sentence to Longley and, pointing to his 200 guards, he told the people he had worked three months to select his men for the occasion. He said he thought he had about the best men around to assist him in the execution.

The sheriff then asked Longley if he wanted to make a talk. Bill said that he did and pulled his hat off and placed it on a chair. Looking calmly over the crowd, Bill Longley addressed the guards and spectators:

"This is a big crowd here to witness the last of me. I know I am surrounded by enemies, but I forgive them for all that they have done against me, and I want them, as well as my friends, to pray for me."

Then, continuing, he said:

"I understand that my brother Jim was in here intending to kill the man who cuts the rope to hang me. If you are in the crowd, Jim, don't kill anybody on my account. I knew that if I was ever caught that I would have to pay the penalty, which I am now paying. I hate to die, but I have killed many a man who hated to die as bad as I do now. I know I am getting my just deserts."

When Longley had finished speaking, he knelt between two priests. He had been confined in the jail at Galveston for 18 months and while there he converted to the Catholic faith. Each priest put his hand on Bill's head and they knelt together in prayer for several moments.

BILL'S COUSINS had bought him a nice suit and he was neatly dressed. Young and fine-looking, with dark hair and long black mustache, and with a complexion as fair as a lady's, he looked so handsome. It seemed a pity he would have to die in such a terrible manner.

After Bill and the priests finished their prayer, Bill rose and walked straight to the trap-door and, bowing to the crowd, said, "Goodbye everybody."

The sheriff immediately placed the cap over his head, the rope around his neck, and bound his hands and feet. Then he got the hatchet and cut the rope which sprung the trap-door. He dropped through and his neck was broken. And thus the career of Bill Longley was terminated.

Mrs. Anderson, the widow of the man whom Longley had murdered, was present at the execution, with her two children. When the doctors pronounced Bill dead, she remarked that she was satisfied. Then they let the body down and placed it in the coffin.

The hanging rope was coiled and placed on Longley's breast and the lid of the coffin was nailed shut. Then a sorrowful father took charge of the remains of his wayward son.

WILLIAM JOHN L. SULLIVAN was born July 10, 1851, the son of Tom Sullivan and Summer McFarlen Sullivan, in Winston County, Miss. He and a brother became orphans at a young age and were beaten and abused by their guardian. They escaped and were taken in by a regiment of Confederate soldiers. At war's end, the two became wards of one of the soldiers, Bill Henley and his wife. Sullivan later became a cowboy, taking herds up the trail to Kansas, and joined Capt. Bill McDonald's Company B of Texas Rangers in 1889. He served for 12 years and wrote a book about his experiences. He died on May 21, 1911, and was buried at the Round Rock Cemetery.

80

STONE FOR AN INDIAN CHIEF

Clarence Wharton

HISTORIAN, ATTORNEY

The raiding days of the Kiowas were now over. Their war chiefs were gone. The tribe which numbered 5,000 at the time of the Little Arkansas Treaty in 1865 counted now about 1,200. Kicking Bird was the head chief and he was doing his best to encourage his people to become farmers.

In the late summer of 1874 Chief Satanta was back in the penitentiary of Texas, wearing his old number, 2107. He was about 65 years old. A feature writer from Scribner's Magazine who saw him in his prison garb wrote — "In the corridor of the penitentiary I saw a finely formed man with bronzed complexion and long flowing hair, a man of princely carriage on whom even the prison clothes seemed elegant. It was Satanta, the great chief of the Kiowas. He had come into the prison workroom where he was supposed to labor, but he did no more than spread himself on a pile of oakum."

For a time after his return to prison Satanta had a hope for release but as the years passed and he had no word from the world outside, he grew morose and showed despair.

When the autumn of 1878 approached and the leaves on the sweetgum on the hills of Huntsville were colored with its touch, Satanta would stand for hours at a window and gaze toward the northwest. It was the time for the annual buffalo hunt and for more than 50 autumns he had ridden with his warriors on this great occasion. He had told the Peace Commissioners at Medicine Lodge, "I do not want to settle down in houses you would build for us. I love to roam over the wild prairie where I am free and happy. When we settle down, we grow pale and die." Now he was settled down for good.

One night in October he opened the arteries in his neck and legs and was found bleeding to death. An attendant took him to the hospital on the second story and stanched his wounds and left him alone on a cot. When the attendant was gone, he dragged himself to a window and plunged headlong to the ground, where he was found dying.

ON THE SAME NIGHT that Satanta died at Huntsville, White Bird, to whom he had resigned his place in the tribe and to whom he had entrusted the magic lance, met his own fate. He and a small party of Kiowas had been permitted to go out on a last buffalo hunt and were accompanied by a detachment of soldiers from Fort Sill. The soldiers were to chaperon them and participate in the hunt.

They crossed the north fork of the Red River and were in Greer County and had camped for the night a few miles from their soldier escort. While sitting about their campfire, they were attacked from the darkness by a party of Texas Rangers. White Bird was killed. The Rangers rushed the camp and scalped him and cut off one of his fingers to get a ring he wore. Only the intervention of the soldiers saved the remainder of the Indians from slaughter.

Satanta, chief of the Kiowas

Satanta's bow was broken now, his bugle silent, his lance had lost its magic.

* * *

ONE EVENING IN DECEMBER 1879, Thomas Byrne sat in the little shack he called his office at his marble yard on Fannin Street in Houston. Byrne had long been the leading tombstone maker for Houston and the country all about. His work adorned many a Texas cemetery.

The day was late and it was time to shut up shop. A tall veiled middle-aged woman came to his door and without announcing her name opened negotiations with him for the erection of a tombstone. She wanted a memorial for Satanta who died in Huntsville in October the year before. She told him where the grave could be found.

Byrne was surprised to get this commission. He had marked the graves of late soldiers of the Confederacy and many a Texas pioneer but this was the first time his custom had been solicited for an Indian chief. Efforts to find out who she was or why she was interested met a stern rebuff. She would pay cash, and wanted to select a stone and give him the inscription. When she had chosen a slab of Georgia marble, she handed him a slip of paper with the inscription, "Satanta, Chief of the Kiowas" to which was added some words in Latin which Bryne did not understand. It would be interesting to know what act of kindness the ruthless warrior had done in his cruel career which merited such a tribute.

The next day his stonecutter inscribed the marble slab and the mysterious woman arranged for Bryne to go to Huntsville and place it. She paid him $127 and went away as quietly as she had come. Who she was, or where from, he never learned. He made an entry in his account book: "Stone for Indian Chief, $127, paid in cash."

The marker stood in the convicts' burial ground in the deep pine woods of Huntsville for 40 years, but has long since disappeared.

––––––––––

CLARENCE RAY WHARTON was born in 1873 in Tarrant County. He taught school from 1888 to 1892, studied law, was admitted to the bar, and moved to Houston where he entered the law firm of Baker, Botts, Baker, and Lovett. His interest in Texas history prompted him to become a writer. He died in Houston on May 1, 1941 and was buried there in Glenwood Cemetery.

81

ISLAND RANCH

Pat Dunn

CATTLE RANCHER

During the war, the enemy took your things and the Confederates "pressed" (confiscated) them. It amounted to the same thing. You never got your things back. It didn't matter whether they were taken by foes or friends. Your harness and things would be gone.

Uncle John Dunn lived close to Corpus Christi. Us kids used to go over to his place and play around there. In those days they would just dig a hole for a well about eight feet square and go down until the sand begin to cave in before they put in any curbing. Uncle John had some ox chains, wagon bows and things he did not want to get confiscated by the Confederates so he took all the best chains and bows and wheels off the wagons and hid them in the well.

They wouldn't let us play around the well. They said there

were lions and tigers in there and they would eat us up. I slipped up there anyway and peeped into the well. If there were any lions and tigers in there, I was going to find out about it. I saw Uncle John's ox rigs in the well and went back toward the barn.

About that time some of the Confederate soldiers came to "press" some of Uncle John's things. They looked at the wagons and harness and saw that there was nothing around but junk. They said, "Damn, Dunn, you're a teaming contractor; you must have better stuff than this. This is just pure junk. We can't use it."

I heard all that and said, "There's some good harness stuff down there in the well." My uncle slapped me and I went into the house crying. I told my aunt that Uncle John slapped me when I was telling them about the harness down in the well. She had little sympathy for me, and said, "No wonder you got slapped."

* * *

DURING THE WAR, ox teams were used to haul cotton from Alleyton near Columbus to Brownsville. Sometimes there were from 20 to 40 wagons in a long train. The man who hauled cotton to the border was paid more money for the hauling than the farmer received for the growing.

One day we had just loaded our wagon with cotton for the trip when my father died. He just died suddenly. The oldest boy in the family was 12 and the oldest girl was 13. My mother decided to haul the cotton to Brownsville and she took me along. I was six then.

We never got past Santa Rosa* because the war ended. The war was over and the Confederate soldiers were coming back. Some of them were in a bad humor. Close to Santa Rosa they met up with a train of wagons coming up

---

* Santa Rosa was a way station on the Cotton Road, six miles north of La Feria in Cameron County. Handbook of Texas.

Patrick F. Dunn, cattle rancher on Padre Island

from the border with loaded with dry goods and shoes and such things. The soldiers broke up the boxes and scattered things all over the ground. They threatened to burn our cotton, but they didn't. They were sure mad about something.

* * *

IN THE EARLY DAYS the range was all free. There were no pastures. Then people commenced to building fences and buying the land. My brother and I had some cattle and we had to go someplace, so went to Padre Island. That was

Dunn's old ranch headquarters after he sold the island

in 1879. At that time, I made arrangements with the law firm of McCampbell and Welch, the attorneys, whom I afterward bought out. I had made arrangements with them in 1878to move my cattle to the island, but didn't go until 1879. A man named Healey had some cattle out there.

From the time I first went on Padre Island in 1879 until 1925 when I sold out to Mr. Robertson and others, no one had possession of Padre Island but myself.

I built pens and shacks for my men to get in. I maintained four stations, you might call them, where I had a little cabin for myself and a place for the cook and hands to sleep in and pens and dipping vats and small pastures to put the horses in, and cattle sometimes. These were just small pastures where we could handle the cattle conveniently.

You can find good water most places on the island within a few feet of the surface. You can often find freshwater near the shore when you cannot find it near the center of the island. Storms brought in saltwater and it stood *in lakes for a long time. If you dig in those places, you'll find saltwater. But nearly everywhere you can go down a few feet and find good water.

My cattle drank from shallow cow wells. We called them tanks. They were shored up on the sides with barrel staves and salvaged wood to keep the sand out and the cattle would kneel to drink. These wells had to be kept cleaned out. The cattle grazed on the island grasses, the same vegetation one finds on the mainland in the sand belt.

There never was much trespassing on the island. Occasionally somebody would want to travel up the beach to Corpus Christi. I had men at Point Isabel to look after that for me. Mainly, people who went over to the island were fishermen.

On one occasion I had a lot of trouble with fishermen about one of my fences. They got to seining in the Gulf and ran into my fence and couldn't sein any further. They took the matter up with federal authorities during the war, said I was keeping them from getting fish to feed the people, and they finally made me put a gate there.

I FIRST MOVED to Padre Island to live with my family in 1884. We lived at the Settlement, 20 miles from the head of the island. I did not live there very long, five or six years. One of my children contracted scarlet fever and got paralysis, so we did not live there anymore, but would go there and stay for a few months.

I would not stay long at one place. I would come to the head of the island and then move on down to the next camp. I think it was about six of these stations (four main ones) that I kept up during the last 49 years.

The water tanks were not all at the stations. The stations were about 20 miles apart and we had water tanks between those stations. I had 75 tanks in 1916 when the storm destroyed them.

The use I made of the island was as a cattle ranch. I also ran a few sheep. The fences that I built there were for my convenience in handling the cattle.

The ranch house, built in 1907, faced east on Packery Channel. It was constructed of salvaged materials from shipwrecks. The cattle pens were made of mahogany driftwood.

The house was a two-story structure with wide porches. The walls were made with planks of Louisiana pine and the floors were made from the hatch covers of freighters. The door hinges were taken from steamer refrigerators. The chairs came from the wrecked steamer "Nicaragua" and hunks of coral rock were used as door stops. Whiskey barrels sat under the eaves to catch rainwater. The wash basin on the porch was a cask with Japanese writing on it. The house was never painted, inside or out.

Once, when Col. William Sterrett, a newspaperman, saw these things, he said, "Pat, everything you've got here is public property. It washed up on the beach and you just put it all together."

PATRICK FRANCIS DUNN was born on Oct. 10, 1858, the sixth child of Thomas Dunn Sr. and Catherine Hickey Dunn, who were married in Dublin in 1849 and left the next day for Texas. Pat Dunn married a widow, Clara Jones and adopted her daughter, Lalla. In 1879, Pat moved cattle belonging to his family (his mother and a brother) to Padre Island, where he operated a cattle ranch until he sold out to Col. Sam Robertson in 1926. He died on March 25, 1937. His wife Clara died in 1910. Both are buried in Rose Hill Cemetery.

82

A PHOTO FOR
QUANAH PARKER

Zoe Tilghman
BIOGRAPHER

Two Texas cattle ranchers whose cattle grazed on Indian lands north of the Red River, Burk Burnett and Dan Waggoner, invited Quanah Parker, chief of the Comanches, to visit the Stock Show at Fort Worth as their guest. He went and was treated with honor. There was less impudence and animosity than he usually encountered from whites and he enjoyed the visit thoroughly. Thereafter he rarely missed a Stock Show.

Quanah could speak English quite well and under the tutelage of his friends he learned the ways of the city. He still wore his native costume. He was described at the time as "A fine specimen of manhood; tall, muscular, gray eyes that looked straight through you; dark skin, perfect teeth. His dark brown hair — not the raven black of the Indian —

he wore in two braids tied with red cloth. He wore a buckskin tunic, leggings and moccasins trimmed with beads. A handsome Mexican blanket was thrown about his body and his hair was decorated with feathers of bright colors and little stuffed birds."

Quanah had seen books at the Indian Agency but in Fort Worth he found boys on the street selling newspapers. Burnett read to him from the paper: news items about the Sioux in Dakota; something about a great queen across the water; something about white men who objected to the cattlemen running their stock on some lands that adjoined the Cheyenne and Arapahoe reservations.

There were so many people in Fort Worth and the cattlemen all seemed to know one another and were greeted in the genial fashion of the cow country. As Quanah wandered about the pavilion of the Stock Show, he was accosted by a man who was looking at the cattle.

"You're Quanah Parker, I reckon, son of Cynthia Ann Parker that was stole off by the Comanches. Well, I saw her once after they brought her home. I hear she had a picture taken in Fort Worth one time, but I don't know who got it."

A picture of his mother! Quanah on a visit to his uncle Silas Parker and his wife Janey had seen the pictures which Janey kept in a little box. There was one of his mother and father, and of a sister.

One day Quanah passed a window where such pictures were displayed. He went in to ask if they had one of Cynthia Ann Parker. The proprietor was bewildered, but polite. No, he said, to take a picture the person would have to come in and sit before the little box. Quanah didn't understand. It was another of the white man's miracles, like the gas lights in the hotel rooms. But he talked with his friend Burnett and told him he would very much like to have a picture of his mother.

"He said there was one made?" Burnett asked. "Well, we'll try advertising in the papers. Quanah didn't understand this, either, so Burnett explained that he would go to the man who made the paper and would put into it a talk, a prayer, which would say that Quanah Parker wanted to get a picture of his mother Cynthia Ann. He would ask anyone who knew of such a picture to write a letter. They were to leave next day so Burnett hastily prepared the advertisement.

Three weeks later, back on the reservation, the Indian agent sent for Quanah. He told him, "I have something for you, Quanah, a letter and a package that came in the mail. It is from Sul Ross, who led the Rangers when they captured your mother. He read your request in the paper, the letter says, and knowing the man who had the picture he got a copy made and sends it to you. It's in the package."

Fumbling with the wrappings, Quanah took out the photograph. There, on heavy cardboard, was the likeness of Cynthia Ann, the face he had remembered through all the years. She was dressed in the ugly clothes of the white women and her hair was cut short as if for someone dead, and little Tau-tai-yah was in her arms nursing.

There was some magic power that held the spirit fast to the cardboard. It was his mother's spirit touching him that made him feel weak in the knees. And what magic, too, that his paper prayer had been heard! He asked the agent to write "and tell this man that my heart is very glad, that it is good of him to send the picture, although it was he who took her away." When Quanah went home he bade Weckeah, one of his four wives, to wrap it carefully in fine buckskin and, soon as she could, she must make a beautiful beaded case to keep it in, this image of the spirit of his mother.

––––––––––

ZOE AGNES STRATTON TILGHMAN was born Nov. 15, 1880 in Greenwood County, Kansas. She married William Matthew Tilghman, who was a friend of Quanah Parker. Her biography "Quanah, the Eagle of the Comanches" was published in 1938.

Quanah Parker, chief of the Comanches

Cynthia Ann Parker and little Tau-tai-yah (Prairie Flower)

83

THIS LAND IS MINE

Robert Maudslay

SHEEP RANCHER

The year 1882 found us, a family of seven, transplanted from the urban center of Manchester, England to the strange wilds of the hill country of Texas. Our dwelling was a hastily constructed frame house of two or three rooms, our "estate" a section of hilly unbroken land covered with cedar and dwarf oak trees.

The village of Bandera was two or three miles distant. The town of San Antonio was 50 miles down an old wagon road over which, in times past, government camels, Texas Rangers, and Army soldiers had traveled from an early fort at Camp Verde, several miles above us, to the door of the outer world, which was San Antonio.

The country at the time of our arrival was unfenced, except for cultivated fields and here and there were a few enclosures for saddle horses and calves whose mothers were supplying the farmers with milk. Livestock was the farmers chief sustenance and so their farms were called ranches, though they were infinitesimal compared to the great ranches I was to know later.

My older brother Harry had come before us to choose our place of settlement. It was probably the beauty of the hills that determined his choice of the Bandera country. Harry was never, at any time, a practical man. If he had been, he might have chosen the rich black land to the east. But Harry scorned to be a farmer. Where, for him, would be the adventure he craved?

Land was cheap in Bandera, which suited our limited capital. And in the hills was color borrowed from the great plains beyond. Life was western, but on a smaller scale. It offered a great deal of romance with little of the danger. And here in these rugged hills Harry could dream of adventure without actually having to face it.

THE WOMEN IN THE FAMILY didn't have Harry's eyes to see the glorious land of adventure. I am afraid they noticed little on their arrival in the romantic city of San Antonio except the intense heat, it being midday in August.

I had not, nor had any of us, learned to dispense with superfluous clothing. We arrived all buttoned up. My hat was a black bowler, or derby, with a very narrow brim. It was nothing less than torture in the August noonday sun. Harry met us and laughed when he saw me. "Take that coat off and throw that damned hat away," he said, and took me to where I could get more suitable clothes.

We camped on Red Bluff Creek that night. This was the first time any of us had spent a night in the open. We could hear tree frogs and crickets, but no other sound disturbed the profound stillness of the night. After living practically all our lives in a great city, and becoming accustomed to its incessant mechanical noises, we found the first night in the woods almost painful in its natural silence.

We were on our way again early the next morning and arrived at our new home long before the sun went down.

Everything was new to us: the type of dwelling Harry had made ready for our arrival, the food we were expected to eat, and the labor we were expected to perform. Our house was built of rough lumber with strips nailed over the cracks. It was on a slight elevation about 100 yards from Bandera Creek, which was our source of water. One can form a very accurate estimate of the amount of water a family uses when he has to carry it in a bucket for a hundred yards. My estimate was that we used more water than any other family on the face of the earth.

Mother would tell me, after I had spent a day clearing the land and chopping wood, "Robert, run down and bring up a couple of buckets of water while you're resting." There are two sides to a request like that, and only one of them is funny.

My mother worked with us in clearing the fields. Perhaps she worked harder than Harry and I at burning brush and roots. I chopped all the trees down and used the logs and some of the brush to build a fence. Barbed wire hadn't made its appearance in the hills yet.

We couldn't get the whole field grubbed out before it was time to plant. We broke up the ground anyhow and planted the grain in between the stumps. This is what might have been expected of Englishmen from Manchester. When it came up, we couldn't get anyone with a machine to cut it. Oh, we were great farmers!

We bought one or two small bunches of cows. Most of them were old ones the owners wanted to get rid of. If any dry cows happened to get reasonably fat, a neighbor up the creek would kill one, sell us the beef, then come around and help us eat it — a most obliging neighbor.

Things went on this way for some time. One day our friend Ike Stevens came around and said, "You boys ought to get out of the cow business. You can't make a success of it in this part of the country." We took his advice, traded the cows off for mares, bought a fine stallion, and commenced to raise horses.

We began to do a great deal better. Nobody wanted to eat horses and it was unsafe to steal them. Horse theft, we found, was a more heinous crime in Texas than manslaughter, while cattle stealing was more or less an honorable diversion.

When the piano we bought in New York arrived, my mother and sisters moved into town and established a private school. The women of the family did exceptionally well with this venture. Today, a number of older citizens of Bandera owe a lot of their academic knowledge to my mother and sisters. From what Harry and I could gather, the Maudslay School in Bandera did a good job with French, music, drawing, and mathematics. But when it came to history, they pretty much dispensed with the American Revolution and the Civil War in favor of a thorough knowledge of the successive kings and queens of Britain.

Harry and I were left to our own devices. This included a great deal of poker-playing, in which we generally lost, and horse-racing, in which we generally won.

FENCING BECAME general all over the country about this time. Albert Maverick and Charles Montague began to put up fences and Mr. Strickland also fenced some of his land. Thereby hangs a tale. Old surveys show that our land and that of Mr. Strickland were supposed to meet. But when the line was run out, it was discovered that our lands were not actually adjoining. There was a quarter-mile-wide strip of land between us, extending the whole of our northern boundary. As for the records, nobody knew this existed. I took immediate advantage of the circumstance. Under the laws of Texas, to stake a claim to this property I had to live on it and make it my home for three years, after which I would get clear title to it. Harry and I put up a very small house on it and I moved in.

Robert Maudslay: Life wasn't like this in Manchester

It was more like a dry goods box than a house. I could stand up in it, barely, and I could turn around in it without scraping its sides. But it would satisfy the legal requirements. I slept in it on occasion and sometimes ate a meal there. I even commenced to dig a well, though I only got down about two or three feet. The land was good land and it would make a valuable addition to our holdings.

It also aroused the greed of another man. Two weeks after my claim had been surveyed and recorded, Tom Stevens rode by to tell us that a neighbor named J——— C——— had moved on to my land and laid claim to it by putting up a shack. This consisted of a wagon bed into which he had thrown an old quilt or two and a few cooking utensils.

I took a horse up there, intending to pull the wagon off my property, and found that the running gear of the wagon had been removed and stakes held it firmly in place. There was no way of hitching to it and pulling it away. I went back to the ranch and reported my failure. Harry filled a can with kerosene and said, "Come on."

At the wagon, Harry shouted, "If there's anyone in there, come out!" There was no answer so he sprinkled the "house" with kerosene and we set it on fire.

My contentious neighbor came by next morning. He asked if I knew who had set fire to his camp and I told him that I did. That evening a deputy sheriff came out to place us under arrest, but instead accepted our promise to appear in court the next Monday. The charge was willful burning of private property. We were placed under a $1,000 bond to appear at the next district court.

THE TRIAL WAS continued several times and Harry and I got quite a lot of free publicity in the Bandera Bugler. We had the sympathy of our neighbors, some of whom told us that J—— C—— had done this before, with the sole purpose of extracting a cash settlement for the land. It was easy money, when it worked.

One day Harry was in George Hay's Saloon when J—— C—— came in and said, "Hello, you damned ——" and similar compliments, then raised a foot to kick the pipe out of Harry's teeth. Harry caught his foot while it was in the air and threw him backwards. J—— C—— grabbed a billiard cue and Harry landed two or three punches before they could be separated. Harry went to the justice of peace and lodged a complaint of assault. J—— C—— was fined $17.50, which added to his hard feelings against us.

Soon afterwards, Sheriff Buck Hamilton asked Harry if he had a gun. Being told that he didn't, the sheriff handed him a six-shooter and said, "Take this one. I think you're going to need it."

Things were getting interesting, and quite to Harry's taste, and perhaps a little to mine. Life had never been like this in Manchester. Harry, not being used to six-guns, was playing with the trigger and it went off by accident. He was in Carmichael's store and at the time J—— C—— was standing just outside. He jumped on his horse and left town, no doubt thinking that he had been shot at. The bullet, however, hit Carmichael's safe and endangered no one but the bookkeeper.

The day of our trial came around and our lawyer advised us to plead guilty. We were fined $100 and costs, which we immediately paid. A civil suit for $200 we just ignored, and judgement went against us, by default. Neither Harry or I had the money, and where there isn't anything, nothing is the result. J—— C—— got nothing.

This land that I "fought" so hard for I lost in a horse race, won it back again, then sold it, making more than enough money to pay for the amusement I had had in keeping it. If you look, you can find on the old Land Office map of Bandera County, sandwiched in between the large rectangles bearing the names of the forgotten land grants of the King of Spain, a tiny almost infinitesimal rectangle that bears the name of Rob't Maudslay. It is proof that an Englishman can acquire a little bit of the original Texas.

ROBERT MAUDSLAY was born in England in 1855. He and his brother Harry, mother and four sisters moved from Manchester to the Bandera area in 1882. His mother and sisters established a private school in Bandera. Robert turned to raising sheep and for more than two decades trailed sheep over much of the Southwest. He retired from the sheep business in 1905 and moved to his sister's ranch in the Bandera hills. He never married. He wrote a chronicle of his experiences not with eye for publication but for his nieces. He died in 1939 when he was 84.

84

GERONIMO IN SAN ANTONIO

Mary Olivia Handy

AUTHOR

Fort Sam Houston in San Antonio sent its last battalion of soldiers to take part in an Indian expedition in 1885. The movement was occasioned by activities of the Apaches under Geronimo and other Indian leaders in New Mexico and Arizona.

Post returns for the last half of 1885 and most of 1886 make regular reference to what was going on in that area.

On Dec. 19, 1885, a battle was fought with Apaches at Little Dry Creek, New Mexico. Several Indians and soldiers were killed in the fight.

On Sept. 10, 1886, Geronimo, Naches* and 30 other Apaches arrived as captives at Fort Sam Houston. They were confined by order of the commanding general, with the Quadrangle of the post serving as a stockade.

---

* Also spelled Naiche or Natchez, son of Cochise.

Apache Chief Geronimo

Geronimo had been induced to surrender by Lt. Gatewood, of the Sixth Cavalry, according to Leo Turner in "The Story of Fort Sam Houston." Geronimo's band was never really captured; they were persuaded to give up by Lt. Gatewood, in whom Geronimo had a great deal of confidence.

They were placed on a special train at Fort Bowie, Ariz., and were escorted by Capt. H. M. Lawton and the Fourth Cavalry to Fort Sam Houston.

One can easily picture the thousands of people who must have gathered around the old passenger railway station on Austin Street the day of Geronimo's arrival. Many would have followed the prisoners and the army escort up Grayson Street to the post.

The Quadrangle and bell tower at Fort Sam Houston

In the fort's Quadrangle, tents were pitched to serve for their shelters during their stay in San Antonio. One can well imagine the feelings Geronimo must have had when the commander of the Department of Texas, Gen. David Stanley, came to call and promised this brave Apache warrior the protection of the army.

There are many stories connected with the Apaches' time in San Antonio. According to one source, while they were staying at the Quadrangle, they were provided with spending money and the dry goods stores of San Antonio sent out wagons with bolts of brightly colored calico that was prized by the Indian women.

Another story said the Apaches were taken on a tour and one of their stops was the Lone Star Brewery, where they were given ice-cold beer. It was said that they could not understand what the beer was, where it came from, and what made it so cold. They were given chunks of ice to taste and Geronimo put his in his pocket. He could not understand what became of it after it melted. *Where did it go?*

Still another story said the Apaches were taken atop the 87-foot-high bell tower in the Quadrangle. They were talking and pointing and deciding which path to take for their journey home when the clock in the tower struck. The Indians were horror stricken. They rushed to the ground, thoroughly shaken and frightened.

The tales may be apocryphal, since there is no proof for their authenticity, but probably if they were not true then other colorful ones likely were. It was only natural that Indians who had been wild and free should find aspects of civilization strange and threatening.

The Apaches remained in their Quadrangle reservation for 40 days, until Oct. 22, 1886, when they were put on a train, with Company K of the 16th Infantry as escort, and sent to Fort Pickens, Fla., to an island 10 miles from Pensacola.

———————

MARY OLIVIA HANDY (Parker) was the daughter of Gen. Thomas Troy Handy who once commanded the Fourth Army at Fort Sam Houston in San Antonio. Mary Olivia Handy later married Harry J. Parker of San Antonio and they had two children. Her book "The History of Fort Sam Houston" was published by the Naylor Company in San Antonio in 1951.

85

CROSSING THE REEF

Leona Gussett
MRS. ROYALL GIVENS

My husband, Royall Givens, was in the insurance business for a long time. But he is best known as a wholesale fish shipper. He was the first man to ship drum from Corpus Christi. He called it "white rock." It was shipped in slabs and there was a huge market for it. He patented the name "Star Brand" in Mexico, where many of his fish products were sold. He did a big business in shipping turtles, which were raised by Mr. Ritter.

Mr. Givens also did a good business in shipping bones. They would be piled in great heaps as high as a house. They were loaded on ships, sometimes making up the entire cargo.

Wonderful fish fries were held at Mr. Givens' fish house on North Beach by the reef. Fifty or 60 young people would gather and spread the supper on the long tables that were used for opening the oyster shells.

My father, Norwick Gussett, had three schooners running between Corpus Christi and New York. They would take out a great deal of wool and bring back cargoes of merchandise. One of the schooners was named the "Leona" for me. It was built in New York at a cost of $30,000. My father allowed many people to make trips to New York on the "Leona" without charge.

The big exposition in New Orleans (December 1884 to June 1885) was well-attended by Corpus Christi people. Mr. and Mrs. W. S. Rankin were married in New Orleans while the exposition was going on. That was on April 16, 1885. Pat Whelan and his daughter Maggie attended the wedding.

At the exposition one could ride on what was, I think, the first electric streetcar ever built. It cost 25 cents to ride just one block. You want to know what the herdies were like? They were like streetcars now only they were drawn by horses. The fare was very low but I don't remember how much. I never would ride in them. We called them "herdies," though the correct name was herdic coaches.

MR. HEATH AND my father ran mule cars from the Miramar, a beautiful hotel on North Beach, out to the Alta Vista Hotel. People would go to Aberdeen on these cars, which were dragged back and forth by two little mules. For a time, we had steam engines operating the streetcars here. They were regular engines, with smoke pouring out as they went down the street. Mr. McKenzie, the house painter, was run over and killed by one of these engines.

Before the railroad was completed, there was no way of crossing the reef except by horseback or carriage of some sort. Once, while the railroad trestle was under construction, my sister Susie and I were taking our younger sister Elise to San Antonio to place her in the convent.

We were crossing the reef in two hacks, the girls in one and the men in another. The horses of our hack fell into a

Horses and wagons crossed Nueces Bay on the "reef road"

hole. The men had to get out of their hack — wetting their good clothes — and carry us girls in their arms to land. Dr. Harry Hamilton carried one of my sisters; I don't recall who carried me, but whoever it was had an armful.

Sometimes women would cross the reef on their horses. When they came to the channel, near the south end of the reef, the horses would have to swim. One day I saved a little boy's life in that channel. He was sitting on the end of a scow, pulling it back and forth, and in some careless manner he fell into the water. His grandmother in the boat screamed for help. I got there in time to rescue him.

LEONA GUSSETT GIVENS was born on May 17, 1868, the daughter of Norwick Gussett and Margaret Evans Gussett. She married Royall Givens, a wholesale fish dealer. Leona Gussett Givens died on Oct. 12, 1948 and was buried in Holy Cross Cemetery.

86

THE KING OF RANCHES

Richard Harding Davis

JOURNALIST, AUTHOR

The inhabited part of a Texas ranch, the part on which the people who own it live, bears about the same proportion to the rest of the ranch as a lighthouse does to the sea around it. To an Eastern man, it appears almost as lonely. It is the loneliness of the life that will impress the visitor who comes from places of closely built houses.

Those who live on the ranches will tell you that they do not find it lonely, that they grow so fond of the great open pastures about them that they become independent of the rest of mankind, and that a trip to the city once a year is all they ask of the big world outside the barb-wire fences.

I am speaking now of those ranch owners who live on the range and not of those who hire a foreman and spend their time and money in the San Antonio Club. They are no more ranchmen than the absentee landlord who lives in London is a gentleman farmer.

King Ranch headquarters and main house in 1890

The largest ranch in the United States, and probably in the world, is in Texas and belongs to Henrietta King, the widow
of Capt. Richard King. The ranch lies 45 miles south of Corpus Christi. The ladies who come to call on Mrs. King drive from her front gate, over as good a road as any in Central Park, for 10 miles before they arrive at her front door. The butcher and baker and iceman, if such existed, would have to drive 30 miles from the back gate before they reached her kitchen. This ranch is enclosed by barb-wire for more than 300 miles, covers 700,000 acres in extent, and holds 100,000 head of cattle and 3,000 broodmares in its various pastures.

This property is under the ruling of Robert J. Kleberg, Mrs. King's son-in-law. He has under him a superintendent, who himself has the charge of 300 cowboys and 1,200 ponies reserved for their use. There are cowboys and then there are King Ranch cowboys, or I should say, vaqueros, as the cowboys on King Ranch are usually called.

It is disconcerting for the man from the East to find that these are not like the mythical cowboys who ride with both legs at right angles, shooting their six-guns into the air to frighten the greenhorn or tenderfoot. The cowboys I saw on the King Ranch stand up and politely take off their sombreros when one is leaving their camp.

The ranch is carefully organized and moves on sound business principles, as much so as any good bank.

One thing the man from the East could not at first understand is how the 100,000 head of cattle, wandering at large over the range, are ever collected together. He sees a dozen or more steers here, a bunch of horses there, and a single steer or two a mile off. Even as he looks at them, they disappear into the brush, and as far as his chance of finding them again would be, they might as well stand 40 miles away at the other end of the ranch. But this is a very simple problem to the ranchman.

Mr. Kleberg, for instance, receives an order from a firm in Chicago calling for 1,000 head of cattle. The breed of cattle which the firm wants is grazing in a corner of the range fenced in by barb-wire, and marked pale blue for convenience on a beautiful map blocked out in colors, like a patchwork quilt, which hangs in Mr. Kleberg's office.

WHEN THE ORDER is received, Mr. Kleberg sends a vaquero on a pony to tell the men near that particular pale blue pasture to round up 1,000 head of cattle. At the same time, he directs his superintendent to send as many vaqueros as may be needed to that pasture to "hold" 1,000 head of cattle on the way to the railroad station.

The boys being sent to the pasture, which we suppose to be ten miles square, will take 10 of their number and five extra mounts each and go directly to that pasture's water-tank. A cow will not wander more than two and a half miles from water, and so with the water-tank as the rendezvous, the finding of the cattle is comparatively easy, and 10 men can round up 1,000 head in a day or two. When they have them all together, they drive them to the station.

At the station, the agent for the Chicago firm and the agent for King Ranch ride through the herd together. If they disagree as to the fitness of any in the herd, an outsider is called in and his decision is final. The cattle are then driven on to the cars and Mr. Kleberg's responsibility is at an end.

In the spring there is a general roundup and thousands and thousands of steers are brought in from the different pastures. Those for which contracts have been made during the winter are shipped off to market and the calves are branded.

It is difficult to imagine one solitary family occupying a territory larger than some eastern states — an area of territory that, in the east, would support a state capital, with a governor and legislature, and numerous small towns, with competing railroad lines and rival baseball teams. And all that may be said of this side of the question of ranch life is that when we are within Mrs. King's house, we would imagine it was one of 20 others touching shoulder to shoulder on Madison Avenue. The distant howl of coyotes in the night is all that tells us that the hansom cabs are not rushing up and down outside the front door.

RICHARD HARDING DAVIS, born on April 18, 1864, was one of the leading journalists of his era. He was a war correspondent who reported from the Spanish-American War, the Boer War in South Africa, the Russo-Japanese War, and World War I. He was also a popular novelist and playwright. His wife Cecil Clark Davis was also famous, as a wealthy heiress and painter. The description of his visit to King Ranch, in 1890, was included his book, "The West From a Car Window." He died on April 11, 1916 and was buried in Leverington Cemetery in Roxborough, Pa.

87

THE BILL COLLECTOR

Owen P. White
WRITER

One afternoon my father, a doctor in El Paso, handed me a bunch of about 20 bills and his eyes twinkled as he told me to go out and collect them. I looked at the addresses and gasped. Every one of them bore a number somewhere on Utah Street. This was a world I did not know.

"Dad," I said, "You don't mean that I'm to go down there, and go in those houses, and get this money from those painted women?"

But he did mean it. He knew what he was doing. He knew that in common with almost every other normal 12-year-old kid in El Paso, my feelings regarding the girls on Utah Street was one of overwhelming curiosity mixed up with some kind of mysterious fear. It was true.

Many times, sneaking out at night, I had walked down Utah Street to take in the sights, but I always kept strictly to the middle of the street. I didn't dare tackle the sidewalks for fear that some of the semi-naked painted ladies, standing in doorways, or leaning out of windows, would grab me, drag me inside, and ravish me. But, "to be or not to be, that is the question." Did I want to be ravished? I didn't yet know. That was something I was beginning to get curious about. That was why my father, who knew I was curious about it, wanted me to go down and collect those bills from those women. He didn't explain it to me, but I got his idea when he said in reply to my protest:

"Of course, son, I want you to go to those places and collect those bills. Why not? Those women won't hurt you. They're not nearly as bad as most people say they are. In fact, many of them are very good and the sooner you find that out the easier it will be for you to get along with them a few years from now when you'll be calling on them for something other than to collect money."

I'LL NEVER CEASE to be grateful to my father for sending me out with those bills. It cured me of curiosity. By calling on the Utah Street ladies between three and four in the afternoon, when they were just getting up, often nursing hangovers, with their warpaint off and face grease on, their hair done up in curlers, the air in their rooms heavy with the odor of liquor and cigarette smoke and stale perfume, I unavoidably came to the conclusion that the beauty of sin, as they peddled it, was entirely mythical.

As for their treatment of me, in the many months that I collected accounts from them not one of those women ever said a wicked word to me. Instead, because I was Doctor White's kid, and they had great respect for him, they were very nice to me. They paid me and I really learned to like many of them. But I was not so deluded as not to know that when they were practicing their profession, they were very tough sisters. They had to be. They had some tough men to deal with. Generally, their dealings were carried on at night. Sometimes, though, due to the early arrival in town of men who couldn't wait, hell would begin to heave in the red-light district in the middle of the afternoon. When this happened, my job became very interesting.

I'll never forget, for instance, the afternoon when Bass Outlaw, a deputy U. S. marshal, Kid McKittrick, and an unknown man started to shoot up Miss Tillie Howard's very high-class establishment.

I was not 200 feet from Tillie's place. I was headed there to present bills to a couple of her girls when the shooting began. I heard a fusillade of shots, a police whistle, a few more shots, and then running feet from Tillie's front door.

DASHING ACROSS the street and into an Italian saloon went the unknown man. Behind him, with a gun in his hand, limping badly but making good time, was Uncle John Selman.* Uncle John crossed the street, pushed open the swinging door of the Italian saloon, and fired one shot. Turning, and seeing me, he asked if my Dad was in his office. "I reckon so," I said. "What's the matter?"

"Bass Outlaw shot me in the leg," said Uncle John, as he hobbled away.

I went into Tillie's place to see what had happened. It was easy to assemble the particulars. Early in the day, Outlaw, McKittrick, and the stranger started to lay the foundation for a spree. By three o'clock that preliminary had been completed, and as the ethics of the enterprise demanded that, after a certain amount of liquor had been consumed, the next step was to shoot up some sporting house. The trio chose Tillie's place as the one in which they would put on this show.

No sooner had they arrived and gotten inside and pulled out their guns and cracked loose at the china bric-a-brac and chandeliers than Miss Tillie, foreseeing a rough time

---

* John Henry Selman, "Old John" or "Uncle John," was an outlaw and lawman, gambler and city marshal. As related here, he killed Bass Outlaw in Tillie Howard's brothel on April 5, 1894. He killed gunman John Wesley Hardin in the Acme Saloon on Aug. 19, 1895. Handbook of Texas.

ahead for everybody, ran out on the back porch and began blowing her police whistle.

Hearing that whistle, Constable John Selman, who was playing seven-up in the Monte Carlo, ran into the alley and started climbing over Tillie's back fence. As Selman threw his leg over the fence, Bass Outlaw, who had come out on the porch to take away Tillie's police whistle, saw it and just for the hell of it put a bullet into Selman's leg. No one bullet ever stopped John Selman and this one didn't either. But it did give him a personal interest in what was going on in Tillie's place.

Selman, limping across the yard, went into the back hall, where he was instantly shot at, and missed. But Selman didn't miss. With his first shot he got Outlaw, who dropped in the hall. With his second shot he destroyed McKittrick in one of the parlors. With his third shot, as we have already seen, he killed the stranger in the Italian saloon.

When I got inside Tillie's, the atmosphere was full of blue smoke, mad women and ear-scalding profanity. The floor was littered with a couple of dying citizens and it was clear that Miss Tillie and her girls didn't give a damn about that part of it. They were hopping mad because the two dying citizens were bleeding all over some costly Oriental rugs.

OWEN PAYNE WHITE was the son of Dr. Alward and Katherine White. He was born at El Paso on June 9, 1879. White married Hazel Harvey in 1920, the year he began work as a columnist for the El Paso Herald. His first book, "Out of the Desert," was published in 1923 and he moved to New York. His "Autobiography of a Durable Sinner" was published in 1942. He died on Dec 7, 1946, when he was 67. He was buried in Cutchoque Cemetery in Cutchoque, New York.

88

BIG DAY IN HAVANA

T. F. Fitzsimmons and Robert Hall

SOLDIERS

T. F. FITZSIMMONS: Sunday, New Year's Day, Jan. 1, 1899 was a gala day in Havana. The First Texas (our outfit) and the Second Louisiana regiments marched into the city early in the morning to witness the raising of the American flag over Morro Castle. At 12 p.m. the Spanish flag was lowered and the Stars and Stripes raised in its place.

The battleships in the harbor each fired a 21-gun salute. All the ships were decorated with American and Cuban flags. It was a grand sight. We expected trouble, but there was nothing but cheers for "los Americanos."

On the morning of our arrival in the harbor, two days before, we met a Spanish transport going out with Spanish soldiers. The Spanish and the American soldiers cheered and waved their hats at each other. The poor fellows seemed to be glad they were going home.

The health of our regiment was never better than it is now. While we were at Savannah, there never was a morning that we did not have one name on the sick report book. Not one name has been on the book since we have been here. Our camp location is a good one. It gets quite warm between 10 a.m. and 3 p.m., but the rest of the time it is very pleasant.

We are not allowed to visit Havana except on special business. Enlisted men are not permitted to go unless they are accompanied by an officer, who is held responsible for their behavior. This country is like Mexico, with the same kind of stone buildings, cobble-stone streets, and no sidewalks to mention. It does seem strange that there are so many Negroes here who can't speak English.

* * *

ROBERT HALL: Jan. 8, 1899, Havana. We were paid off the other day, when there was a hot time in the old camp that day because we were not allowed to go into town.

Everything is very dear here. Eggs are worth ten cents each and butter sells for 60 cents a pound, and it is stuff not fit for a dog to eat. Land is sold at $500 an acre and most of it is poor land at that — rocks and hills. Every hill you see has a little fort on top of it.

The girls here are the prettiest I ever saw.

The Cubans sure yelled when they saw us coming. They think the Americans are the only people and have got so that they won't take Spanish money at all. A Spanish one-cent coin is as large as an American half-dollar. If you get an American dollar changed into Spanish money, you will have more money than you can carry.

The Cubans say it was the Spanish who blew up the "Maine". They sure hate the Spaniards. The Cubans were so happy the day the Americans took charge that they put out American and Cuban flags on every home. They threw us cigars in the parade and gave us stuff to drink. Some of them even kissed the mane and tail of Gen. Lee's horse. They went crazy. I never saw the like.

Some of the Cubans are half-starved and have hardly any clothes on them. All the houses are made of stone. I have not seen a frame house since I have been here. Some of the people cook on top of their houses.

The Cubans sure have funny stuff to drink. Two drinks will put you to sleep for the rest of the day.

Havana is full of Americans looking for jobs. The big rich bugs are buying or getting hold of most of the land. If there is any money to be made, they will make it.

I don't know when we will ever go home. Gib Rogers has his discharge and is working up town for fifty dollars a month. I am getting tired of army life. They can't turn me loose any too soon. One of the soldiers in the Second Louisiana regiment shot another soldier over a game of craps. The body was buried under a tree.

———

TOBIAS FRANCIS (TOBE) FITZSIMMONS was the first lieutenant of Company E, the former Kenedy Rifles, of the 1ˢᵗ Texas Volunteer Regiment. Fitzsimmons, born on Dec. 4, 1872, was the son of Joseph E. Fitzsimmons and Eleanor Reynolds Fitzsimmons. He died on July 8, 1938 and was buried in Holy Cross Cemetery. ROBERT REID HALL, the son of Amelia Reid Hall and John A. Hall, was born July 10, 1881. He served in the Spanish-American War as a member of Company E, First Texas, formerly the Kenedy Rifles. Hall was a longtime county commissioner. Bob Hall Pier on Padre Island was named for him. He died on Nov. 23, 1960 and was buried at Rose Hill Cemetery.

89

VALLEY OF LONG HOLLOW

J. Frank Dobie
AUTHOR

Papa used to recall how Ramirenia Creek was a running stream when he first knew it — before the lands along it were overgrazed, thus making them shed rather than retain the rainfall. When I was a boy the Ramirenia and the Lagarto creeks no longer ran constantly but they had good waterholes. Then the waterholes filled with sand and we had to bore wells and put up windmills in pastures that were once bountifully supplied with creek water.

One day while Papa and I were waiting in the Primm pasture for another rider, I got down off my horse and picked up a rounded stick. It was sharp at one end with a groove in it just below the head. Papa said it was a stake pin.

Some rider had staked his horse on the prairie where I stood, not a bush in sight to tie a horse to. A person would have a hard time now finding in that area a spot of land free enough of mesquite and other brush to stake a horse in.

Growing up on the ranch, no play world could have been more interesting than the one we Dobie children made for ourselves. With pegs, twine and sticks we built big pastures and stocked them with spools, from which my mother's sewing machine had used the thread, for horses; with tips of cattle horns, sawed off in the branding chute in the ranch corrals, for cattle; and with oak galls for sheep and dried small shells for goats. The goats could not be branded, but we branded the other stock with pieces of baling wire heated red-hot.

Our ranch house was in a grove of live oaks on a plateau overlooking the valley of Long Hollow. For most of its distance, this hollow used to be a drainage way, its bottom grassed over in places, carrying water only after hard rains, though it could get on a boom now and then.

When I first knew it, the valley was a cornfield. Then it was turned out as a part of what we called the Horse Pasture, where the milk cows and saddle horses were kept. In time, this old field grew into a dense thicket of mesquite and huisache.

Thousands of times I have looked across Long Hollow and something from those vistas remains deep inside me. One spring the bluebonnets on Long Hollow were up to my stirrups. They bloom that high inside me every spring.

The house had a paling fence around it and in the yard were more flowers — roses, chrysanthemums, cannas, violets — than any other ranch in that part of Texas had. The garden, very prolific, was where vegetables grew. They and the flowers were irrigated from a cypress cistern and a dirt tank in which a windmill, back of the kitchen, pumped water.

The yard was bare of grass, in the tradition that guarded against snakes. Occasionally a rattlesnake was killed in it.

My father tended the flowers as well as the vegetables. He set out orange trees, which never bore. He laid out a croquet ground in the shade of oaks. He could do anything.

J. Frank Dobie: The stillness of day and night was broken by windmill lifting rods.

He liked cutting up meat and the meat he butchered was all we had. It was ample. Like many other ranchmen, he never hunted. He hoped his eldest son would choose a career better than ranching — that of a clean-collared banker, perhaps. He paid 8 and 10 percent to his banker and liked him.

Back of the house was a caliche rock smokehouse and on behind the smokehouse was a big stable combined with corn crib, hay loft and rooms for tools, saddles and buggies. Along the rear end of it grew a row of pomegranates. Their fruit was a treat. Near them a stout mustang grapevine twined up into the Coon Tree, an oak which a chicken-stealing coon had been seen or shot. High up across the branches, we children had a platform — "the house in the Coon Tree" we called it.

BEHIND THE COON TREE, next to the barn, were a shed and three pens. The smallest was for the milk calves, which we boys rode; the largest for driving the saddle horses into and for the milk cows. Except in winter, when two or three were fed, there were 12 or 15 cows, all of range breeding, more various in color than productive of milk.

The third pen held hay ricks and fronted the horse stalls, but only the buggy horses and work teams were fed. Before daylight somebody — and in time that job was mine — caught the night horse out of the little pasture in front of the house and rode to bring in the remuda* from the Horse Pasture.

Many a morning I walked stooping over to the ground every few steps trying to skylight a night horse taking his sleep standing up. He always had a drag-rope around his neck, and I would try to get hold of it before waking him.

The sandy ground in front of the big stable was paved with caliche. Red ants bored through the caliche and

---

* Remuda was a vaquero word for horse herd or string of remounts.

colonized below. They have a vicious sting. We saddled our horses on the caliche or close to it. While we were saddling, the horses would stamp the caliche in order to knock off the red ants crawling above their hoofs.

After I went off to college I half awakened before daylight every morning to the sound of horses stamping their feet on the caliche. I could hear the plopping down of saddles on horse backs and the metallic clinking of cinch rings and spurs. I never hear those sounds before daylight any more, but the memory of both the actuality and the half-dream is a part of me.

The jackdaws — grackles, as called now — that nestled in the oaks about our house; the calves sucking their mothers and playing about them in pasture; the cows, chewing cuds in the milk pen; the sandhill cranes fluting their long cries on a winter evening; the coyotes serenading from every side right after dark; my horse Buck pointing his ears when I walked into the pen and seeming to ask if I were going to ride him or Brownie; the green on the mesquite in early spring so tender that it emanated into the sky; the stillness of day and night broken by windmill lifting rods; the south wind in the tree tops; the rhythm of a saddle's squeak in the night — these the land gave me. Its natural rhythms and the eternal silence entered into me to remain as long as I remain.

J. FRANK DOBIE was born on Sept. 26, 1888 in Live Oak County, the first of six children of Richard and Ella Byler Dobie. His early life on the Dobie ranch became the foundation for his books, including "A Vaquero of the Brush Country," "Coronado's Children," "The Longhorns," "The Mustangs," and many others. Dobie died on Sept. 18, 1964 and was buried in the State Cemetery.

90

SELLING TEXAS LANDS

George H. Paul
LAND PROMOTER

The George H. Paul Company bought four combination dining cars and we obtained Pullman cars as we needed them to bring people from all over the country to see the lands that were available for sale in South Texas. Special trains were run regularly every two weeks for four years.

Our agents all over the country would interest people in making the trip and trains would bring them to Kansas City, where they would board the South Texas Special. If a person bought property, then the price of the train fare was deducted from the purchase price of the land.

When we first started, people in South Texas were doubtful we could successfully colonize the barren cattle country and turn it into farmland. But I guess that we had a pretty good day in the development of most of the towns and territory in the region. During four years, from 1907

"Homeseekers" gather in front of the George H. Paul excursion train at Robstown

through 1911, we brought more than 300,000 persons to the Corpus furnish and all the other available teams Christi area and many of them bought land and established farms. The towns followed the farms.

One of the great problems we had to contend with in those early days of selling Driscoll Ranch lands around Robstown, and Taft Ranch lands in San Patricio, was transportation.

In 1907, when we first started, there were not more than half a dozen automobiles in Nueces County. We would not have used automobiles to show the land anyway. They could not be driven through the brush, even after we had removed the largest brush from the section lines after the survey.

We had to use horses and vehicles of various kinds, just everything we could find. There were three livery barns in Corpus Christi, one in Alice and one in San Diego. They could furnish quite a few spring wagons that would hold

George H. Paul, land promoter from Iowa

eight persons besides the driver. They had a few carriages that would hold three or four besides the drivers. On most trips, we would take all the buggies these livery barns could from Corpus Christi to San Diego and across the river north to Skidmore and Mathis, including Sinton, Taft and Gregory. All these vehicles would arrive at Robstown either the night before our train came in or early that morning. On a typical trip, by the time we left Kansas City, we knew how many people we would have to have conveyances for and we would wire our Corpus Christi sales manager and he would start lining up these vehicles.

One morning our train was standing on the siding at Robstown. We were making ready for a trip to the country to look over the land. It was a beautiful sunny morning. We had a very spruce elderly gentleman with us from Nebraska. He had a long silky white beard and carried a fine gold-headed cane.

The gentleman was just wandering around, getting acquainted with the sights of -Robstown. He stopped at the corner of a little park across the tracks from the depot. There was a very luxurious specimen known as a joint cactus, which grows in joints and easily breaks off.

The Nebraska gentleman stopped and, I suppose to see what it was really like, took a whack at it with his heavy cane. It seemed like most of the cactus joints came loose. He was covered with sticky joints. He had them in his clothes, so many they were almost impossible to remove, but it seemed like most of them went into his beard.

He did not make the trip to the country to look at land that day. He and one of the porters spent most of the day trying to eliminate those cactus joints from his beard. They used every possible method but they finally had to resort to scissors. That beard never looked the same.

ON OUR FIRST trip in January 1909, we had just made a good start selling the Driscoll lands south of the railroad. We had finished most of the land north of the railroad in 1908 and went over to San Patricio and sold the Taft Ranch lands, while Col. Driscoll was making up his mind to sell the lands south of the track. Then we bought those lands and had them surveyed and ready for sale.

We were well started on those lands on this first January trip in 1909. Each agent always had a new map showing which lands had been sold and what was still available for sale.

As we started out that morning, we had between 40 and 50 teams in our caravan. They were started out in a line and three men on horseback rode back and forth so as to be in touch with the agents and check up on anything the buyers wanted. We drove slowly and stopped a great deal of the time to show what we had to offer.

We had cards printed that the buyers could sign for the purpose of purchasing any of the unsold lands. The cards specified that they could have a complete showing of the

particular tract they were buying before entering into
any definite contract. Salesmen often sold lands off the map
before we were that far along. Then the buyer was given as
much time to look over the land when we reached it as he
wanted.

On this particular morning, when the caravan reached a
point about a mile south of Robstown, we had a 40-acre
tract for sale. A Mrs. Cynthia Barnes from Indianola, Iowa,
said she would like to buy that 40 acres, but she wanted a
driver with her to have time to drive over it a bit. When he
had done so, she signed the card.

Others had been looking over their maps and they could
see that the land looked quite similar and that it was mostly
a matter of location.

Before Mrs. Barnes' card had been filled out, the
horsemen had gone back with orders for the next tract of
880 acres and then another one for 160 acres. They all had
to report to the sales manager to make sure they weren't
selling the same land twice. The result was that before the

teams moved again, we had signed cards covering 3,000 acres.

It took a lot of driving to allow each buyer to examine his purchase to his heart's content. Then several of them would leave the caravan and come back to my office on the train and enter into formal contract. I always stayed at the train office for that purpose on the excursion dates.

I did so much driving over the lands at other times that I could talk intelligently regarding each tract, even show them just where each little swale, or draw, was located.

Our excursions always reached Robstown on Friday mornings. We spent Friday and Saturday looking over the lands and surrounding territory, to give the new people as good an idea of what the country looked like as possible. Saturday evening the train was taken into Corpus Christi and set on the siding there for Sunday. I never allowed anyone to show land on Sunday.

MANY OF THE PEOPLE hoped to make that part of their trip a sort of sightseeing vacation so I always hired an excursion boat called the Pilot Boy for all day Sunday. Those who wanted to attend church services stayed in Corpus Christi but the rest of the crowd was taken for an all-day excursion on the Pilot Boy. They crossed Corpus Christi Bay and went out into the Gulf of Mexico, which was quite an experience for people who had never seen saltwater before.

We always used a couple of things in persuading people to make the trip to investigate our land. We had all our agents schooled on these points. We told them to be sure to tell the prospective customers just enough to make them feel there must be something worth seeing.

When the agent felt that point had been reached, he would say, "If this land is as good as I say, you would like to have some of it, wouldn't you?" If the prospective customer said that he believed he would, the agent made him the proposition. If he would go on the next trip to

Texas, and should he find that he, the agent, had overdrawn the story in any way, we would pay all his expenses. I can truthfully say we were never asked to make good on that promise.

Another thing that had a great influence was the fact that we knew that some people were sure to feel that when they got so far from home among strangers, they might be high-pressured into buying something they would regret later.

All our agents were instructed to tell their people that "Mr. Paul will never ask you to buy." They explained that we simply showed the lands and left it to the customer to make his decision. I never asked anyone to buy. I simply visited with them as I had the opportunity. The agent was the one who would ask them if they had made up their mind, but the agent was instructed to never urge or coax them to buy. The land sold itself.

———————

GEORGE H. PAUL came to South Texas in 1907 to sell ranchland to Midwest farmers. His company sold an estimated half-million acres during the land-rush era. Paul was known as the father of Robstown and was instrumental in the founding of the towns of Driscoll, Taft, Sinton, Gregory, and St. Paul. He suffered business reverses later in life and died in poverty in Omaha, Neb., in 1965. He was buried in the Elm Grove Cemetery in Washington County, Iowa. There were no surviving members of his family.

91

THE 'GOOD INDIAN'

Robert G. Carter

LIEUTENANT, FOURTH U.S. CAVALRY

After "coming in," Comanche war chief Quanah Parker lived at the Fort Sill Reservation. To placate him and keep him on the good road, so that he might follow the white man and be a "good Indian," he was given land, horses, mules, cattle and a substantial two-story house to live in. This house had a large star on the roof, presumably to distinguish it from the other houses. It was 12 to 15 miles from the town of Lawton, Okla.

Quanah Parker leased his land to cattlemen for grazing purposes and in this way accumulated a large fortune, for an Indian. He rode in state in a four-mule ambulance with his wives, of whom, at one time, he had seven.

He came to Washington many times. In 1905, at Theodore Roosevelt's second inaugural, I saw him ride up Pennsylvania Avenue in the inaugural column with other "good Indians." Most of them, like Quanah, had dipped their hands in the blood of many a white settler.

On Feb. 10, 1908, John Stephens, a member of Congress from Texas, introduced a bill to appropriate $1,000 to fund a memorial for Cynthia Ann Parker. He offered the following as his reason: "In view of the public service rendered by this Indian (Quanah Parker) to the white people of the Texas frontier, in causing his tribe to quit the warpath and live on the reservation, and in consideration of the suffering of his mother for so many years as a white captive among the savages."

This measure was introduced at the request of Quanah, who was then in Washington, in behalf of his mother. She had died about 1864 along with her infant daughter Prairie Flower (Quanah's sister). Both were buried in Fosterville Cemetery near Poynor in Henderson County. The measure was passed as part of the Indian appropriations bill. Quanah then had ample means to erect a memorial.

TEXAS AUTHORITIES REFUSED to give Quanah permission to remove the bodies of his mother and sister to his new home in Oklahoma. One night he and C. W. Birdsong, Indian agent and his son-in-law, smuggled the bodies from the graves and brought them to Cache, some 15 miles west of Lawton, near Fort Sill.

Quanah died on Feb. 22, 1911 of an attack of asthma and rheumatism. He left three wives and 15 children. He was reputed to be the wealthiest Indian in the country, through the generosity of the government. He was buried at Post Oak Mission Cemetery, near Lawton, on Feb. 24, 1911.

The reburial of his mother had been postponed for the following Sunday, and it had been planned that Quanah would perform the ceremony. His sudden death interrupted those plans.

At sunrise on the morning of his death, the real Indian burial ceremony began for Quanah. Three times during the night, the favorite of his three wives, "Too-Nicey," rose

Funeral of Quanah Parker at Post Oak Mission Cemetery near Cache, Okla., on Feb. 24, 1911

and loudly called to the Great Spirit for her chief. At five o'clock, she cried out, "This is the time I always build a fire for him." At six o'clock, the Medicine Man, Marcus Poco, conducted a sunrise funeral, making supplications to the Great Spirit, and also to the white man's God, to accept the spirit of the dead chief. The Indians chanted their funeral dirge. More than a thousand of them were in attendance.

The body of Quanah was dressed in his old buckskin suit. At noon the burial party wended its way among the hills to the little Indian cemetery. Rev. A. J. Becker, a Mennonite missionary, conducted the service in the manner of the whites. Following this, the Indians sang the Swan Song, the Medicine Man made one final appeal to the Great Spirit, and the body was lowered to rest beside that of his mother.

Items placed in the coffin included a deerskin bag containing his favorite feathers, war bonnet, trinkets and jewelry. Among the latter was a diamond brooch valued at

$450 which was the present of cattlemen who had grazed their stock on the Comanche range and became rich.

NOCONA, A TOWN NAMED for Quanah's father, is in Montague County, a few miles south of Old Spanish Fort on the Red River. Not far away is the town of Vernon on the Pease River where Nocona was killed and Cynthia Ann was recaptured by Sul Ross's Rangers. The town of Quanah in the Panhandle is the seat of Hardeman County. It is some miles east of Blanco Canyon, which I know well.

Has anybody heard or known of any other towns or county seats in Texas being named for any officers of the Fourth U.S. Cavalry? It was they who risked their lives and sacrificed their health to drive out the savage bands of Comanches. It was they who helped open up that wild and desolate region to settlement, civilization, and material prosperity, which the Comanches, under Quanah Parker and other "good Indians," sought to prevent with their bloody raids, their burning, plundering, and savage orgies.

———————

ROBERT GOLDTHWAITE CARTER was born on Oct. 29, 1845 in Bridgton, Maine. He was a lieutenant in the Fourth Cavalry during Col. Ranald S. Mackenzie's initial campaign against hostile Comanche bands in the Llano Estacado. In the battle of Blanco Canyon on Oct. 10, 1871, Carter and five soldiers held off a large force of Comanches while the rest of the detachment retreated. For that action, Carter was awarded the Congressional Medal of Honor. The Comanche war chief in that battle was Quanah Parker. Nearly 50 years later, Carter wrote a book on this campaign titled "Tragedies of Cañon Blanco." He died in Washington, D. C., on Jan. 4, 1936 and was buried in Arlington National Cemetery.

92

HORSES, BUGGIES
AND CADILLACS

Carlyle Leonard

HOUSING PROJECT MANAGER

You could rent a rubber-tired buggy and horse at Pitts Livery on Mesquite Street in Corpus Christi. On the hill was Beynon's Livery Stable where the hacks were kept. Julius Parrish and old man Ford drove stylish hacks. They sat up on top of the hack and two shining brass lights were on each side of the driver.

Hauling in the early days was done by drays. These were flat bodies with only two wheels and one horse. The hauling in Corpus Christi was done by Ellis and Brown, two men who came from Jamaica, or by Gabe Greene. Ellis would drive his horse to his dray ever day but Sunday. On that day he would curry his horse, hitch him to his buggy and drive down Chaparral. Ellis always led parades on horseback.

Pitts Livery on Mesquite Street in Corpus Christi

We used to know everyone in town who owned an automobile. If we saw a Hudson coming down Chaparral, we knew it was Mrs. Maude Miller, Roy Miller's wife. If we saw an open Benz with the brass shining like a twenty-dollar goldpiece, we'd know that it was Mr. Driscoll. Mr. Grim could be heard before we saw him, in his chain-driven car, or Dr. Arnold with his three-wheel job. One of the first cars in town was Dr. Spohn's Cadillac in 1905.

If there were young fellows in a Hudson, you knew it was Morris Lichtenstein and his young friends. If you were near Artesian Park and heard a four-cylinder Cadillac, moving slowly and almost talking, you would know that it was Judge McDonald, or Mr. Oppenheimer or Sam Guggenheim.

At Irishtown, past the Courthouse, were the old families, the Vetters, Shaws and Fitzsimmons. The Vetters, who lived in the 1100 block of Chaparral, were carpenters. They had their own pier that ran out into the bay behind Westbrook Court. We used to go out on Vetters' pier to watch an airplane take off from North Beach.

There was a crabbing hole where the ship channel is now. We boys would go there and catch blue crabs by the sack full. Benny Anderson's mule yard occupied one side of the bayou and Spohn Sanitarium the other side. North Beach was the Gold Coast. I remember the beautiful home of Judge McDonald before it was so badly wrecked in the 1919 storm.

Old man McClane, who was the sheriff during Reconstruction, lived in front of the Courthouse. Dr. Burke lived across the street and in the same block lived Mr. Martin Luther. On the sidewalk in front of the courthouse one could see where Sheriff Mike Wright had the old pistols imprinted in the wet cement. They were still there after old man Sherman, or maybe it was Lehr, laid the walk.

WHEN I WAS A BOY we used to go to Mrs. Ralter's to get yeast to make our bread. She lived in the same block of Chaparral Street where Mayor Dan Reid lived.

The old Artesian Park had a deep well that smelled like rotten eggs. The water was supposed to cure all kinds of ills. People came with jugs to drink the water and take some home. The Tribbles rented a building in front of Artesian Park and started a market, something like our present shopping centers. The Church of the Good Shepherd stood where Biel's Grocery Store was later. Dr. Sykes and Mr. Robinson lived on one corner and the Heath family on the other. Mrs. Rankin had Rankin's Rooming House on Mesquite, south of Artesian Park. Cooper's Clean Bakery was where K Wolens was built later. Across the street was a Chinese laundry. As a boy, I lived in a house on the corner where W. T. Grant's was built, cattycorner from Cooper's Clean Bakery.

Dr. Turpin had a little white house where Loving's Clothing Store was later, on the east side of Chaparral. Down the street to the south, on one corner, stood Guggenheim & Cohn's and on the other corner was Lichtenstein's. In those days you could shop on Saturday night. Past Cooper's Alley was Sidbury's lumber company. One of the things they built was cypress cisterns. A cistern can be a very dirty thing. Like the old chimney sweeps, we had cistern cleaners.

You'd never believe that men had barrels on two wheels and would go to the standpipe operated by Mr. Garcia to get water to sell for 15 cents a barrel. Then you'd have to pour ashes in the water to keep the wiggletails out. In the old days, our electricity was generated by Mr. Gibbons, across the street from the Eureka Laundry.

The famous Market Hall stood where City Hall was built later, at Mesquite and Peoples. Here were Dreyer's and Gutierrez's meat markets, the fire station, and upstairs was a big hall where dances and banquets were held. The volunteer fire department was headed by Mr. Shoemaker, whose blacksmith shop was on Mesquite Street across from the State Hotel. Most of the fire equipment was at Market Hall but hose houses were all over the city.

As one sauntered up Chaparral on a spring morning, when he got to the 1000 block, he might see Judge Timon going to the courthouse and Mr. Crabbe going to the post office. Then at night, before the streets were paved, you could hear clip-clops as Sheriff Wright and his deputies rode their horses on the dirt streets at all hours of the night.

CARLYLE LEONARD was the grandson of pioneer barber Will Leonard, who came to Corpus Christi from New Orleans in 1867 and opened a barbershop on Chaparral, which some said was the first in town. Leonard's father was also a barber. Leonard was born in 1901 and worked at the Nueces Hotel, Lichtenstein's, and was the manager of the D. L. Leathers Housing Project. He died on July 6, 1977.

93

MR. JOHNSON
KILLED MY CAT

Theodore Fuller
SOLDIER

My parents said that town was no place for a dog, but cats were admissible. We were not alone in this, for in a range of three or four blocks on Corpus Christi's North Beach there were many cats but only one dog roamed our neighborhood.

I claimed our cat as my own. Since I was not yet of school age, I had more time to devote to it. We got him as a playful kitten and I learned to rig all sorts of attractions for him. Marbles, balls, or objects suspended or dragged at the end of a string were used to play with the little fellow.

He never seemed to mind my teasing him. When I discovered that he could turn over in mid-air, I would hold him upside down, with his four feet in the air, and drop him. By going lower and lower, I found that he could do this trick as long as he was held higher than his own height. I would tease him with food by holding it higher than he could reach.

When he was grown, he stayed away from home for longer periods of time and mama explained that grown cats were like that. While kittens remained close at hand, big cats liked to stay out from time to time. I eventually became accustomed to his absences.

One morning three or four boys came toward us from up the street. It was Saturday. One of them, an older boy, was carrying something. I went out to meet them. They had what had been my cat, which was a mangled gory mass. The boys watched me as they dropped the remains at my feet. They said that Mr. Johnson killed my cat, that he shot it with a shotgun because it had been sucking eggs in his hen house.

I could not comprehend that this ugly mass was the little animal that had been so playful. Only mama and I were at home that morning. As I was lying on the bed crying, she called a neighbor boy and paid him to take the cat away and bury it.

I WAS NEARLY doubled in age when Mr. Johnson offered "Brother," my older brother, a one-day job for both of us. I no longer felt hate for Mr. Johnson but there was a lingering residue of dislike. Papa was present when Brother told me of the job. Papa asked me if I really wanted to work a day for Mr. Johnson. His question was posed in a way that I could easily have gotten by with a lame excuse. But it brought a quick rationalization and I agreed.

Mr. Johnson busied around and had no time for friendly exchanges. I found that I could face him with none of the old feelings of hate and rancor. Afterwards, in our rare encounters, I could offer him the same greeting as I did the other grown men.

* * *

MAMA TOLD ME to look out for the ice man. She wanted 50 pounds. We had to tell him because Mama didn't like to use those cards which the ice company furnished. She felt that it was nobody's business how much ice she wanted on any given day.

The cards were diamond-shaped and had 12½, 25, 50 and 75 printed on the corners. It was fastened in the center and the amount one wanted was turned to the top. It could be seen from the street. A full block of ice was 300 pounds. Cut into thirds gave a hundred, halved by 50, and so on. It cost a nickel for 12½ pounds, a dime for 25. Home ice boxes usually held up to 50 pounds.

I spotted the ice wagon two blocks away. I ran down to meet it. The kids had just taken all the little chips of ice and were leaving the wagon. I had to wait until the man chipped off another block with his ice pick for delivery to the next house. The present piece of ice in the wagon was down to 50 pounds. He would on the next stop have to bring out a 300-pound block from under the canvas cover. That would mean a lot of chipping. I nibbled chips all the way to my house.

After the ice wagon Mama sent me to Vannay's Grocery on Chamberlain Street for a bottle of vanilla and some ice cream salt. I was ecstatic. I knew what that meant.

Brother and I didn't mind turning the ice-cream freezer but would always swear that it was hard to turn long before the ice cream was stiff enough to be ready. The one that wasn't turning the handle would sit on the toe sack which covered the top of the freezer. We usually made it just before supper. Mama would pack it so that it would hold until dessert time. Mama made it so rich that it made the creamery ice cream seem bland and watery.

* * *

AS I REMEMBER IT, the Morgans lived on a corner of Staples Street and Buford, or maybe it was the corner of

Staples and Morgan Street. Mr. Morgan was a well-to-do farmer with lands somewhere out by the Alta Vista Hotel. He also had some kind of business interest in town.

There were several Morgan boys of grade-school age. If you attended Edward Furman Elementary School in the teens, there was probably a Morgan in your class.

It was Christmas Eve 1915. From the sidewalk came a call for Mr. Morgan. It was not late and the weather was clear. A streetlight lit up that corner of the street. Mr. Morgan came out his front door. Having come outside from a lighted room, he would not have seen the man at the edge of the street as easily as the man could see him. Two shots were fired.

All this we learned the next day. The 30-30 caliber rifle shell cases provided the only clues. The assassin faded into the shadows by the time the alarm sounded.

This had a shocking impact on my six-year-old mind. I had heard of death before but it had come from quiet and respectful voices. Death was a peaceful event that followed illness. This was my first knowledge of a murder, a violent death. Why should a man have to die when he had not even been sick? Why should somebody want him to die? What a horrible word — murder.

My mother thought of the children. "Christmas should be a happy time. It will be a long time before those poor children will have a merry Christmas."

———————

THEODORE (TED) FULLER: In 1913, when he was five, his family moved to Corpus Christi from West Texas. Ted, his brother, father and sister survived the 1919 storm but his mother and aunt were drowned. Theodore Fuller went on to become a lieutenant colonel in the U.S. Army. He served on the staff of Gen. Omar Bradley in World War II and after the war he was stationed in London as a military attache in the U.S. Embassy. He died in 1990 in Sylva, N.C. He is buried in Arlington.

94

FLU DIARY

Anita Lovenskiold
SCHOOLGIRL

September 3, 1918. We cleaned up the house and then went to mass and received Holy Communion for the boys "over there" and for some other things. We have been going ever since they left.

September 15. We got dressed and went to Josephine Gay's then went kodaking. "We" included "Joe" (Josephine) Gay, Lucille Emmert, Katherine and myself. We sure had some fun. Some of the soldiers from Camp Scurry wanted their pictures taken but Katherine and Joe didn't take them; they only pretended to. On the way home we had to pass a truck and the boys said they would give us a ride if we would take their picture. Joe and Katherine once again made believe they took it, but there wasn't any film in the camera.

September 21. We are going to the dance tonight. I hope I will enjoy it but I doubt it. Sometimes I nearly die with mortification and embarrassment; I wish I could overcome my shyness. We went to the dance with Uncle Tom Southgate and we took Lucille Emmert, and Grace and Claudine Toups. I danced every dance but half of one and the fellow couldn't keep step so we sat down and talked.

One soldier I danced with wanted to come see me. I told him I was going someplace and that Dad didn't want us to have visitors (boys). He wanted me to put one over on Dad, but I didn't. He wasn't bad-looking but he had light hair and blue eyes and I like dark hair and dark eyes.

September 23. It was my day to get the bread. I went out through the park and found the nicest pocketknife with a white pearl handle. Only it wasn't real pearl.

September 28. We got up a little after nine and Katherine went down to Dad's (dentist office). I stayed home and did the house and kitchen work both. We each made 50 cents. It's grand to have some money of your own.

September 29. We got home from the dance last night about 12 o'clock. I really did enjoy myself. I danced every dance, but of course I did not especially care about all those I danced with. Some of them were ugly.

"Remember, Anita," I had to remind myself, "looks are only skin deep."

OCTOBER 5. HOW DEAD things are. The boys at the army camp are all under quarantine. Nothing else seems to be lively. I went down to Dad's to work for him all day.

When I came home Mama had heard that Charles Wheeler was very sick. Sometime after that Moise Weil rang up and said Charles was dead. Oh, it made us feel so bad. He died of the flu at Camp Pike, Arkansas.

October 6. I went over to Mrs. Wheeler's and of course I had to cry as Mrs. Wheeler was crying, and reminding me of the good times that Charles, Ella, Katherine and I used to have.

October 7. We came home from school about 12 o'clock, had dinner, and was starting back to school when the phone rang. It was Uncle Tom saying that he had just received a telegram that Uncle Lee Lovenskiold in San Antonio was sick.

Mama and Papa seem worried about Uncle Lee, although Charlie is there with him and taking care of things. They closed all the picture shows in town.

October 8. Uncle Lee died last night about 9 o'clock. Uncle Tom rang up and told us. As soon as we received the message we went to mass and Holy Communion. I came home and got breakfast.

Mama phoned the sisters about school and they said that we wouldn't have school, that all the schools were ordered closed. Everything is closed and the army camp is quarantined on account of the Spanish influenza.

October 10. They brought Charles home this morning. They said he looked awful because of the pain he had suffered. They opened the coffin at the undertaker's but they wouldn't leave it open.

They sang "Nearer My God to Thee" and Dr. Austin said the service. It was a military funeral. The coffin was draped with a large American flag.

October 21. I got up rather late this morning, as I did not go to mass. It was about 8:30, then I cleaned the house and went down to Dad's office to help him.

It was quite a busy day. I think Dad is trying to make me some kind of a "professional lady." He was going to give me the job of extracting a tooth from an old Negro woman but she said that if I did try to take out her tooth that I wouldn't be able to pull it out because she would be laughing so hard.

We came home sometime after six o'clock. Papa gave me $2 to get some writing paper for me and Katherine because he said we had been "good girls."

There was another military funeral today. There are so many deaths and the casualty lists are something dreadful. I hope Barrie and John are all right and they will come home.

* * *

NOVEMBER 11. OH, WHAT a grand and glorious day is today. We have received the news that the war has ended and the Kaiser has left Germany. This morning about five o'clock the whistles blew, the bells rang, and music began to play.

We got up and got ready for mass. About the time mass was over we heard music in the streets and a lot of yelling so we went to the front of the hill. It was a parade and we sure did some running to catch up. I lost my money and goodness knows how many hairpins. I would not go back and look for them. After the parade was over, I found my money. I wasn't even looking for it, just saw it on the sidewalk.

———————

ANITA LOVENSKIOLD was the daughter of Dr. P. G. Lovenskiold, dentist, mayor, and descendant of an early pioneer from Denmark. Anita kept a diary. She later married Jesse Jolly and had four children. She died in Baton Rouge, La., in 1983 when she was 80.

95

THE WATER KEPT RISING

Anna Priscilla Sorelle

MRS. CYRUS EUGENE FARLEY

Sept. 13, 1919. On Saturday morning, we were aware
that there was an uneasiness in the air. Our home was about
a hundred feet from the water's edge in Port Aransas. As
the day wore on, the tide began rising and the wind picked
up, growing stronger. Late in the afternoon we met our
neighbors, the Chester Currys, by the water's edge and
discussed the situation.

After a while I got my bucket and went to milk our cow,
Old Jersey. It was to be the last time for several months, as
we left her on the island.

Later in the evening we were sitting in the living room
and heard a roar of water as if a large wave was passing by.
We talked about it, but Cyrus, my husband, said, "Oh, it
isn't anything. It can't be any worse than the storm we had
in 1916."

I don't think anyone on the island went to bed that night,
but Cyrus, and he slept, too. But not me. As time went by, I

could hear the water lapping up against the floor. I told Cyrus I thought we should leave before we were trapped. There was a low place between our home and town. I had to insist, but he finally consented to go. He kept saying that we would be back before breakfast.

We had on our everyday clothes. We didn't even take our money, since Cyrus was so sure we would soon be back. We did take our sweaters. By that time, it was pouring and we had to wade through water waist-deep to get to town.

Part of the town was under water. We couldn't get to grandpa's house, so went to Uncle Will's (William Farley Jr.). His house was on a higher elevation and when we arrived there were about 50 people already there. A terrible feeling of impending tragedy was in the air.

THE WATER KEPT rising. By daylight on Sunday it was up on the porch. More people had come in during the night and we were all just milling around, trying to decide what was the best thing to do.

The water was still rising so people decided it would be best to leave before it got too deep. We would go on to the sand hills. Uncle Will and Cousin Mae (Lorena Mae Curry Farley) brought out all of their clothes and quilts. All who could get the clothes on did so.

We were following the orders of the older men. The men carried the children on their shoulders and the women held on to each other when they couldn't make it alone. The water was so swift when we stepped out in the yard it was all we could do to keep our feet on the ground. As we left town, going toward the sand hills, the water was turbulent and the wind so fierce we had to battle to get through.

There was a crowd of about 70 pushing and trying to stand up in the strong tidal waves. After an interminable time, we had traveled about a mile to the top of the highest sand hill we could see.

The spray was so thick and the air so full of flying water we could only see a few yards ahead of us. We finally dug into the crater on top of the hill. These craters are scooped out by the continual winds on the coast.

We lay down on the sand, snuggled against each other to keep warm. We covered the best we could with the quilts, but still we shivered, our teeth chattering so there was not much talking. We lay there and wondered what our fate would be. The sand hill would shake and quiver as if someone was pushing it around.

Late in the afternoon some of the men made their way over the crater's edge and looked down the hill to see if the waters were receding. They reported that they thought they were going down a little. We would try to jump and walk a little in the bottom of the crater to get our blood to circulate. It was so cold it seemed we would freeze to death.

With the arrival of darkness, it seemed the wind was dying down and the water beginning to subside. The men thought that we had better try to get back to town if possible. Some went to scout ahead to see if we could go. They returned and said we might get to the first house nearest the hills and there, at least, we would be in out of the weather.

We began the struggle to walk against the wind and among the storm debris, with the men carrying children, the women stumbling, falling and trying to get up again.

When we reached the home of Uncle Newt Curry, we were a wet, bedraggled, and unsightly crowd. The water had been about four feet deep in the house and it left behind a mess of slimy mud.

Our first move was to find food for the children. In the pantry there was flour in a cloth sack, which had become a solid paste on the outside but the inside was dry. There were a few potatoes and canned goods. We used it all and each got a little. We also had coffee.

We had to stand or sit on wet beds and chairs all night. The mud was two inches deep and had an unpleasant odor. With daylight on Monday we were anxious to see if our property was left. We found there were only a few houses left standing. We were even more thankful to be alive.

We heard a cow lowing and, sure enough, there was Old Jersey coming down from the hills. The women with babies were happy at the prospect of getting some milk for their children. Where our home had been was swept as clean as if a bulldozer had passed over the place. Cyrus and I had nothing left. Since there was no food and not enough shelter for 500 residents, there was nothing to do but evacuate. The Coast Guard had floated an auxiliary boat and a dinghy up to the sand hills when the water was still rising and these vessels were the only means of getting off the island. We knew we would have to leave with the first boatload out.

When we returned to Port Aransas on Nov. 1, a month and a half after the storm, we went to our lot and found a gold hatpin and silver spoon. All we could see of what had been our car was part of the bumper sticking out of the sand. The swirling water had washed away the sand from underneath, letting the car sink into a hole, and then covered it up again. My cedar chest with the gold pieces that Cyrus had gotten in tips from the people he had taken fishing was gone.

Cyrus went to Wichita Falls and worked on a pipeline. I stayed at Mama's at San Marcos. We came back to Aransas Pass and had Old Jersey moved over by barge. She was the only property we owned in the world.

ANNA PRISCILLA SORELLE FARLEY was born Dec. 27, 1896 in San Marcos. She married Cyrus Farley of Port Aransas in 1915. He died Nov. 21, 1963 and she died Sept. 12, 1982. Both are buried in Prairie View Cemetery in Aransas Pass.

96

OH, MOMMA!

Lucy Caldwell
TEACHER

Sept. 21, 1919.

Dear Momma: Where shall I start? I guess with the storm. Oh, that I could forget it! As I told you in my wire, the army boys who helped to clear away the debris say that the only thing which compares with it is devastated Belgium. A week ago, I wrote you from the Nueces Hotel in Corpus Christi, telling you what a beautiful place it was and how I was enjoying myself on the beach.

You also recall that I stated in my letter that I was not going bathing that night as there was a peculiar restlessness of the water. The waves weren't high and the wind was not strong, but the water gave one the impression of a child denied something and chafing in a suppressed manner. That was Saturday night.

I slept soundly till about two a.m. when I was waked by a strong wind and rain. I thought it nothing more than a common occurrence on the seashore and after a short time went to sleep. Again, I was waked by a terrific crash which proved to be the crashing in of some of the windows on the fourth floor of the hotel. From this time on there was no sleeping for anybody. Doors were slamming and windows were crashing with the increasing wind and rain. People were deserting their rooms for the halls because of flying glass.

By early daylight the lobby was a swarm of people inquiring about trains and trying to get service cars. By nine a.m. the phones were dead. The rain was falling so thick that you could hardly see across the street. The wind was hurling the water from the bay in such torrents that it was almost impossible to stand on the street. When I say that water was hurled, I mean it literally, for the wind threw the water as you would dash a bucket of water on a fire.

By ten a.m. the hotel authorities announced that no trains were leaving, that no phoning could be done and no telegrams would be accepted. The elevator ceased working and in another hour the lights went out. We realized that the storm had reached a terrible stage as residents of the city and visitors occupying other hotels on the beach were flocking into the Nueces for safety, each telling of some building having been swept away.

ALTHOUGH WARNED to keep away from windows, we saw that the wires were down, telephone poles were gone, not a bathhouse was in sight, not a fishing pier, the garage near the hotel was gone with 60 cars in the bay, the concrete service station was gone, also the dancing pavilion and bowling alley. All of the timber of which these buildings were constructed was piled in front of the Nueces Hotel. Next came the entire wreckage of the Pavilion Hotel, a portion of which struck the plate glass front of the dining room, crashing in a large portion. Instantly the water began pouring into the dining room.

You can imagine the confusion and excitement — everybody grabbing food, rushing through the water to the second story, families getting together, porters trying to get baggage upstairs. Pandemonium reigned.

To add to the horror of what we could see ourselves, refugees were rushing in, wet, hatless, and some with much of their clothing gone. Each had a more horrible tale than the preceding one — of floating on doors and mattresses, of helping to rescue women and children, of seeing bodies float away from the houses which were swept into the bay. Entire families came in weeping telling of seeing their house swept away, others came in after having seen the remainder of their families swept out of sight.

In the meantime, the hotel doors and windows were crashing in, the bedrooms were being soaked and the water in the lobby was rising. Still the storm raged and still the refugees came, and still we wept for them. At six p.m. the storm started with greater fury and by eight o'clock there was a mass of human beings imprisoned in the hotel, without a drop of water for drinking or sewerage, and without a light except matches, most of which refused to strike.

From about ten p.m. to 2:30 a.m., the storm reached its point of most intense fury, the water on Chaparral stood 10-1/2 feet, and in the hotel lobby it stood even with the top of the desk. You understand that the hotel lobby is several feet higher than the street.

At 2:30 the water began to recede. The hotel lobby was a pitiful sight — the handsome furniture floating in the water. Also floating into the lobby came pieces of houses, beds, baby buggies, tops of autos, cigars, sacks of flour, portions of boats. It was said that a dead horse floated in, but I did not see it.

By the middle of the afternoon the hotel assistants were in their bathing suits. They spent the entire night in the water of the lobby diving to make sure that no bodies were

Peoples Street outside the Nueces Hotel after the storm

in the water. We spent the night huddled on the floor in the halls, with no light except that from matches. The babies cried, the women mourned and the men tried to watch the storm and quiet the women and babies. Children cried for food and water, but nothing could be had. The storm broke about 2:30 and the water began to recede. Many dozed for a few hours from sheer exhaustion. I didn't sleep.

What a sickening sight Monday morning. The water was still two feet in the lobby and several feet in the street. The beach was a solid mass of wreckage: houses, cars, boats, street cars, railroad track, horses, cows, seagulls. I am truly thankful I was imprisoned in the hotel and did not see the human bodies in the wreckage.

Every store, bank and office from the bluff to the beach (except the courthouse, jail and post office) was practically ruined.

On the beach proper were left the Nueces Hotel, a part of the Spohn Sanitarium, a part of the hospital for convalescent soldiers and a wall here and there to mark some familiar spot. It is impossible to conceive of it without seeing it.

Monday morning about 10 a.m. Maj. McCann, a former flyer who was a guest in the hotel, collected a party of men, waded to the bluff and returned with buckets of water, bread, cheese, canned goods and, cookies, which he obtained from grocers in that portion of the city. We all revived a little from our long fast.

All day the refugees poured in. Many who had spent the night in the hotel waded up to the bluff to find shelter with friends and relatives. All day into the hotel poured men and women, trying to locate some relative who could not be found and who was seen last floating in the bay. One man was brought in who had floated with his wife and baby for eight hours and finally lost them. A boy came in who had seen his mother, father and five brothers and sisters drown.

By Monday afternoon the local Red Cross was in operation and stations were established at the City Hall, Courthouse, high school and Presbyterian Church. Practically every pound of food in the city was in the hands of this organization. Nothing could be bought — money was worth nothing.

By Tuesday morning, the water had receded sufficiently to admit our reaching the Red Cross stations by wading in mud and slime above the ankles. All of the men and women who were able to do so trudged to these stations for food and many of us gave all assistance that we could. I was assigned to the courthouse to help in serving food and distributing clothing and candles and matches. Remember, the city was in total darkness.

Oh, Momma! I cannot describe to you what I saw there. People huddled together, hungry, almost naked, shivering, barefooted, some without a stitch of underwear, hatless, men with women's middy blouses on for shirts, women in men's trousers, one woman with a child wrapped in a flag, men and women in bathing suits, women with their hair down, some with toes cut off, hands cut off, teeth knocked out, limbs broken or cut, one woman with typhoid fever, men with children half naked, the mothers having been drowned, women shrieking for lost ones, men prostrated from trying to save their families, and families with everything which they had tied up in a pillow slip.

On the floor of the courthouse they lay with nothing under them or over them till the relief trains began to come in. And the horror of horrors was the morgue in the basement of the courthouse. Rescue parties came in every hour or two, bringing in corpses from a distance of 15 or 20 miles. Sometimes they would have two, sometimes as many as 20. And, oh!, the condition they were in. Arms and legs off, heads almost severed, all the hair gone, swollen beyond conception and black from the oil, hair entangled with seaweed and bodies so mutilated that identification was impossible. At one time there were 83 unidentified bodies in the morgue.

THERE WAS NOT a casket in the city available after the storm, so until the relief trains could bring in coffins, the courthouse lawn was a carpenter shop for making rough wooden coffins. I saw men whose hands were absolutely minus the outer skin due to constant washing in disinfectants for protection in handling the dead bodies. Stout men fainted and had to be relieved by others.

Tuesday night I slept a little in a room, the windows of which did not blow out. Wednesday morning the Western Union office opened and I stood on the walk in the mud and rain for two hours to file my telegrams to you. The only trains whose tracks were standing were those to San Antonio by way of Brownsville and Laredo and many went that way. On Thursday, the SAAP and the SAU&G* by detouring through Alice and Robstown went to San Antonio. They took six trains over. I made application three

---

* San Antonio & Aransas Pass Railroad; San Antonio, Uvalde & Gulf Railroad.

times for a permit to go on these trains but was refused each time because I was classed as a "refugee not on charity."

It was announced on Friday morning that a train would leave some time during the day for San Antonio by way of Robstown through Sinton and Beeville and that a limited number of tourists might go. I obtained a passport and reached Sinton where I wired you again.

As a result of the awful experiences of the preceding days, my nerves were in a shattered condition. Consequently, on receiving my first assurance from you that you had heard from me, I broke down completely in the Western Union office. But as there were seven coffins containing bodies of victims from Port Aransas, awaiting identification, and as the depot was full of pitiful refugees, no note was taken of my distress at all.

I am thankful to be alive and comfortable. I leave in the morning for Karnes City and follow my route from there. I am now out of the devastated area, but it is all that you can hear discussed. Had one told me that I should have witnessed such a scene, I should have said "No, such a thing is impossible."

––––––––––

LUCY CALDWELL was born on April 15, 1882, the daughter of Whitfield S. Caldwell and Mary Robertson Caldwell. Lucy Caldwell was a 37-year-old teacher from Terrell, Texas on vacation and staying at the Nueces Hotel when the 1919 hurricane struck and devastated the city. She wrote a lengthy letter to her mother describing the storm and its aftermath. She died in 1945 at the age of 62.

97

THE TALKING SKELETON

Ike Elliff

DEPUTY SHERIFF

It was a hot and sluggish day in the office of Sheriff Ben Lee in Corpus Christi on Sept. 1, 1931. "Something's going to happen before long," I predicted, looking out the window with my mind on the sultry weather. At that moment I heard excited voices in the hallway, a mixture of Spanish and English. Something was about to happen all right.

Pat Dunn, a rancher I had known for years, walked in with one of his ranch hands, a man named Juan. I knew there was something important about this visit.

"This is the sheriff's office, Juan," Dunn told the man. "Tell them what you saw."

The story was that Juan was working cattle 10 miles south of Corpus Christi on the Oso near the Don Patricio Causeway. He noticed that the cattle were shying away from something in the brush. He thought it was a rattlesnake but when he went to look, he found a human skeleton.

Sheriff Lee told Deputy Jim Shaw and me to check it out. We followed Dunn's car to his ranch. I knew this remote section of the Gulf Coast well. It was seldom invaded by anyone other than ranch hands looking for stray cattle.

At the site, Juan pointed to an old automobile top, but I had already seen the bleached bones scattered around. Closer examination revealed short light blond hair about the skull. The hair left no doubt that the skeleton was that of a man. A gaping hole in the back of the skull was mute evidence the man had been murdered.

Shaw and I agreed that the vaquero had stumbled on the evidence of a murder that provided a baffling mystery. Who was this blond man who had been so ruthlessly done to death? Who was the killer? What was the motive and which way should we turn to look for clues? The underwear and socks offered no clues; the elements had destroyed any laundry marks that might have led to an identification.

SEARCHING OVER THE SITE, we found a scrap of newspaper from the Houston Post-Dispatch and an empty envelope addressed to Fred Sinclair of Sinclair Metal Works, at 102 Chaparral in Corpus Christi. I had known Sinclair for years and knew he could not have been involved in such a crime.

We gathered our clues and the bones of the murder victim and returned to Corpus Christi. We left the skeleton in charge of justice of the peace B. G. Moffett and undertaker Maxwell P. Dunne.

We kept the story of the murder quiet. Moffett ruled that the man had come to his death at the hands of some unknown assailant. One thing that came out of the coroner's examination was that the murdered man's left arm was three inches shorter than his right arm.

We had something to work on. The shorter left arm brought to my mind some vague memory of an experience I had had with a man so afflicted, but I could not remember who, when or what the circumstances were.

I began to search my notes on past cases and the name of Alfred J. Steinbach caught my eye. I knew immediately he was the man I had been thinking of.

I had been sent to investigate this young man. A girl he had been seeing named Mary Moulter told Sheriff Lee that he was a suspicious character, that he didn't have a job but always had money.

In my investigation then, I found Steinbach at a rooming house where he shared a room with a man named V. Don Carlis. Steinbach, about 20 years old, told me he was writing a book, that his home was in Cincinnati, and that his father sent him an allowance each week.

I quickly concluded that Mary Moulter's suspicions were entirely groundless. But when I had talked to Steinbach, I noticed his left arm was considerably shorter than his right.

Now, I recalled that Steinbach's hair was light blond. I went to the Osborne rooming house where he had a room and Mrs. Osborne told me she hadn't seen him since early July. We told her nothing about finding the skeleton. She could add few details to what I already knew. She said he had few friends and had roomed with Carlis since coming to Corpus Christi. She said Carlis told her Steinbach left for San Antonio.

I decided we needed to know more about Carlis. Mrs. Osborne said he was a quiet man, about 45, who worked as a mechanic at Binz Service Station on Water Street, and that he used to work for Sinclair Metal Works. I was beginning to tie some threads together in my mind. We believed the murdered man was Alfred J. Steinbach, a young man writing a book who roomed with V. Don Carlis.

We went to see Fred Sinclair but didn't tell him about the skeleton. Sinclair said Carlis worked for him in 1927

The 1914 Nueces County Courthouse where the "talking skeleton" case went before the jury

and 1928 then again in 1931. We went to the Binz Garage on Water Street and asked for Carlis.

"I am Carlis," said a tall man who carried himself with an aloofness not expected of a garage mechanic. We told him we were looking for a young man named Steinbach. I watched his reaction closely. He showed no more surprise at my question than if I had asked for a match. "I am looking for him too," he said. "He owes me $125. I've been trying to collect from his father but I am not having much luck."

He said he had last seen Steinbach on July 7. He said he thought he had left for Canada. I told Carlis that he would have to go with us for further questioning.

It was night now. Deputy Shaw and I had been working fast since we found the bleached bones that morning. We had Carlis in jail but we had no evidence against him. If we told him about finding the skeleton and accused him of murdering Steinbach before we had any evidence, we would probably get nowhere with this quiet stoical man.

Maxwell P. Dunne, the undertaker, called Steinbach's father, who said he would bring his son's dental chart.

Shaw and I went back to the Binz Service Station. Frank Binz's son, Henry, said he went with Carlis to the Don Patricio Causeway to put an axle on a car. He said Carlis told him he had been hunting near the causeway and found a human skeleton.

Shaw and I were startled. We had kept the news of the skeleton quiet, yet here was a statement that Carlis knew of human bones in the patch of mesquite where the man we believed to be Steinbach had been found.

THE CASE WAS TAKING SHAPE. We knew that Carlis roomed with Steinbach. He had worked for Sinclair and an envelope addressed to Sinclair was found by the bones. And Carlis told about seeing a skeleton in that very area.

Dunne got permission at the Binz Service Station to inspect Carlis's tools. He found a ballpeen hammer that fitted perfectly into the hole in the skull. And there were bloodstains and a strand of blond hair still on the hammer.

We went back to talk to Carlis. We learned he had been in prison and used several aliases. We told him Steinbach was dead and accused him of killing him.

Carlis, still calm, said he had something to say. He said he and Steinbach were out riding when his car broke down and another car came along, three men jumped out, one of them shot Steinbach, and they took off. He said he didn't think anyone would believe his story so he hid Steinbach's body in the brush. The body was found on Tuesday. Carlis was interviewed on Wednesday. The father arrived on

Thursday and the dental chart positively showed the body was his son's.

Carlis was charged with murder. When the trial date came around on Nov. 9, there was widespread interest in the case. The courtroom was packed. Halfway through the trial, there was a scream and spectators rose from their seats. Dunne the undertaker was wheeling a gurney with the skeleton into the courtroom.

District Attorney D. S. Purl said Steinbach had returned from the dead to tell the jury of his fate. "Look at my teeth, look at my left arm, look at these pictures. You see, I'm Alfred Steinbach," the bones of the dead man seemed to be saying. "Look at these nicks in my ribs. That's where I was shot. See this round hole in my skull? That's where the murderer hit me with a ballpeen hammer."

The district attorney did his work too well. The jury found Carlis guilty and he was sentenced to 99 years in prison. But bringing the dead man's body into the courtroom attracted national attention and cries that the trial was unfair, that the skeleton inflamed and prejudiced the jury. The case was reversed and remanded for retrial.

There was no skeleton in the second trial and Carlis, though he was found guilty, was sentenced to eight years in prison.

––––––––––

RAYMOND DOUGLAS (IKE) ELLIFF was born on Aug. 18, 1903. His parents were Joseph Elliff and Maria Acebo Elliff. His grandfather was Josiah (Si) Elliff, founder of a ranch at Banquete. Ike's brother, William Leo, also worked as a deputy sheriff in the 1930s. Ike married Pinie Marie Rumley in 1926. He died on June 14, 1959, at the age of 59, and was buried in Rose Hill Cemetery.

98

STORM ON THE ISLAND

Louis Rawalt

FISHERMAN, BEACHCOMBER

Many nights I slept on the sand with only a piece of tarpaulin around me when I was fishing away from camp. It was one of the times when I had gone alone to a spot 35 miles below our shack that the car stalled. No amount of tinkering could get a sound out of it. There was nothing to do but start walking. It was 70 miles to Corpus Christi Pass where someone lived who had a car. The tide was exceptionally high and I had little hope that any fishermen would venture down the beach that day.

It was early morning when I started. A little before sunset I reached our shack. Viola, my wife, was visiting my people in Kingsville. The place had an empty feeling. I ate, drank some coffee, and rested for a few moments before starting again. The tide was rising rapidly. It looked as though a storm was brewing. If I didn't get the car out of the reach of the water, I wouldn't have a car.

This thought kept my bare feet plodding through the sand all night. It was dark as pitch. Sudden squalls blew in, keeping me drenched most of the time. But with the first gray light of morning, I could see by the familiar outlines of the dunes that I was only a few miles from the pass.

Bill White, another fisherman, was cooking breakfast in his tarpaper shack when I knocked at his door. I was too tired to eat but as I gulped down scalding cups of coffee, I couldn't help crowing over the fact that four years before I had been given six months to live. Yet in the past 24 hours I had walked 75 miles.

During the previous year I had acquired a fishing partner. We called him Shorty and if he had another name I never knew it. He was a good man on the end of a net, and it relieved Viola from some hard work. She had found a bale of cotton washed up on the beach and subsequently launched a quilting project. Shorty set up his tent a little beyond our shack and we established a pleasant and profitable partnership.

Then the Gulf staged a real shindig. We had several scares that year, 1933, and Viola kept our important possessions packed in boxes against the time we might have to run.

IT WAS ONE of the most perfect of island days on Friday before the storm hit on Tuesday (Sept. 5, 1933). The water was flat and blue. The skies were clear and the southwest wind was warm and gentle. Shorty was expecting weekend guests and Viola, thinking they might visit us, unpacked the boxes and made the house cozy and neat.

I was fishing early Saturday morning when I noticed the swells were coming over the beach in an erratic rhythm. Far out over the water the sky had an ominous look. Wild life deserted the beach. A squall hit with sudden intensity. I pulled in my line and went into the shack. Viola was still sleeping. I woke her and told her to get ready to go to town, that I thought there was a storm on the way. Sleepily, she started mumbling about repacking everything. I walked to the porch and looked out. The tide had risen so fast that it was already hazardous to travel the beach.

"You won't have time for that," I told her. "We'll have to go now or not at all."

Shorty came in. He had also seen the signs. There was no need to tell him. Another squall hit as we were getting into the pickup where we were squeezed in together. The beach was almost impassable where the long sweeps crowded us up into the soft sand and shell. But the Model-A came through and in late afternoon we reached the house of friends in Corpus Christi.

I checked with the Weather Bureau and found that a storm in the Gulf of exceptional force was headed straight for the Texas coast. They expected it to hit on Monday. After getting Viola settled, Shorty and I began to talk about returning to the island and going down the beach at low tide that night to save our equipment. We decided to go and, over Viola's protests, we refueled the Ford and drove back over the causeway to Padre.

THE ISLAND WAS a place of darkness and fury that night. It rained incessantly and the wind blew in gusts that threatened to topple the pickup. We had gone a mile or two down the beach when we both had to admit that it was hopeless to try to go farther until daylight. We drove the Ford up into the edge of the dunes and sat there all night trying to sleep, our legs cramping and the water reaching nearer with every heave of the Gulf.

When morning came, the rain let up a little. We shoved and shoveled our way through the dunes and to the grasslands in the center of the island. It took all day to reach the shack, driving through pools of water left by the night's deluge. It still rained and the wind blew.

We left the truck behind the dunes and walked over to the house. The water was running under it so deep it was over our knees as we waded up to the steps. We estimated

444

that the tide was four or five feet above normal. I knew that unless some miracle happened, the shack was not going to stand much longer.

I went inside and dumping a pillow out of its case started grabbing some of the valuables and putting them into the pillowcase. I tossed in a box containing several old coins I had found, the stem-wind gold watches I had found in a wooden box on the beach, and my collection of arrowheads and spear points.

I was looking around at all the rest of our furnishings and equipment, wondering how much to take, when a giant roller hit the shack with terrifying force. I felt the floor sway and buckle under my feet. The water was running up through the cracks when I went out the back door with a pillow case in one hand. The steps had washed away.

As I jumped off the porch into the water that was now over waist-deep, I caught sight of a can of gasoline that I was counting on to use for the return trip to town. I caught the can as it floated by me and waded out of the maelstrom. Shorty, having collected his belongings from the tent, was waiting for me in the truck.

I put the gasoline in and looked back at the house. It had toppled over and was being beaten to pieces by the waves. When I started to place the pillowcase on the seat, I discovered I had grabbed the wrong one. I had salvaged only a pillow and a can of gasoline which might not even be enough to get us back to town.

Darkness was coming on fast. The storm grew in intensity. We would be lucky if we got out of it with our lives.

Fortune was kind to us that night. By following our recently made tracks back up the center of the island, we made our way to the north end of Padre. There we found the waters of the Laguna Madre lapping over the plank troughs of the Don Patricio Causeway. Could we make it? The choice had to be made quickly. We would try.

The Don Patricio Causeway to Padre Island before it was destroyed in the 1933 storm

I nosed the Model-A onto the planks and we inched our way over the water. Wind tore at us and the rain poured down in torrents.

It was daylight by then — a liquid gray daylight in which everything blended and wavered like the scenes in an underwater film. At the ship channel we found that the swing
bridge had been torn partly loose. The ends of it were two feet higher than the planks of the causeway. A barge was anchored nearby with several men aboard. They came to our rescue. Climbing from the barge to the causeway, they lifted the Ford and set it on the bridge. Then they set it down at the other end. We finally reached the comparative safety of the mainland.

Later we learned that during the next hour after we had crossed the causeway was reduced to a total wreck. The planks were torn loose and flung into the air. Some of them were found weeks later on King Ranch 20 miles away.

The hurricane of Sept. 5, 1933 left a scene of devastation everywhere. Padre Island was cleared of everything for a hundred miles. The contours of the beach were changed and there were 30 channels cut all the way from the Gulf to the Laguna Madre.

Within a week after the storm, we were back on the island. We got there by loading our car on an improvised raft and poling it across the Laguna Madre. Driving the beach was hazardous. It was stripped with deep ruts and covered with logs and debris. The passes were filling up with sand, and we were able to drive through them, although we drove through water two feet deep in places.

At the site of our former shack there was nothing. Nothing, that is, except an old ice-box half sunk in the sand. Shorty's tent had caught around the ice-box and on examination showed its only damage to be a small rent. In searching about the campsite, he found all the things he had left with the exception of a small stew kettle. As I said, Viola and I found nothing. Out of all the supplies, the equipment, the bedding, the clothing, not a sign of anything. Yet Shorty found everything he owned except for a 35-cent kettle.

The ways of the sea are strange. They say that whatever it takes away from you it brings back. I'm inclined to think that it does. The next few months the tide carried in the lumber and piling for us to build a bigger and stronger house.

LOUIS ENOCH RAWALT was born in 1898. He was a veteran of World War I, the survivor of a gas attack. In 1927, he was hospitalized from his old wounds and given months to live. He married Viola Mae Bell and they moved to a squatter's shack on Padre Island. They had two children. Rawalt died on Jan. 27, 1980 at the age of 81 and Viola Mae Bell Rawalt died on Nov. 8, 2010, at the age of 106. Both are buried in Rose Hill Cemetery.

99

GET-AWAY MONEY

Bill Duncan
REPORTER, EDITOR

One day in 1935 Mom came back from the well with oil spots on her skirt. She had a little vial of crude oil to show us. I don't know, but I always supposed it was a gusher. We lived two miles south of the discovery well, back in the brush. The well was a mile north of where the Flour Bluff school was built later.

Months before, the Schlumberger crews had been setting off small depth charges all over the countryside, taking sonic readings of the substrata and leaving behind little potholes that quickly filled with groundwater, crawdads, and children's feet.

Oil landmen were everywhere, talking about fabulous riches and swearing that one-eighth royalty was all that was allowed by law. However, the natives were avaricious enough and smart enough to learn that they could get a bigger share of any production potential, depending on how bad the bidder wanted the mineral rights.

There weren't many owners of large blocks of land at Flour Bluff in the 1930s but of those few, like my father and mother, they thought of the oil-lease payments they received as "get-away money."

We used ours to move to a ranch at Three Rivers, 75 miles north, in 1937. It was a small boy's paradise. The Atascosa and Frio rivers formed the western boundary of the ranch and this became my natural habitat.

Huge live oaks were hung with Spanish moss and draped with mustang grapevines. The floors of leaf mulch carried a dank smell of the earth. Ridges of big mesquites were festooned with mistletoe. Hackberry trees were ideal for making Indian-quality bows. All this was a wonderful dream-come-true for a young boy.

I always thought I was overworked as a boy. Dad would see us expending large amounts of energy playing touch football or barnyard hockey and quickly look for a more productive use of our energy. So now it's hard for me to equate this overwork with the seemingly endless periods of underemployed time that I spent in our private outback.

I CARRIED A SLINGSHOT and picked up oval stones on the hills away from the river. I practiced on any target, animate or not. I shot mockingbirds and woodpeckers and rain crows, everything. And I tasted them all. I would build a small fire, cut a green branch, singe them a little, and eat them.

Woodpeckers have a sort of sweet-tasting yellow meat. I remember that because I had to force myself to take the first bite. I don't remember what the others tasted like.

I didn't see it then as anything more than exploratory. I think I didn't kill more than a couple of non-game species. Now I'm sure I would be horrified to see any kid do such a thing for any reason, but we learn.

We learn that it takes two to hunt squirrels. You can get out in the river bottoms before daylight and take a stand under a likely tree and wait for daylight and the squirrels to come out chitter-chattering and flourishing their tails.

Or you go out later, in tandem, and one guy walks maybe 75 feet in front of the other. The shy squirrel scrambles around the tree limb, keeping it between him and the hunter. He doesn't see the following hunter, who zaps him.

It's not all about killing. Some of it is just being motionless, snugged down in a thicket among the centipedes and spiders. You see the mama skunk trailing her black-and-white offspring across a clearing. You hear the rustling of leaves and loud footsteps and know that something big and dangerous, maybe a bear, is approaching. You feel silly when you see a rooting armadillo. You hear a strange clacking noise and see two diamondback tortoises mating.

We all need some get-away money.

———————

WILLIAM EDWARD (BILL) DUNCAN was born on March 22, 1925, the son of Sidney Duncan and Ruth Pipkin Duncan. Bill Duncan was one of a handful of students who attended the first Flour Bluff school on land donated by his grandfather. The family moved to a ranch at Three Rivers near the end of the Depression. In high school, Bill Duncan was a football quarterback. He was later hired by the Corpus Christi Caller-Times and became managing editor of the afternoon paper, the Times. He died on March 10, 2006 and was buried in the Duncan Cemetery at Flour Bluff.

100

FIELDS AND FENCES

Roy Bedichek
NATURALIST

I have been looking over a 200-acre plot of fenced land and trying to compare the life it now supports with that which it supported for thousands of years when the first white man occupied it 100 years ago. This land has been living on its own fat and finally on its own vitals, consuming its capital instead of the interest alone, as it did in the year 1846 and before.

In spring and early summer the abandoned field of 50 acres is blanketed with poverty weed; in later summer and early fall with Mexican tea, a species of croton which even hungry goats refuse to eat.

Judging from the native vegetation growing on an adjacent highway, there were no less than a hundred different species of flowering plants and shrubs, as well as a dozen different grasses thriving here before the pasture land was intensively grazed, the field was fenced, and the first plow disturbed its long-accumulated humus. Relatively few vegetable species have survived, which means that the variety of animal life also has been proportionately reduced. Variety has been sacrificed to produce cotton, corn, oats, and to graze sheep, goats, and other domesticated animals.

In the 200 acres under fence there are now about a hundred chickens, fifty turkeys, twenty head of neat cattle, three or four horses, and little wildlife to speak of, but even this domestic stock is not supported from the land on which it is confined. From year's end to year's end the food which nature supplies from the depleted soil has to be supplemented with store-bought provender, grown elsewhere, processed, sacked, transported great distances, and at last dished out as an individual purchase and hauled 20 miles.

It is this elaborate organization which permits animal life to subsist at all on these famished acres, and which gives people the illusion that the land is providing something besides space in which the animals may move around.

IT IS TRUE THAT EVEN IN pre-pioneer times fire restricted the variety of life on prairies and plains for the benefit of grazing animals valuable to the Indians such as the antelope and buffalo. But annual autumn fires had no such disastrous effect upon natural life as fencing has had, since the flow of grazing life was unimpeded and the fertility of the land itself little impaired.

In pre-Columbian times, on the creek skirting this tract, there were beaver dams which multiplied the number of species, both animal and vegetable. With the extermination of the beaver, floods have swept their old check dams away and scoured banks and channel bed. Swollen to madness by the increasing runoff from its tilled watershed, the little stream ground and tore away all obstructions, year after year, until the channel throughout its length from hills to river valley is swept clean as a floor. Present owners, or some of them, along its course are constructing concrete dams to take up again the work which the beavers left off 75 years ago. I think they are locking the door after the horse has been stolen.

As the period of abuse lengthened, the creek grew temperamental and had spells of refusing to run at all during long summer droughts, drying up into stagnant pools which are death traps for aquatic life. Blow followed blow during successive years. The decline was so gradual that it was long unnoticed; and even now it requires the perspective of a whole century to bring before the mind's eye the full extent of the catastrophe.

DEER WANDERED ACROSS this acreage in pre-Columbian times, taking mast in the fall or nibbling tender shoots in the spring, but wounding nothing to its hurt. Opossums, coons, skunks, snakes, fish, frogs, beaver, predators and preyed-on, and man himself had reached an equilibrium when the first fence appeared; and year after year there had been no diminution in the amount of life or, what is more important, in the variety of life immediately dependent upon the creek and the acres along its borders.

Instead of the fifty-odd turkeys now liberally subsidized, this plot of ground in pre-pioneer times served merely as a part of the range for flocks of wild turkeys who stayed not long unless there happened to be a pest of insects and then they not only stayed but brought in reinforcements until the pest was checked.

Mobile life flowed in and concentrated only when an excess of other life justified such concentration. Monopoly by any one form of life was prevented and less fortunate forms were given a chance to recuperate. Nature, left alone, multiplied forms: from the infinite number of mutations called forth, a few are continually chosen to slake the eternal thirst for variety. She abhors not only a vacuum, but monotony also. Free and unlimited fencing has interfered with the healthy circulation of natural life, congested and confined it in pockets, restricted its channels, and developed conditions analogous to hardened arteries in the human circulatory system. In the present instance, the fence has frustrated nature, and nature retaliates with poverty weed and Mexican tea.

In the free circulation of life there is always moderation, nothing too much, no robbing or senseless gorging. The acres now under fence were as rich at the end as they were at the beginning of any period, a year or a hundred or a thousand years.

AS FOR HUMAN LIFE, this plot of ground supported the minute fraction of an Indian. If "one" is made the numerator of this fraction, the denominator will, I think, run into at least six figures. But whatever the size of the denominator, it can be multiplied by one thousand to get the fraction of an Indian this same plot of ground would now support with fences down, present population removed, and domesticated life permitted to seek its own competitive level.

This is a fundamental, irremediable impoverishment, differing from the devastation of war, which, being wrought mainly on the works of man, is by man quickly repaired. It is all recorded statistically. Cold columns of figures set forth the facts, but no Isaiah, or poet of desolation, has burned the truth into the public mind. The "plan of salvation" presupposed a "conviction of sin" and this necessary basis has not yet been laid.

The curse which blighted these 200 acres has been multiplied a million times. Texas, topographically, is an inclined plane tilted toward the Gulf of Mexico which still has in its yawning chasms room for unlimited consignments of soil fertility. In periods of excessive rainfall the regurgitations of bloated rivers spill over the continental shelf. In droughty seasons, sweepings of vast erosions are blown by violent winds clear from the plains

The fence has frustrated nature and had a disastrous effect on the natural life cycles of the land

miles out to sea. Natural life has been more profoundly affected by fencing than by any other of man's devices, ancient or modern, for it is the fence which enabled him to multiply at will those species which minister to his wants, while suppressing plants and animals which do not. From the walling about of a desert waterhole by an Arab nomad to the throwing of a prefabricated net of barbed wire over the great plains and prairies of North America, the fence has fenced off or fenced in certain natural life from one resource or another that it must have to survive, and has given priority to other forms favored by the fence-maker.

TEXAS IS CERTAINLY THE MOST fence-conscious state in the Union, and I am one of the most fence-conscious individuals in it. A fence-war burst upon my childhood with a shock I can still feel. At sundown I saw stretching for miles across the gently rolling and virgin prairie a lately completed barbed-wire fence, four shining strands of galvanized Glidden held up by cedar posts peeled and weathered to the shade of old ivory and set solidly eight feet apart. It was the first real fence I had ever seen and I had watched the workmen building it, wide-eyed with wonder.

But at that, it was an interest mingled with fear instilled by half-heard murmurs against fencing up the country. Men sitting around the general store on Saturday afternoons didn't like it a bit.

One day I took a long look at the wonderful fence and went to bed thinking about it. Next morning at sun-up I rushed out to have another look. During the night a frightful transformation had occurred. Each tightly stretched strand had been cut between each pair of posts and the wire had curled up, giving the line a frizzled appearance. I was speechless. I couldn't for the moment call any one to come and see what had happened.

As a result of this fence-cutting, an old, smoldering feud flamed up in the community. There were mysterious riders at night, moving along in such close formation that you could hear stirrups popping against each other as a group approached in the darkness. Law and order, however, finally prevailed and the fence was rebuilt.

Then there was a period of big pastures. The prairies were still virgin. There were endless swells of greenery in spring stretching away to the horizon, parched in summer, brown and sere in autumn and winter. There was still riding-room, space to follow a pack of hounds chasing jackrabbits. But every time a dog ran afoul of one of those cursed fences and split his back from neck to tail, my hatred flamed against them. I sympathized with the fence-cutters.

The more extensive fences, that is, field-and-pasture fences, in the rougher portions of the Edwards Plateau, were of stone or rail before Glidden's time. The building of the stone fences was a task for Hercules. Some idea of the cheapness of labor in that period may be gained by the knowledge that it was profitable to enclose five-dollar-an-acre land in a fence weighing not less than a ton per linear yard. It is true that there was a little offset in the cost of this enormous task, since some of the land selected for fields had to be cleared of loose stone anyway.

A FEW OF THESE FENCES have been kept in repair and still serve, but most of them are tumbled down along property lines. Sometimes one finds a fence-museum out in the cedar brake; a stretch of disintegrated stone fence paralleling an old rail fence rotted down, while alongside these relics of other eras runs a string of shining barbed-wire fence, five strands stretched tight and stapled to stalwart posts firmly tamped into two feet of dirt or rock.

Yes, I sympathized with the fence-cutters. I didn't know then how true my instinct was. Wire fences meant not only the doom of the sport of chasing jackrabbits, but of natural vegetation at a time when there was no generally diffused knowledge of its conserving function, no science to mitigate or put off the disaster, and no social consciousness to impel the use of such science even had it been available. Topsoil muddying creeks and rivers caused little comment; great gashes in the earth appeared, wounds from which it will never recover, but no one cried out against this havoc. Soon there was five-cent cotton, tenantry, women worked to death, and undernourished children reared in shameful

457

ignorance. It has been estimated that Texas expended 30 million tons of rich soil for every bale of cotton marketed.

Much has been written of man's inventiveness in destructive devices outpacing his sense of responsibility. But the inventions and appliances of peace are often just as disastrous and for the same reason. There was no serious discussion of the social implications and of the sensible use of barbed wire, as the terrific assault began — only general jubilation over the solution of the fencing problem.

SAMSON AND HERCULES must assemble the material for a stone fence, but brute strength is not enough. There is an art involved, the art of chinking. I was taught this by a robust Italian farmer who built the best stone fences in the country. They are worth going miles to see.

The art of chinking is an ancient one, even here in the new world. The stone fence grows more beautiful with age. Wood, even cedar, decays; wire fences are ugly to begin with and become progressively more unattractive; iron fences, besides having a military aspect, rust, and paint only makes them more offensive.

The weathering of stone fences, the look of age, venerable and nerve-quieting, is time-created. Without losing evidence of their human origin, they come to harmonize with natural features of the landscape, pleasing because they are plainly indigenous. Another generation or two may clear away surviving segments of these fences, as the last generation sawed up the priceless red-cedar logs of pioneer cabins.

Fences of cedar also survive, both worm and stake-and-rider, antedating in some cases the fences of stone. I know a stake-and-rider fence nearly a hundred years old with hardly a blemish in it. The lot and yard fences around homesteads are of cedar, hand-hewed and set upright so close together that a cottontail rabbit must hunt for a hole and then pinch himself a little to get through. This cutting, hewing, fitting, driving, and binding palings to form a vermin-proof fence, while not involving the backbreaking labor of stone-fencing, was still an enormous undertaking. Many of these pales, built by early settlers, remain sound and close-knit. They were fashioned from mountain cedar which lasts like bone.

The word "fence" is a contraction of "defence" which suggests that enclosures in the beginning were constructed for the purpose of keeping things out rather than for keeping them in. The vineyards of sacred literature, as well as the cultivated fields of the American frontiers, were fenced against stock which roamed at large. But now in all civilized countries stock is fenced in instead of out. This makes fences a concern of no small importance to the naturalist, as the construction of these artificial barriers radically change the flora and fauna native to the land.

ROY BEDICHEK was born in Cass County, Ill., in 1878. In 1884 his family moved to Falls County, Texas. Bedichek attended rural schools and Bedichek Academy, established at Eddy by his father. In 1898 he entered the University of Texas and began work in the office of the registrar, John Lomax. He was a reporter for the Fort Worth Record and taught in high schools in Houston and San Angelo. In 1910 he married Lillian Lee Greer; they had three children. Bedichek returned to Austin in 1913 and became secretary of the Young Men's Business League, which later merged with the chamber of commerce. In 1917 he began work with the University Interscholastic League. As director of the league he made it a success. In 1948, at the age of 70, he took a leave of absence to write "Adventures with a Texas Naturalist." That was followed by "Karankaway Country." He died on May 21, 1959.

BIBLIOGRAPHY

Adams, Robert. *Learning by Hard Licks*. Based on oral history interviews conducted by Marie Blucher from March 1939 to September 1940; Corpus Christi Central Library. Also in *Recollections of Other Days*, edited by Murphy Givens and Jim Moloney, Nueces Press. Corpus Christi, 2013.

Allen, John Taylor. *Early Pioneer Days in Texas.* Wilkinson Printing Company, Dallas, 1918.

Almond, Joseph. *The Joseph Almond Diary*, on microfilm at the Corpus Christi Central Library, was transcribed and privately printed by Sharry Reynolds and Robyn Reynolds-Vaughn in 2002.

Anderson, Andrew. *Recollections of Capt. Andy Anderson.* Biographic files, Corpus Christi Central Library. Also in *Recollections of Other Days*, edited by Murphy Givens and Jim Moloney, Nueces Press. Corpus Christi, 2013.

Bacon, Elizabeth. See Custer.

Baker, Jonathan Hamilton, *Diary of a Trail Drive*, reprinted in *Wranglin' the Past, the Reminiscences of Frank M. King*. Trail's End Publishing Company, Pasadena, Calif., 1946.

Barry, James Buckner. *Texas Ranger and Frontiersman: The Days of Buck Barry in Texas, 1845-1906.* Edited by James K. Greer. The Southwest Press, Dallas, 1932.

Bedichek, Roy. Adventures With a Texas Naturalist. Doubleday, 1947.

Blessington, Joseph P. *The Campaigns of Walker's Texas Division by a Private Soldier.* Lange, Little & Company, New York, 1875.

Bollaert, William, *Arrival in Texas in 1842.* Colburn's United Service Magazine and Naval and Military Journal, November 1846, London.

Boyd, Mrs. O. B. *Cavalry Life in Tent and Field.* J. Selwin Tait & Sons, New York, 1894.

Burnam, Jesse. *Reminiscences of Capt. Jesse Burnam.* Southwest Historical Quarterly, 1901.

Caldwell, E. H. *The Caldwells of Corpus Christi,* edited by Robert J. Caldwell, privately printed. Corpus Christi Central Library.

Caldwell, Lucy. Her letter to her mother, Mary Caldwell, was written from the Gunter Hotel in San Antonio a week after the storm. It was published in the Caller-Times on Sept. 20, 1950. Also in *1919 The Storm* by Murphy Givens and Jim Moloney, Nueces Press. Corpus Christi, 2009.

Carter, Robert Goldthwaite. *Tragedies of Cañon Blanco, A Story of the Texas Panhandle.* Gibson Brothers Printers, 1919.

Castro, Henry. See Sowell.

Cates, Cliff D. *Pioneer History of Wise County: from Red Men to Railroads—Twenty Years of Intrepid History.* Decatur, Texas, 1907.

Cazneau, Jane (Cora Montgomery). *The Eagle Pass: Life on the Border.* George P. Putnam & Company, 1852.

Cude, W. F. *Trail Drivers of Texas.* Edited by J. Marvin Hunter. Jackson Printing Co., San Antonio, 1920.

Custer, Elizabeth B. *Tenting on the Plains, or General Custer in Kansas and Texas.* Charles L. Webster & Co., 1887.

Davis, Andrew A. *The History and Reminiscences of Denton County.* Ed. F. Bates. McNitzky Printing Company, Denton, 1918.

Davis, Richard Harding. *The West From a Car Window.* Harper & Brothers, 1892.

DeShields, James T. Cynthia Ann Parker. Printed by the author in St. Louis in 1886.

DeWees, William Buford. *Letters from an Early Settler of Texas to a Friend,* Louisville, Ky., 1858

Dixon, Olive K. *Life of "Billy" Dixon*, Plainsman, Scout, Pioneer. P. L. Turner Company, Dallas, 1927.

Dobie, J. Frank. *J. Frank Dobie Writes of His Boyhood in Live Oak County*. Corpus Christi Caller-Times, Jan. 18, 1959. Also in *Recollections of Other Days*, edited by Murphy Givens and Jim Moloney, Nueces Press. Corpus Christi, 2013.

Dodge, Col. Richard Irving. *Our Wild Indians: Thirty-Three Years' Personal Experience Among the Red Men of the Great West.* A. D. Worthington & Company, Hartford, 1890.

Dodson, Ruth. *The Gamble Brothers*. Copy of the article in manuscript form in the author's possession.

Domenech, Abbé. *Missionary Adventures in Texas and Mexico, A Personal Narrative of Six Years' Sojourn in Those Regions.* Longman, Brown, Green, Longman. London, 1858.

Duganne, A. J. H. *Camps and Prisons: Twenty Months in the Department of the Gulf.* J. P. Robens, New York, 1865.

Duncan, Bill. Article, Corpus Christi Times, Oct. 20, 1980.

Dunn, John B. *Perilous Trails of Texas* was first published in 1932, edited by his daughter. It was re-published by Nueces Press in 2015, edited by Murphy Givens and Jim Moloney.

Dunn, Patrick F. *Pat Dunn and Padre Island.* Compiled from a deposition in Cameron County (*Lizzie Havre v. Pat Dunn*, April 1928), reprinted by Pauline Reese, *History of Padre Island;* thesis, 1938. And from interviews conducted for the Corpus Christi Caller by Ernest G. Fischer in 1927.

Duval, John C. *The Adventures of Bigfoot Wallace.* Claxton, Ramsen & Haffelfinger, Philadelphia, 1871.

Dwyer, Thomas A. *Horse and Mule Raising in Western Texas.* Pamphlet: A Brief Description of Western Texas, San Antonio, 1872.

Elliff, Ike. His account of the investigation, as told to Forrest H. Beck, was included in the manuscript of "Pathfinders of Texas" by Mrs. Frank DeGarmo.

Farley, Anna Priscilla. See Sorelle.

Fitzsimmons, T. F. (Tobe) and Hall, Robert. Letter from Cuba to Fitzsimmons' parents. Corpus Christi Caller, Jan. 13, 1899. Robert Hall's letter from Cuba, dated Jan. 8, 1899, was written to Hall's friend, Lee Talbott. Corpus Christi Caller. January 1899.

Fremantle, Arthur James Lyon. *Three Months in the Southern States. April-June, 1863.* Published in London in late 1863 and in New York in 1864 by J. Bradburn.

Fuller, Theodore. *When the Century and I Were Young.* A copy of Fuller's privately printed autobiography is in the Corpus Central Library.

Gillett, James B. *Six Years with the Texas Rangers, 1875 to 1881.* Yale University Press, New Haven, 1925.

Givens, Leona Gussett. From interviews by Marie Blucher in November 1938 and February 1940. Corpus Christi Central Library, biographical files, Local History Room.

Grant, U. S. *Personal Memoirs of U. S. Grant.* C. L. Webster & Company, New York, 1885-86.

Handy, Mary Olivia. *The History of Fort Sam Houston.* The Naylor Company, San Antonio, 1951.

Hardin, John Wesley. *The Life of John Wesley Hardin, From the Original Manuscript Written by Himself.* Smith & Moore, Seguin, Texas, 1896.

Hatcher, Mattie Alice. *Letters of an American Traveler, Mary Austin Holley, Her Life and Works, 1784-1846.* Southwest Press, Dallas, 1933.

Hill, Dr. Robert T. *The Story of Fort Griffin.* Dallas Morning News, June 5, 1931. Reprinted in *The Story of Lottie Deno,* by J. Marvin Hunter.

Hitchcock, Ethan Allen. *Fifty Years in Camp and Field: Diary of Major-General Ethan Allen Hitchcock.* G. P. Putnam's Sons, New York, 1909.

Holley, Mary Austin. See Hatcher.

Holloway, Carroll C. *Texas Gun Lore.* The Naylor Company, San Antonio, 1951. This book was republished in 2014 by the Copano Bay Press, edited by Michelle M. Haas and titled "Guns of Texas."

Houstoun, Mrs. *Texas and the Gulf of Mexico or Yachting in the New World.* G.B. Zieber & Co., Philadelphia, 1845.

Hoyt, Henry F. *A Frontier Doctor.* Houghton Mifflin Company, 1929.

Jarvis, Nathan S. *Surgeon Notes on Frontier Service.* Journal of the Military Service Institution of the United States, Vol. 39, 1906.

Johnson, James T. From *Trail Drivers of Texas.* Compiled and edited by J. Marvin Hunter. Jackson Printing Company, 1920.

Lane, Lydia Spencer. *I Married a Soldier or Old Days in the Old Army.* J. B. Lippincott & Company, Philadelphia, 1893.

Lee, Nelson. *Three Years Among the Comanches; The Narrative of Nelson Lee, Texas Ranger.* First published in 1859, it was republished in 1957 by the University of Oklahoma Press, with an introduction by Walter Prescott Webb.

Leonard, Carlyle. Article. Corpus Christi Caller-Times, April 27, 1952.

Linn, John J. *Reminiscences of Fifty Years in Texas.* D. & J. Sadler & Company, New York, 1883.

Longstreet, James. *From Manassas to Appomattox: Memoirs of the Civil War in America.* J. B. Lippincott Company, Philadelphia, 1896.

Lovenskiold, Anita. Copy of her diary for 1918 is in the author's possession.

Lubbock, Francis Richard. *Six Decades in Texas, or, Memoirs of Francis Richard Lubbock*. Edited by C. W. Raines. B. C. Jones & Company, Printers, Austin, 1900.

Lufkin, Edwin B. *History of the Thirteenth Maine Regiment*. H. A. Shorey & Son, Publishers, Bridgton, Maine, 1893.

Lundy, Benjamin. *The Life, Travels and Opinions of Benjamin Lundy*. W. D. Parrish, Philadelphia, 1847.

McConnell, H. H. *Five Years A Cavalryman or Sketches of Regular Army Life on the Texas Frontier*. J. N. Rogers & Co., Jacksboro, Texas, 1889.

Manci, Rev. V. L. *Letter on Indianola Storm*. The Woodstock Letters, Vol. 5, No. 1, Jan. 1, 1876.

Maudslay, Robert. *Texas Sheepman, the Reminiscences of Robert Maudslay*, edited by his niece, Winifred Kupper, published by the University of Texas Press, 1951.

Maverick, Mary. *The Memoirs of Mary A. Maverick*. Alamo Printing, San Antonio, 1921.

Merriman, Eli T. *Growing up at Banquete*. Columns in the Corpus Christi Caller-Times in April 1936.

Mills, W. W. *Forty Years at El Paso, 1858-1898*. Drawings by Tom Lea. Carl Hertzog Company, El Paso, 1962.

Morrell, Z. N. *Flowers and Fruits in the Wilderness*. Commercial Printing Company, St. Louis, 1882.

Moses, J. W. Columns printed under the pen name of "Sesom." San Antonio Daily Express, various dates between 1887 and 1890. Also, *Texas in Other Days*, edited by Murphy Givens. Friends of Corpus Christi Library, 2005.

Noakes, Thomas J. *The Diary of Thomas J. Noakes*. Entry dated July 2, 1858. Transcribed copy of the original in the Corpus Christi Central Library. Also in *Thomas Noakes Diary*, edited by Murphy Givens and Jim Moloney, Nueces Press. Corpus Christi, 2019.

Noel, Theophilus. *Old Sibley Brigade,* published in Shreveport in 1865, and *Autobiography and Reminiscences of Theophilus Noel*, published in Chicago, 1904, by the Theo. Noel Company.

North, Thomas. *Five Years in Texas, or, What You Did Not Hear During the War.* Elm Street Printing Company, Cincinnati, 1871.

Nott, Charles C. *Sketches of Prison Camps; a Continuation of Sketches of the War.* Anson D. F. Randolph, New York, 1865.

Olmsted, Frederick Law. *A Journey Through Texas or A Saddle-Trip on the Southwestern Frontier.* Dix, Edwards & Company, New York, 1857.

Paul, George H. A compilation from articles in the Robstown Record, Oct. 31, 1957, and the Corpus Christi Chamber of Commerce magazine, October 1940.

Peoples, John H. *Letter from Peoples.* Corpus Christi Star, March 24, 1849.

Priour, Rosalie Hart. Unpublished memoirs of Rosalie Bridget Hart Priour, Corpus Christi Central Library.

Rawalt, Louis. A copy of his unpublished memoirs, *Island of Reprieve*, is in the author's possession.

Rea, William L. *District Judges of Refugio County.* Hobart Huson. Refugio Timely Remarks, 1941.

Reagan, John H. *Memoirs, With Special Reference to Secession and Civil War.* The Neale Publishing Company, New York, Washington, 1906.

Redmond, Henry W. *Letters to William Mann.* Texas Indian Papers, 1846-1859. Dorman H. Winfrey. Texas State Library, Austin, 1960.

Richardson, Rupert Norval. *The Frontier of Northwest Texas, 1846 to 1876: Advance and Defense by the Pioneer Settlers of the Cross Timbers and Prairies.* The Arthur H. Clark Company, Glendale, Calif., 1963.

Rodríguez, José María. *Memoirs of Early Texas.* Passing Show Printing Company, San Antonio, 1913.

Santleben, August. *Early Staging and Overland Freighting on the Frontiers of Texas and Mexico.* Edited by I. D. Affleck. The Neale Company, 1910.

Schwien, Anna Moore. *When Corpus Christi Was Young*. Memoirs compiled by Marie Blucher from oral history interviews, Nov. 8, 1938 to May 15, 1941; Corpus Christi Central Library. Also in *Recollections of Other Days*, Nueces Press, Corpus Christi, 2013.

Siringo, Charles A. *A Texas Cowboy, or Fifteen Years on the Hurricane Deck of a Spanish Pony*. Siringo & Dobson, Chicago, 1886.

Smithwick, Noah. *The Evolution of a State or Recollections of Old Texas Days*. Gammel Book Company, Austin, 1900.

Sorelle, Anna Priscilla (Farley). *The 1919 Hurricane as I Saw and Experienced It*. A copy is in the author's possession.

Sowell, A. J. *Early Settlers and Indian Fighters of Southwest Texas*. B. C. Jones & Company, Austin, 1900.

Steele, Mrs. Jean. *The Mexican and Indian Raid of '78*. Based on a pamphlet of affidavits prepared at Corpus Christi after the event. Texas Historical Association Quarterly, 1901-1902.

Sullivan, William John L. *Twelve Years in the Saddle for Law and Order on the Frontiers of Texas*. Boeckmann-Jones Company, Printers, Austin, 1909.

Sutherland, W. G. Compiled from various columns by Sutherland in the Corpus Christi Caller from 1925 to 1930.

Swisher, John Milton. *Swisher's Memoirs*. Edited by Rena Maverick Green. The Sigmund Press, San Antonio, 1932.

Tilghman, Zoe. *Quanah, the Eagle of the Comanches*. Harlow Publishing Company, Oklahoma City, 1938.

Trueheart, James L. *The Perote Prisoners*. Edited by Frederick C. Chabot. The Naylor Company, San Antonio. 1934.

Wallace, William Alexander Anderson (Bigfoot). See Duval.

West, John C. *A Texan In Search of a Fight; Being the Diary and Letters of a Private Soldier in Hood's Texas Brigade*. Press of J. S. Hill, Waco, 1901.

Western, Thomas G. *Texas Indian Papers, 1844-1845.* Dorman H. Winfrey. Texas State Library, Austin, 1960.

Wharton, Clarence Ray. *Satanta, the Great Chief of the Kiowas and His People.* Banks Upshaw and Company, Dallas, 1935.

White, Owen P. *The Autobiography of a Durable Sinner*, G. P. Putnam's Sons, New York, 1942.

Whiting, Daniel P. *A Soldier's Life*. Nueces Press, Corpus Christi, 2011.

Wilbarger, J. W. *Indian Depredations in Texas.* A facsimile reproduction of the original, published in 1889. The Steck Company, Austin, 1935.

Williams, R. H. *With the Border Ruffians, or Memories of the Far West, 1852-1868.* E. P. Dutton, New York, 1907.

ALSO AVAILABLE FROM NUECES PRESS

1919 – The Storm

Corpus Christi – A History

A Soldier's Life

Great Tales from the History of South Texas

Recollections of Other Days

Perilous Trails of Texas

Columns   2009 – 2011

Columns 2 2012 – 2013

Columns 3 2014 – 2015

Columns 4 2016 – 2018

Streets of Corpus Christi Texas

Thomas Noakes Diary of War & Drought

Signed copies are available from

www.nuecespress.com

www.ingramcontent.com/pod-product-compliance
Lightning Source LLC
Chambersburg PA
CBHW070945150426
42812CB00067B/3324/J